The Archdiocese of

CHICAGO

A Journey of Faith

The Archdiocese of
CHICAGO
A Journey of Faith

EDWARD R. KANTOWICZ

CONSULTANT EDITOR

JOHN J. TREANOR

PARISH AND SCENIC PHOTOGRAPHY

TINA LETO

BOOKLINK

THE RECENT CELEBRATION OF THE BEGINNING of the Third Millennium of the salvation won by Our Lord Jesus Christ encouraged all Christians to consider anew how the providence of God has guided his Church for two thousand years. God's providence works in ways great and small, in times good and bad. God's providence has been at work in and through the Archdiocese of Chicago for over 160 years.

This illustrated history of the Archdiocese shows the workings of God in and through his faithful people. It features the story of our parishes, schools and other institutions; but it is basically a story of grace. Millions have cooperated with the Lord in creating and sustaining this Archdiocese. Millions more will continue and build upon this history in the years to come. Catholics were the first Europeans to visit and settle the southern shore of Lake Michigan, before the United States existed. Catholics came as immigrants to build up the city of Chicago, as they came and built up other great American cities.

Our history is a story of faith, courage and charity; it is also a story of sin and betrayal of the Lord. A spiritual author has said, "The Church is always God hung between two thieves... to be a member of the Church is to carry the mantle of both the worst sin and the finest heroism of soul..." The Archdiocese is the local or particular Church that God uses to make us saints. In her we find all the gifts we need, along with the need to share them as universally as possible. This book shows how we've used Christ's gifts or squandered them, how we've hoarded them or shared them. It's the story of our life in Christ, a story more beautiful even than the marvelous pictures and poignant words that have been brought together to create this book.

I hope that many Catholics of the Archdiocese and others will rejoice in this book, use it and share it. May it prompt us to new gratitude to Almighty God and to a new sense of purpose. May God, the Father of Our Lord and Savior Jesus Christ, continue to bless us abundantly and bring us to delight in his ways.

Sincerely yours in Christ,

FRANCIS CARDINAL GEORGE, OMI

ARCHBISHOP OF CHICAGO

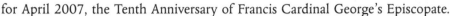

PLEASE ALLOW ME TO INTRODUCE YOU to this wonderfully edifying book on the history of our local Catholic Church, *Archdiocese of Chicago, A Journey of Faith*. This project has been a labor of love for the Staff of the Archdiocese of Chicago's Archives and Records Center as we prepare for April 2007, the Tenth Anniversary of Francis Cardinal George's Episcopate.

History is the story of past people, places and events told from the vantage point of the present. Over time the present becomes past and history is rewritten from a new perspective with fresh insights gleaned from new documentary sources not available to previous scholars. The *Archdiocese of Chicago, A Journey of Faith* looks afresh at the illustrious and sometimes tumultuous history of the Roman Catholic Church from our present vantage point, the beginning of the third millennium after the death of our Lord, Jesus Christ. This illustrated coffee table book contains photographs, images and stories never before assembled in one volume. It chronicles the rich historical legacy of our Archdiocese's missionary roots, its growth as a fledgling Diocese that encompassed the whole State of Illinois, to its present boundaries of Lake and Cook Counties. The esteemed Chicago Historian, Edward R. Kantowicz, weaves a fascinating portrait of the local parishes, lay persons, priests, bishops, events and faith that have conspired to make our history unique.

This project would have never been completed without the assistance of the entire Staff of the Archdiocese of Chicago's Archives. In particular, I must commend Margaret O'Toole, Chief Processing Archivist and Julie Satzik, Assistant Research Archivist, for their incredible research skills and knowledge of our collections. Their efforts made this story come alive. I am also grateful to Maria Elena Moreno-Villagomez, my Administrative Assistant, for her project management skills that kept us on deadline. In addition, I must not forget Rebecca Ulmer, my former Associate Archivist, who started this project with me and left to care for her new son Max. The beautiful images of our parishes and church art are themselves the artwork of Tina Leto and Kevin Craig, our esteemed photographers. Of course, there would be no story told without our good friend and colleague, Edward R. Kantowicz. I am grateful for his knowledge, friendship, patience and kindness during the course of the project and my years in Chicago.

I trust you will enjoy our story and share it with your family and friends. Surely the faith of our fathers and mothers is a precious gift, not only to us but to those around us as well.

JAC TREANOR

CONSULTANT EDITOR AND ARCHIVIST

Present at the Creation

Fr. Marquette statue at the portage between the Chicago and Des Plaines Rivers

Chicago Catholics were "present at the creation" of their Midwestern boomtown. In 1833, the same year that the community on Lake Michigan incorporated as a town, a group of French, Irish, and British Catholics organized St. Mary's parish. Ten years later, the city was designated a separate Catholic diocese; the first resident bishop, William J. Quarter, arrived from New York on May 5, 1844. However, Catholics had actually lived at the swampy prairie site that the local Miami Indians called "Chicagou" for a century and a half before its incorporation as a town and its organization as a diocese.

FRENCH CHICAGO

The first European who landed in Chicago was a Catholic priest. In September 1673, Fr. Jacques Marquette, S.J., a French Jesuit, along with Louis Joliet and four other companions, discovered the portage between the Des Plaines and Chicago Rivers. As they dragged their birch bark canoes over this land bridge, they envisioned a canal connecting the watersheds of the Mississippi River and Lake Michigan. Father Marquette returned to the site a year later and spent the winter of 1674–75 in a rude cabin near the portage. Like many a later Chicagoan, he contracted a deadly virus in the brutal cold and died the following spring while returning northwards to his base at St. Ignace, Michigan.

According to Ulrich Danckers, an amateur historian who has meticulously researched "Early Chicago" as a labor of love: "During the next 25 years many other missionaries, traders, and military men followed the pathways opened by Marquette and Joliet. . . . By the year 1700 both a mission and a trading post stood on land that is now almost at the center of the city." Father Francois Pinet, S.J., founded *La Mission de l'Ange Gardien* (Guardian Angel Mission) in 1696, surrounded by a Miami Indian village. This was almost three-quarters of a century before the establishment of the better known California missions.

Guardian Angel Mission lasted only until about 1702 or 1703 when it was abandoned due to frequent Indian raids. Throughout the eighteenth century small-scale but fierce warfare raged incessantly across the center of North America as the French and their English rivals made and broke numerous alliances with Indian tribes and confederations. Nevertheless, various French traders and missionaries lived on the banks of the Chicago River from time to time throughout the century. After the French and Indian War and then the American Revolution settled the European contest for control

OPPOSITE
Downtown Chicago from
St. Mary of the Angels

Mosaic of Fr. Marquette in the
lobby of the Marquette Building

Portrait of Mark Beaubien
From Gilbert J. Garraghan S.J.,
Catholic Church in Chicago,
1673–1871

of the Midwest, more permanent settlement could begin in Chicago. A French-speaking mulatto with an Indian wife, Jean Baptiste Point de Sable, built a log cabin near the mouth of the Chicago River about 1784 and remained there as a prosperous farmer until 1800. He is widely heralded today as Chicago's first non-native, long-term settler. Probably born near Montreal, Quebec, Point de Sable (or Pointe du Sable, as it is sometimes written), was a "free Negro" and a Roman Catholic. The Chicago pioneer and his Indian wife Catherine had their marriage solemnized by a Catholic priest at the mission of Cahokia, Illinois in 1788 and later their daughter also had her marriage blessed by a priest at the same settlement. Despite the long Catholic presence in Chicago, there was no priest resident there at the end of the eighteenth century.

After American ownership of the mid-continent had been won, the U.S. government erected a military post, Fort Dearborn, near the mouth of the Chicago River in 1803. The fort was destroyed and its garrison massacred at the beginning of the War of 1812 but the government rebuilt it in 1816. In the meantime, some English-speaking settlers, both British subjects and American citizens, had filtered into the tiny settlement. Most notable among the newcomers was John Kinzie who bought Point de Sable's farm on the north bank of the river shortly after the older settler had moved on to Missouri territory in 1800. The majority of traders and farmers who lived around Fort Dearborn, however, were still French-speakers, such as Antoine Ouilmette (sometimes spelled Wilmette) and the brothers Jean Baptiste and Mark Beaubien. The latter two men both lived in the Chicago area until their deaths in 1864 and 1881, respectively. Much more than Point de Sable, the brothers Beaubien can be termed fathers of Chicago, in the most literal sense. Between them they fathered 42 children by a succession of Indian, French, and English wives.

Bronze bas-relief of Fr. Marquette
and the Indians in front of the
Marquette Building

Imagined site of early Chicago with cabin and profile of Jean Baptiste Point de Sable.

From Alfred T. Andreas, *History of Chicago,* courtesy of Chicago History Museum

PARISH AND DIOCESE

On April 16, 1833, Bishop Joseph Rosati of St. Louis, whose far-flung diocese included most of the American Midwest, received a petition from Catholics living in Chicago asking that he send a resident priest to minister to them. The petition to Rosati was signed by 36 men and listed the number of family members belonging to each, for a total of 128 Catholic individuals. Judging by their last names, the petitioners numbered 21 French, 13 Scottish or English, and 2 Irish. Many of the signers had Indian blood or were married to Indian women. The petition was written in French. Chicago incorporated as a town that same year, on June 18. A minimum of 150 settlers was required for incorporation. If the minimum number were present in Chicago, the 128 Catholics would have comprised an overwhelming majority. Even if more Chicagoans were present in 1833, as some historians have estimated, Catholics formed a significant presence in the new town.

Bishop Rosati responded to the Chicago petition immediately and sent a newly-ordained, French-born priest, John Mary Irenaeus St. Cyr. Arriving in Chicago on May 1, 1833, he said Mass for the first time in Mark Beaubien's log cabin. Fr. St. Cyr and his eager flock formed St. Mary's parish and quickly built a wooden church building at the corner of Lake and State streets. St. Mary's church was one of the first buildings in the United States built by the so-called "balloon-frame" method. Instead of employing skilled carpenters to laboriously fit together heavy wooden beams with mortises and tenons, a light-weight frame was hastily assembled from pine boards and nailed together. The balloon frame was cheaper and quicker to erect and also easier to break down again or move intact. Accordingly, St.Mary's church migrated twice, first to Michigan and Madison and then to Wabash and Madison.

Fr. St. Cyr ministered not only to his original flock of petitioners in Chicago but to about 400 others, including Indians and African-Americans, in the surrounding area. The last Indians, however, were forced to migrate westwards in 1835 and St. Mary's lost some of its original parishioners, such as Antoine Ouilmette who left with his Indian wife. In 1834, the Chicago area came under the jurisdiction of a newly-formed diocese at Vincennes, Indiana, but Fr. St. Cyr remained for two more years until October 1836 when he returned to St. Louis and was replaced by a priest from Vincennes.

In 1843 Chicago became a separate Catholic diocese, embracing the whole state of Illinois. William J. Quarter, an Irish-born priest working in New York City, was assigned as the first resident bishop. Arriving in the city on May 5, 1844, he discovered that his congregation had replaced the wooden balloon-frame church with a more substantial brick and masonry "cathedral," in the neo-classic style then current in American architecture. The new St. Mary's, on the southwest corner of Madison and Wabash, was still unfinished on the interior and had a debt of $3,000 hanging over it.

Finding his religious compatriots impoverished and debt-ridden, Bishop Quarter called on the resources of international Catholicism, inviting religious orders of women and men to establish schools, hospitals, and other institutions in the city. The women came first. Indeed, before Bishop Quarter left for Chicago, he personally greeted a group of Irish-born Sisters of Mercy when their boat docked in New York harbor in December 1843 and persuaded them to come west to

Fr. John Mary Irenaeus St. Cyr, first pastor of Old St. Mary's

RIGHT: Bishop William J. Quarter
BELOW RIGHT: Pages from Bishop Quarter's diary

his new diocese. Led by twenty-four-year-old Sr. Agatha O'Brien, R.S.M., the Mercy Sisters arrived in Chicago on September 23, 1846 and almost immediately founded St. Francis Xavier Academy for women and Mercy Hospital, next door to St. Mary's cathedral on Wabash Avenue. Three-quarters of the $4000 purchase price of the property was donated by the Association for the Propagation of the Faith, a missionary society in Lyon, France. The sisters shrewdly bought property on the outskirts of the city as well, which eventually permitted them to expand Mercy Hospital into a modern health care institution and to extend the work of St. Xavier Academy into higher education. The Mercy Sisters and other orders that followed them did the kind of work later made famous by Hull House and the social settlement movement, organizing employment bureaus, industrial schools, and homes for "wayward women." As historian Suellen Hoy has concluded, they "minister[ed] to the most despised of Chicago's immigrant poor, while the founders of Hull House were still only girls themselves."

Ten years after the Sisters of Mercy began their work in Chicago, the celebrated Jesuit Order of priests arrived, led by Fr. Arnold Damen, S.J. In 1857 Father Damen established Holy Family parish to serve the "shanty Irish" squatting in hovels out on the prairie west of the city. He built a massive Gothic church that survived the Chicago Fire and briefly was the tallest building in the city. Holy Family parish housed separate elementary schools for girls and boys, and in 1870 the Jesuits opened St. Ignatius College, which still exists today as an elite college preparatory school and which eventually spun off Loyola University.

In the meantime, Bishop Quarter had literally worked himself to death. His *Diary*, one of the oldest documents in the Archdiocesan Archives, reveals the rigors of a pioneer bishop who traveled an entire state in his ministry. Less than a month and a half after his arrival in Chicago, he set out to visit the rest of his diocese. On June 15, 1844 he wrote: "The roads were very bad; swam the horses over the LaSalle river; . . . had some difficulty in passing the sloughs; had to apply rails to lift the carriage out of them twice; found a steamboat ready to sail down the Illinois river; stopped at Peru." After just four years of this regimen, Bishop Quarter died on April 10, 1848. He was only forty-two years old.

PRESENT AT THE CREATION

The early presence of Catholics in the Midwest made a difference. It is not just a historical trivia question or a matter of bragging rights. The

DIARY OF A FRONTIER BISHOP

WILLIAM J. QUARTER
Born in Kings County (Offaly), Ireland, January 24, 1806
Emigrated to the United States, 1822
Ordained for the Diocese of New York, September 19, 1829
Appointed first bishop of Chicago, February 1844
Consecrated March 10, 1844
Arrived in Chicago, May 5, 1844
Died April 10, 1848

15th [June, 1844]. On this morning the Bishop set out, in company with Rev. Mr. De St. Palais for Juliet [sic], with the intention of visiting a portion of the Diocese. Arrived at Juliet about 8 P.M.; said Mass next day and preached at 10:30 A.M.; preached again at Vespers; met there the Rev. Mr. Carroll, of Alton; set out for Ottawa (17th), accompanied by Rev. Mr. Carroll, de St. Palais, de Pontavice, and Mary McMahan, sister of Rev. P. McMahan. Mr. Sutliff, of Juliet, drove the carriage. The roads were very bad; swam the horses over the Au Sable river; stopped that night at Verniets, within nine miles of Ottawa; reached Ottawa next day, early; had some difficulty in passing the sloughs; had to apply rails to lift the carriage out of them twice; found a steamboat ready to sail down the Illinois River; stopped at Peru.

19th. Walked to La Salle; saw the Church and clergymen.
20th. Left next day in steamboat Rositan; stopped a short time at Peoria, and at the different villages along the Illinois where the boat could find a landing; observed many villages *almost entirely submerged in water* owing to the recent *extraordinary floods.*

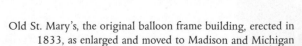

Old St. Mary's, the original balloon frame building, erected in 1833, as enlarged and moved to Madison and Michigan

Old St. Mary's, the brick building erected in 1843 as Chicago's first cathedral

Catholic Church did not suffer as much prejudice and hostility in Chicago as it did in Puritan Boston or Knickerbocker New York, where Catholics were viewed as alien latecomers to a well-established Protestant society. The Illinois legislature, in an 1845 law elaborated by amendments in 1861, empowered the Catholic Bishop of Chicago to hold title to all church property in his diocese as a "corporation sole." The corporation sole status (though not unique to Illinois) is far more favorable to hierarchical authority than the incorporation laws of New York, Pennsylvania, or most other eastern states. It allowed Chicago bishops to avoid the problems of lay trusteeism that plagued their East Coast colleagues. Though groups of laymen often took the initiative in organizing a new parish, they were always required to hand over the property title to the bishop. In the legal sense, Chicago Catholics were never congregationalists.

The educational and social institutions established by the Sisters of Mercy, the Jesuits, and other religious orders initially served the whole community, not just Catholics. Historian Timothy G. Walch has cogently pointed out: "As the first of their kind, these institutions initially operated in public capacities and often received monetary support from municipal and state governments." The pioneering role of Catholics in Chicago created a fund of good will and prestige for the Church that was often depleted but never completely exhausted over the years. It also instilled a sense of confidence in Chicago Catholics, which has remained a distinguishing mark of the Church in the Midwest's metropolis.

Nonetheless, the relationship between Chicago Catholics and other communities in Chicago was also competitive from the start. The petition for a resident priest at St. Mary's, addressed to the bishop of St. Louis in 1833, begged for a pastor "before other sects obtain the upper hand, which very likely they will try to do." As Catholic numbers increased, the community became more inward-looking, hostility from non-Catholics heated up, and Catholic institutions devoted more of their services to Catholic families and individuals. The state of Illinois ratified the separation of Catholic educational facilities from the rest of the community by creating a public school fund financed by property taxes in 1855. A provision of the 1870 constitution flatly prohibited the use of this fund to support any religious schools.

The history of the Catholic Church in Chicago, therefore, was filled with tensions and paradoxes. Despite the cooperation and good will at the beginning and a sense of self-confidence throughout, Chicago Catholics have also experienced much struggle and turmoil and faced many challenges.

Chicago Catholic history can best be divided into three time periods: an ethnic, separatist phase, from the establishment of the first national parish in 1846 to about 1916; a denominational phase from 1916 to 1963; and, finally, an outreach phase, from 1963 to the present.

Left to right: St. Xavier Academy, Convent of the Sisters of Mercy, and St. Mary's Cathedral

It's fortunate that early Chicago Catholics had built up a fund of goodwill and self-confidence, for in the latter half of the nineteenth century they faced immense challenges. Bishop Quarter's immediate successor, the Belgian-born Jesuit, James Van de Velde, S.J., took one look at Chicago and began petitioning Rome to get him out of there. He lasted two-and-half years before finally receiving a transfer to warmer parts of North America. Bishop Anthony O'Regan stayed a little longer but he too kept trying to convince Rome to accept his resignation. O'Regan found that an "episcopal visitation [of his farflung diocese] was almost one continual succession of breakdowns." He left after four years. O'Regan's succesor, Bishop James Duggan, cracked under the strain and had to be removed to an asylum.

Chicago was not only rough, but disaster-prone. In 1871, the city burned down. The fire began on a hot, windy night in early autumn in the stable of an Irish Catholic widow, Katherine O'Leary, on the near West Side. At first, the wind swept the fire westwards towards Holy Family Church and St. Ignatius College. According to legend, Holy Family's founder, Fr. Arnold Damen, S.J., implored the Blessed Virgin to spare his church and promised to keep seven votive lamps lit in front of her statue in perpetuity. The wind shifted, the Jesuits' church was saved, and the lamps still burn at Holy Family. The conflagration destroyed most of the city. St Patrick's church, just east of Holy Family, was also spared as the fire simply side-swiped it, but St. Mary's cathedral in the city center and the Gothic Holy Name parish church on the residential north side weren't so lucky. St. Mary's bought a Protestant church at 9th and Wabash, spared by the fire, but Holy Name was rebuilt and became the diocese's new cathedral.

The most important challenge facing Chicago Catholics, however, was a tidal wave of immigration flowing into the city. In the long century from 1821 to 1924, 55 million Europeans crossed the Atlantic looking for new homes, one of the greatest population movements in world history. Roughly 34 million, or

Mother Cabrini window at
Assumption Church (Illinois St.)

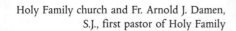

Holy Family church and Fr. Arnold J. Damen,
S.J., first pastor of Holy Family

After the fire, St. Joseph's church and priory

REST IN PEACE, BISHOP DUGGAN

On a beautiful spring day in 2001, the Fourth Bishop of Chicago, James Duggan, was interred in the Bishops' Mausoleum at Mount Carmel Cemetery in Hillside, Illinois. It was his second burial. He died on March 27, 1899 in St. Louis and was buried shortly thereafter in Calvary Cemetery, Evanston, Illinois. His sad and tragic life explains the long hiatus between his two burials.

James Duggan was born in Maynooth, County Kildare, Ireland on May 22, 1825. He came to the United States in 1842 to finish his seminary training at St. Vincent's Seminary, Cape Girardeau, Missouri, and was ordained in 1847 for the Archdiocese of St. Louis. His gift for languages and great skill as an orator distinguished him among his clerical colleagues, and he was named Vicar General of St. Louis in 1854. On January 21, 1859, at the age of 34, he was appointed Bishop of Chicago.

Just ten years later, Bishop Duggan was removed from office and remanded to a sanatorium run by the Sisters of Charity in St. Louis. He spent the next 29 years in confinement until his death in 1899. He was described in one history as "hopelessly insane." Yet the diagnosis and treatment of mental illness have changed dramatically since the nineteenth century, so it is impossible to say with any degree of certainty what ailed the Bishop.

One of James Duggan's colleagues described him as having a "delicate disposition." If so, he was in the wrong place at the wrong time. Chicago in the 1860s was a rough frontier boomtown, and the American nation descended into Civil War during this decade. Both of Duggan's immediate predecessors as Bishop of Chicago had resigned their posts after serving just a few years. Following their example, Bishop Duggan traveled abroad for an extended period to seek relaxation and cure. Upon his return, he abruptly closed the seminary and dismissed four priests, some of whom had been his closest advisors. On April 14, 1869, the Vatican removed Duggan and sent him to a mental hospital. With the hindsight of 130 years, we can conclude that Bishop Duggan succumbed to a massive case of job-related stress. Had he lived a century later, he probably would have avoided a long confinement and been treated with medication and other forms of therapy.

The stigma of mental illness prevented the inclusion of Duggan's remains with those of other early Chicago bishops when the Bishops' Mausoleum was erected at Mount Carmel Cemetery in 1912. Attitudes towards the mentally ill have changed since then, however; and in the first year of the new millennium Chicago's Fourth Bishop was finally laid to rest among his peers. May he rest in peace!

ABOVE: Combination church/school building, St. Clement's

about three-fifths of these, came to the United States. Chicago, centrally located and bursting with job opportunities, attracted more than its share. In other cities, one or two ethnic groups predominated, such as the Irish in Boston, the Germans in Milwaukee, or the Scandinavians in Minneapolis. Chicago welcomed any and all comers. Not all of them were Catholics. Swedes, Norwegians, Danes, and many Germans were predominantly Lutheran, and a great number of German and Russian Jews also came to the city. Catholics, however, were numerous and diverse, with Irish and Germans predominating at mid-century, later followed by southern and eastern Europeans.

Bishop Quarter prudently acceded to the wishes of new immigrants for separate development as ethnic groups. In 1846 he authorized the establishment of two German parishes in the city, St. Joseph's and St. Peter's. Separate parishes for French-speakers soon followed, and as other Catholic immigrant groups flooded into the city throughout the nineteenth century, they too were permitted to organize separate parishes. This concession to non-English-speaking immigrants was necessary for the retention of religious faith among them. Though the Catholic Mass was conducted in a language equally incomprehensible to all, in Latin, the sermon and other religious services were delivered in the vernacular languages. Furthermore, a local parish was far more than a place of worship; it was also a community center, where immigrants could congregate and inter-marry with people of the same language and customs. Throughout the nineteenth century, therefore, each Catholic ethnic group built a separate community in Chicago.

SCHOOLS CAME FIRST

While building their ethnic communities, Catholics generally began with a school rather than a church. In parish after parish, priests and people built the school building first, as a unifying force for parishioners to rally around, with church services held in the basement until a more suitable house of worship could be built. By the end of the nineteenth century, three-quarters of the 114 Catholic parishes in the city of Chicago included a school. Eventually these schools formed the largest private school system in North America. At their peak in

Holy Name church, rebuilt after the fire
and named cathedral of the diocese

Mother Maria Kaupas   Sister Agatha Hurley   Mother Theresa Dudzik

FOUNDING MOTHERS
FATHERS AND BROTHERS TOO

Religious orders of Sisters exercised a decisive formative influence on generations of Chicago Catholics. The Chicago Church relied heavily on women, and men too, who professed vows as members of religious orders.

Two of Chicago's Ordinaries, the city's second bishop, James Van de Velde, S.J., and the current archbishop, Cardinal Francis George, O.M.I, have been members of religious orders. Order priests founded parishes for the various ethnic groups of Chicago, and Brothers staffed many high schools.

But without the Sisters, the parochial school system of the archdiocese would never have come into existence. Nor would Catholic hospitals, orphanages, or other social services have come to be. The pioneers of these religious orders of Sisters, from many different ethnic groups, were truly "founding mothers" of the Chicago Catholic church.

One of the founding mothers, Frances Xavier Cabrini, has been declared a saint and several others have been beatified. Yet few are well known. Most were nearly anonymous and faceless behind their robes and veils, and it is often difficult even to retrieve their real names.

St. Frances Cabrini

Sisters of Charity of the Blessed Virgin Mary (BVMs) celebrate their 125th anniversary (1958) at Holy Name Cathedral

Class photo from Mother of God parish school, Waukegan

1965, the Chicago Catholic schools enrolled over 300,000 children in city and suburbs. Only two public school systems in the country – those in Chicago and New York – were larger. Throughout the nineteenth century, however, it would be a mistake to describe Chicago Catholic educational facilities as a "school system." Catholic elementary schools were "parochial" in the literal sense, that is, organized, funded, and administered by local parishes, not by the diocesan authorities or a central school board. The pastor built and maintained the school building, hired a religious order of sisters to teach, negotiated their salaries and provided them room and board.

Women religious were absolutely essential to the operation of Catholic schools. It is no exaggeration to say that without the nuns there would not have been very many Catholic schools in the United States, for sheer financial reasons. The pioneering

St. Patrick High School for Girls

Old St. Patrick's Social Center

Monument for Civil War Colonel James A. Mulligan, Calvary Cemetery

historian of American Catholic schools, Fr. James Aloysius Burns, pointed out in 1912 that "the teaching Brother worked for about one-half the salary of the male teacher in the public school; but the Sister could live on one-half the Brother's salary. If a school was to be opened, therefore, Sisters were usually employed as a matter of course." Teaching Sisters lived a frugal, semi-cloistered existence. By the rules of their orders, they were forbidden to attend secular entertainments or to set foot on the street alone. They owed obedience not only to their female religious superiors but also to the local pastor and to the bishop's delegate for women religious. From another point of view however, historian Mary Ewens reminds us, "in many aspects of their lives, nuns in nineteenth century America enjoyed opportunities open to few other women of their time: involvement in meaningful work, access to administrative positions, freedom from responsibilities of marriage and motherhood. . . ." In any case, the Sisters decided what to teach and how to teach it, and each religious order developed its own distinctive religious style and culture. James W. Sanders, a recent historian of Catholic education in Chicago, summed up the situation well: "More uniformity in textbooks, curriculum, and methods of instruction existed among the schools of a single religious order, even when spread over the entire country, than among the schools of different parishes within Chicago."

In addition, the Catholic schools were divided along ethnic-linguistic lines. Instruction in many, if not most, subjects of the school curriculum, was conducted in the language of the parish. Bishops considered Catholic schools vital instruments for maintaining religious faith from generation to generation; immigrant Catholics also deemed schools essential to preserve their language and culture. Education and religion were foundation stones of the separate Catholic communities in Chicago.

Old St. Patrick's parish, c. 1880

St. Alphonsus altar servers,
early 20th century

THE LEAGUES OF NATIONS

Not just education, but every aspect of Catholic life and worship was subdivided along ethnic lines. In Chicago, the Irish, Germans, and Poles formed the largest, "major leagues" of parishes and other institutions, whereas Bohemians (Czechs), Slovaks, Lithuanians, Italians, French-Canadians, Croatians, and Slovenians comprised the "minor leagues." The three major leagues and most of the minor ones built such a wide range of Catholic institutions that they could provide nearly all the services their members required – religious, educational, recreational, social-welfare – without recourse to either non-Catholics or Catholics of other ethnic groups. The one area of life that largely escaped this ethnic subdivision (and it is an important exception) is employment. Catholic immigrants sought jobs wherever they could in Chicago's industrial landscape, and neither the Church nor individual ethnic groups made any collective effort to build separate factories or business establishments.

The Irish, originally imported to dig the Illinois and Michigan Canal, spread themselves widely across the Chicago area in pursuit of both unskilled and skilled laboring positions and simply claimed the diocese's territorial parishes as their own. Many territorial parishes, though officially open to any Catholic who lived within their boundaries, bore distinctive Irish names such as St. Patrick, St. Jarlath, St. Bridget, or St. Columbkille. Parishioners spoke English at all non-liturgical events of the territorial parishes, for the Irish had largely lost their native language before arriving in America. This fact

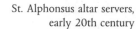

St. Alphonsus school orchestra, 1897

alone set the Irish parishes apart from other ethnic parishes and gave the Irish-Americans a head start in the race for economic mobility, political influence, and Church leadership.

Irish-American priests and nuns, though not opposed to Irish nationalism, did not emphasize it, for in nineteenth-century Ireland nationalism and Catholicism had gone hand in hand and Irish-Americans tended to take both for granted. Irish Catholic leaders focused instead on nurturing an upwardly mobile, American middle class. By the end of the nineteenth century, numerous Irish-American males had pursued professional training as doctors or lawyers or had secured stable jobs in government. Ambitious Irish-American women virtually took over the teaching faculty of the Chicago public schools. In 1902, for example, two-thirds of the candidates who passed the Normal exam for public school employment were graduates of Catholic secondary schools. The Irish Catholic schoolteacher was as much a fixture of Chicago life as the Irish Catholic cop or politician.

Germans, who arrived in America with slightly more resources and skills than the Irish, were also spread widely across the city in a variety of skilled, unskilled, and professional occupations. Yet their residential stronghold lay on the North Side. St. Michael's, just west of Lincoln Park and St. Alphonsus on Lincoln Avenue, both staffed by the Redemptorist religious order of priests and the School Sisters of Notre Dame, were the largest German parishes in the city. The most distinctive feature of the German league was its orientation towards charitable work and social action, a legacy of German Social Catholicism in the old country. All the various ethnic leagues established orphanages, but the German Angel Guardian Orphanage on the North Side, administered by a mixed board of priests and laymen and staffed by sisters, was an acknowledged leader in its field of social work. Many German priests and lay people played leading roles in the St. Vincent de Paul Society (a charitable organization) and later in the Catholic Action movements of the first half of the twentieth century.

The Polish league formed the largest group of non-territorial parishes, clustered around the hallmark heavy industries that earned Chicago its 'big shoulders" reputation late in the nineteenth century. Since Polish immigrants were primarily

Girls play on a swing, Angel Guardian Orphanage, 1910s

St. Hedwig Orphanage, mid 20th century

peasants, arriving in Chicago later than the Irish and Germans with few marketable skills other than a capacity for backbreaking labor, they sought employment as unskilled laborers in large industrial enterprises. Polish neighborhoods and parishes clustered around the Union Stockyards, the South Chicago steel mills, and the tanneries, foundries, and lumberyards along the south and north branches of the Chicago River. The greatest number concentrated on the Northwest Side between the north branch of the river and Milwaukee Avenue. St. Stanislaus Kostka, the oldest Polish parish in the city, and most of the other Northwest Side Polish parishes were staffed by the Resurrectionist order of priests and a number of orders of Polish-speaking nuns who were fiercely devoted to the preservation of Polish language and culture.

Polish pastors attempted to rule their parishes and the Polish league in an authoritarian manner, like feudal lords. Instead of the mixed clerical-lay orphan society that ran the German orphanage, for example, a committee of Polish pastors exercised complete control over St. Hedwig's Orphanage and the three Polish cemeteries. Nevertheless, the spiritual and social life of the Polish-American parish turned out to be a delicate compromise between priestly commands and selective responses by the parishioners, as historian Mary Cygan has detailed in

Angel Guardian Orphanage, 1907

St. Stanislaus Kostka altar servers, 1883

her case study of one Chicago Polish parish. The Polish pastor conducted a door-to-door canvass of the parish every year during Lent, collecting an annual parish registration fee from each family. When the family paid the minimum fee, the priest gave each family member a registration card and reminded him or her to perform the Easter duty, that is, to go to confession and receive communion at least once during the Easter season. Family members were required to hand in their cards when they made their confession. If a family failed in this obligation two years in a row, it was "stricken from the parish registry" and thus denied the right to baptize its children or bury its dead in the parish. This effectively cut them off from the Polish Catholic community. Polish parishioners rarely dared to neglect the Easter duty for the consequences were so severe, yet many adults failed to attend Sunday Mass regularly and the minimum registration fee often served as the only financial contribution to the parish. Many parents sent their children to the parish school for only the minimum two years required to prepare them for First Communion. Lay people charted their own courses in even the most tightly-knit and authoritarian of the ethnic leagues.

Most of the other Catholic groups from Eastern Europe, such as the Lithuanians, the Slovaks, and the Croatians, resembled the Poles in many ways, clustering around heavy industries on the South and West Sides. Like the Poles, also, they tended to be strongly Catholic and nationalist. Bohemians were the exception, less Catholic and more divided than the other Eastern European immigrant groups. Remembering the persecution of Jan Hus and other reformers in the Czech lands of the Hapsburg Empire, a majority of Bohemians had rejected the Catholic Church, styling themselves "freethinkers," or agnostics. These freethinkers maintained their own

Polish Roman Catholic Union parade marking the 44th quadrennial national convention, October 1946

St. Stanislaus Kostka first graders, 1892

Baptismal photo, Mother of God, Waukegan

institutions, separate from the Catholics, conducting weekend language schools and establishing the Bohemian National Cemetery. Only about 17% of Bohemians in Chicago at the end of the nineteenth century attended Bohemian Catholic parishes.

The Italians too were different from both the Irish and German mainstream and the East European nationalist leagues. Spread fairly widely throughout the city and inner suburbs, the Italians had two important clusters of settlement on the Near West and Near North Sides. Their occupations resembled those of the Irish at an early stage of their settlement in Chicago, mainly unskilled labor but with a certain amount of entrepreneurial flair and a disposition to start small businesses. Their parishes were large and nearly all Italians were baptized as Catholics, but the religious practice of the immigrant Italians, especially the men, tended to be nominal and occasional. Though the whole community might turn out for an annual saint's festival, few men attended Sunday Mass regularly and most families did not support the parish

Groundbreaking for Holy Cross (S. Hermitage) church

Italian wedding at St. Philip Benizi

financially. Italian indifference to the institutional aspects of Catholicism had deep roots in the nationalist *Risorgimento* which pitted the Italian state against the temporal power of the Vatican. In the case of both Italians and Bohemians, nationalism and Catholicism were antagonistic, conflicting forces, whereas among the Poles and the Irish nationalism and religion buttressed each other.

NO GROUP TOO SMALL

No Catholic ethnic group was too small to build its own community. The Belgians, for example, numbered no more than a few thousand individuals in Chicago at the beginning of the twentieth century. They were scattered across the city, many of them working as janitors in apartment buildings in all corners of Chicago. In 1903 a Belgian-American, Ernest Des Plenter, wrote a letter to Archbishop James Edward Quigley asking where he could find a Flemish-speaking priest so that his father could confess in his own language. Archbishop Quigley made inquiries and found a Belgian-born Jesuit, Fr. Ernest De Schryver S.J., teaching at St. Ignatius College. At Quigley's request, Fr. De Schryver organized the parish of St. John Berchmans, which subsequently served as a magnet for Belgians throughout Chicago. Had such a small ethnic group waited another decade they surely would not have succeeded in organizing their own national parish. Quigley's successor, Archbishop George William Mundelein, was a confirmed Americanizer and a prudent financial manager. He would never have consented to such a risky enterprise as a Belgian parish in Chicago. James Edward Quigley, however, was determined to leave no ethnic group wandering around the city looking for a congenial parish community. Historian Charles Shanabruch has accurately described Quigley's administration in Chicago [1903–1915] as "one long peace treaty" among ethnic groups.

The ethnic "peace treaty" even extended to the city's most downtrodden group, African-American ex-slaves. Most black citizens, of course, were Protestant evangelicals, but Chicago did have some migrants from black Catholic areas in Louisiana and Missouri, and some African-Americans were attracted to the larger, more "respectable" religious denominations such as the Episcopalians or the Catholics. Reputedly, the first black Catholic, Mrs. Eliza Armstrong, arrived in Chicago with her daughter during the Civil War in 1863, and was joined by her husband after the war. In the next few decades, several hundred more black Catholics settled in Chicago and were segregated in the narrow strip of territory just south of downtown called the Black Belt.

In 1881 the pastor and assistants of St. Mary's church reached out to the black Catholics around them, forming the St. Augustine Society and celebrating Mass for the African-Americans in the

Archbishop James Edward Quigley

Most Rev. James E. Quigley, D.D.
Second Archbishop 1903-1915

Noah and the Flood,
St. John Berchmans church

St. Monica School

basement of St. Mary's. In 1889 a black priest, Fr. Augustine Tolton, took charge of the congregation and began raising money for a separate black Catholic church. Tolton, born a slave in Missouri in 1854, had escaped to Quincy, Illinois with his mother during the Civil War. Local priests encouraged his desire to become a priest, finally sending him to Rome when no American seminary proved willing to admit him. He was ordained in 1886 and served for three years in his native Quincy before coming to Chicago at the request of Archbishop Feehan. Like Bishop Quarter, the city's first bishop, Chicago's first black priest worked himself to death. He raised enough money to begin construction of St. Monica's black Catholic church at 35th and Dearborn. [St. Augustine was the son of St. Monica. Both were from North Africa and many believe they were dark-skinned.] Though the church building was never completed, the congregation moved there in 1893. Four years later, on July 9, 1897, in the midst of a killer heat wave, Fr. Tolton dropped dead. He was "America's first black priest whom all could recognize as a black man." [Two previous priests with African blood, the Hurley brothers of New England, had generally passed for white.]

For the next dozen years, St. Monica's remained a distinct community as a mission of the neighboring St. Elizabeth's parish. In 1909 it again received a resident pastor, a white priest, Fr. John Morris. The parish, which now numbered about 400 families, started a parish school in 1912, taught by nuns from St. Katharine Drexel's religious order, the Sisters of the Blessed Sacrament. In 1917, Archbishop Mundelein asked a missionary religious order, the Society of the Divine Word, to take over St. Monica's and in 1924 the parish was consolidated with St. Elizabeth's, which had lost most of its white parishioners as the Black Belt expanded. St. Monica's/St. Elizabeth's was a segregated parish, but most ethnic groups at the time were segregated, at least in part of their own volition. As the author of a doctoral dissertation about St. Monica's, Helen Kathryn Rhodes, has concluded, "a 'de facto' segregated black parish with a black priest was practically the best that Chicago's black Catholics could expect given prevailing social circumstances." For a brief few, heroic years in the late nineteenth century, while Fr. Tolton was alive, they had both.

Fr. John Augustine Tolton, first African-American priest in Chicago

DIMENSIONS OF ETHNICITY

Archbishop Quigley envisioned an ideal parish encompassing a square mile of the city's turf. In actual fact, however, many ethnic parishes jostled these territorial parishes, and each other, in most inner city neighborhoods. If the city were actually divided into square mile quadrants on a map in the year of Quigley's death, 55 out of the 200 or so possible quadrants would have more than one Catholic parish. In 1916 the Catholic Church in the city of Chicago consisted of 93 Territorial (mainly Irish) parishes with 235,600 members; 35 German parishes with 62,700 parishioners; and 34 Polish parishes, counting 208,700 parish members. The minor leagues accounted for an additional 53 parishes and 139,200 parishioners. The 646,200 active members of the Catholic Church in Chicago formed about 30 percent of the city's population (counted as 2,185,283 in the 1910 census).

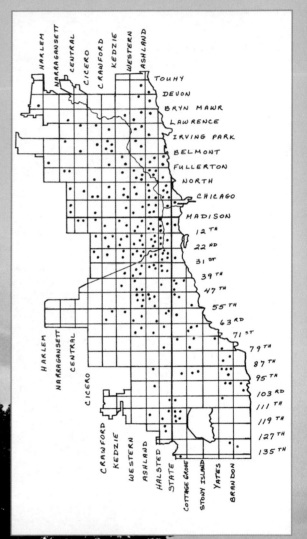

Division of Illinois into dioceses

Location of Chicago parishes, 1916

The diocese of Chicago had originally encompassed the entire state of Illinois. When it was raised to the status of an archdiocese in 1880, the southern parts of the state had already been separated into the dioceses of Alton (which later became the dioceses of Springfield and Belleville), and Peoria. The Rockford diocese, established in 1908, took in the northwestern quarter of the state. By the time of Archbishop Quigley's death, the Chicago archdiocese consisted of six counties – Cook, Lake, Will, DuPage, Grundy, and Kankakee (the latter four became the nucleus of the Joliet diocese in 1949).

Ethnic leagues extended beyond the boundaries of Chicago into these other counties as well. The inner, industrial suburbs, such as Cicero or Blue Island, were barely distinguishable from the city, with Polish, German, and Italian parishes clustered near industrial sites. Satellite cities such as Kankakee, Joliet, and Waukegan reproduced the ethnic divisions of Chicago in miniature. Even the rural areas included German and Polish farm communities, such as Gross Point or Posen, that had established their own parishes in the nineteenth century. Ethnic divisions were all-pervasive, wherever one looked throughout the archdiocese.

The term "ethnic leagues" was always more than a figure of speech. Though these leagues enjoyed no formal, legal status in either Church or civil law, they often functioned as corporate entities. The Polish pastors, for example, frequently met to set policy for the Polish cemeteries and orphanages, and to assess all the Polish parishes for joint building projects. Individual pastors commonly made loans to pastors of new parishes within their league. When St. Mary of Perpetual Help parish in Bridgeport was divided in 1910, Rev. Stanislaus Nawrocki loaned the pastor of the new St. Barbara parish, his brother Rev. Anthony Nawrocki, $28,000 from parish funds. The entire operation remained, literally and figuratively, within the family.

From left: Romanesque, St. Bridget,
Neo-classical, Ss. Cyril & Methodius,
(Hermitage), Baroque, St. John of God

THE GOLDEN AGE OF CHURCH ARCHITECTURE

The Catholic leagues of nations not only remained separate from each other, they looked different, as each ethnic group chose church architecture that reflected its own history and culture. The Catholic church building, adorned with statues, murals, stained glass, and golden altar vessels, was often the only place of beauty in a raw, immigrant neighborhood, an oasis of quiet and harmony amidst industrial cacophony. As historian Ellen Skerrett has argued eloquently in her lectures and essays, the church and its surrounding environs encompassed a sacred space that elevated the minds and hearts of believers.

The Chicago Fire of 1871 presented an opportunity for church-building, just as the Great London Fire of 1666 had given Christopher Wren his chance to pierce the skyline with graceful Renaissance spires. Chicago Catholics, however, did not yet have homegrown architects to capitalize on the opportunity. So the bishop commissioned a Brooklyn Irishman, Patrick C. Keely, to rebuild Holy Name Cathedral, and

Byzantine, St. Basil   Romanesque, St. Monica

Keely also designed the first Polish parish, St. Stanislaus Kostka. The German league imported architects from Milwaukee and St. Louis to rebuild their churches. Not until the 1890s did conditions ripen to produce a golden age of Catholic Church architecture in Chicago.

A vanguard of local architects emerged in the 1890s to serve the ethnic leagues and manipulate the historical styles so popular at the time. In all, 40 individuals or firms built 165 full-scale churches in Lake and Cook counties between 1891 and 1945. Most of the forty were native Chicagoans, born after the Civil War, apprenticed with one of the important architectural partnerships, and making their livings largely on church work for Catholics and other denominations. Seven architects (or partnerships) built the lion's share (79 of 165 churches). The most noteworthy were Henry J. Schlacks, who started his practice in the German league but eventually built for all the major groups; a partnership of two German Lutherans, Henry W. Worthmann and John J. Steinbach, who built the largest and most magnificent of the Polish churches; and the Irish-American Joseph W. McCarthy, who worked in the later time period (after 1916) as Cardinal George Mundelein's favorite architect.

If one knows how to read the architectural styles, a walker in the city can learn something of the history of the Catholic ethnic leagues. Chicago's Irish churches, whose congregations represented mainstream Chicago Catholicism, employed the greatest variety of styles, reflecting the changing fashions in church architecture over the decades. Thus, the earliest Irish churches built after the Fire, such as St. Anne and St. James on the South Side, St. Jarlath on the West Side, and Holy Name Cathedral were all designed in a high Victorian Gothic style. James J. Egan's design for St. Bridget's of Bridgeport, however, built in the 1890s, reflected the Romanesque revival ushered in by Henry Hobson Richardson's Trinity Episcopal Church in Boston. The magnificent basilica of Our Lady of Sorrows, on the West Side, showed the classical influence of the 1893

Victorian Gothic, St. Charles Borromeo

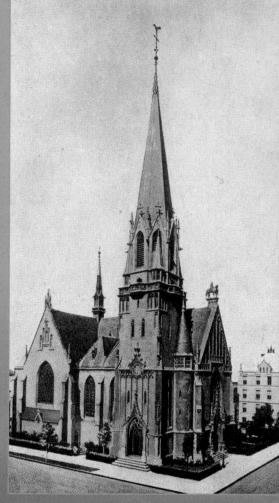

German Gothic, St. Martin of Tours

Chicago World's Fair. The single, most common style among the Irish churches, however, remained the Gothic. Though the Irish would rarely admit it, this style summed up their aspirations for respectability in the eyes of Victorian Protestants.

The German Catholics favored Gothic even more heavily, building nearly two-thirds of their churches in that style. Two of Henry Schlacks's designs, St. Martin of Tours on the South Side and St. Paul's on the West Side, provide handsome examples of German Gothic workmanship. An unsystematic look around the Chicago area suggests that German Lutherans also favored Gothic. In this way both Catholics and Protestants harkened back to the days before Martin Luther, when German Christianity was still united.

The social meaning of Gothic expressed in the previous paragraph is admittedly very speculative, but the preference of the Polish league for Renaissance and Baroque forms seems more clear-cut. The glory days of the Polish Commonwealth came in the sixteenth and seventeenth centuries when it formed the largest state in Europe, stretching from the Baltic nearly to the Black Sea, from the Oder River deep into White Russia and Ukraine. The Polish princes imported Italian architects and artisans to build their palaces and churches in splendid Renaissance and Baroque styles.

The Polish churches in Chicago, particularly the magnificent edifices that Worthmann and Steinbach built along the Milwaukee Avenue corridor on the Northwest Side, reflected the Renaissance glory of Polish Catholicism. Fully half of the Polish churches employed classical forms; only three Polish churches in the archdiocese were built in Gothic. St. Mary of the Angels, with a soaring dome to rival St. Peter's in Rome, is the ultimate example of the Polish Renaissance style.

Fr. Francis Gordon C.R., a leading member of the Polish Resurrectionist order, commissioned this building. [Fr. Gordon was Polish; he did not change his name; he was descended from Scottish soldiers who had settled in Poland during the Wars of Religion following the Reformation.] The church testifies to his daring ambition and the generosity of his parishioners. Built over an eight-and-a-half year period around World War I, it cost over $400,000.

Other ethnic groups and denominations also adopted architectural styles that reflected their national heritages. For obvious reasons, Italian Catholics favored Renaissance designs; English Protestants often imitated the London church of St. Martin-in-the-Fields, designed by Sir James Gibbs; Greek, Russian, and Ukrainian Orthodox congregations usually built in the Byzantine style of Constantinople. Many Jewish synagogues also adopted Byzantine forms, in order to emphasize their Middle Eastern roots and to distinguish their houses of worship from the more common Catholic and Protestant styles. Like the Polish Catholics, Polish and Russian Jews avoided the Gothic style. In a distinctive Chicago pattern, Romanesque design served as a lowest common denominator for smaller, poorer ethnic groups. So, for example, both the African-American St. Monica's and the Belgian St. John Berchmans parishes built in Romanesque style.

In an eclectic, but not random, variety of styles, church steeples joined factory smokestacks to dominate the skylines of Chicago ethnic neighborhoods. The church buildings of each immigrant nationality nearly jostled one another as they proclaimed to God and mankind, "Here we are!"

The schismatic Fr. Patrick Crowley

DIVISIONS AND UNITY

The Archdiocese of Chicago, during its ethnic phase, was organized in a series of ethnic leagues that were virtually sub-dioceses or quasi-denominations. In the Lutheran church, such ethnic leagues actually became independent synods and were counted as separate, self-governing denominations in the United States. Chicago Catholics also took religion and ethnicity seriously, playing for high stakes and creating a combustible mixture that made ecclesiastical leaders nervous.

The first archbishop of Chicago, Patrick Feehan, (Chicago became an archdiocese in 1880) worked mightily to satisfy all the city's numerous Catholic groups, establishing 140 new parishes from 1880 to 1903, a record never equalled by any other Chicago bishop. Nevertheless, late in his life, he faced a rebellion by some of his Irish-born pastors. This cabal of "F.B.I." (foreign-born Irish) resented the influence of American-born Irish priests on the archbishop, particularly the prominence of Peter Muldoon, chancellor of the archdiocese. When Feehan announced Muldoon as his choice for auxiliary bishop in 1901, a major controversy ensued which did not end until one of the Irish-born ringleaders, Fr. Patrick Crowley, had been excommunicated, and Muldoon had been prudently transferred to the new diocese of Rockford.

Polish Catholics also mounted a schism that dragged on through Archbishop Feehan's administration. The parishioners of Holy Trinity parish on the near northwest side resented the dominance of the Polish Resurrectionist Order, and particularly the pastor of neighboring St. Stanislaus Kostka parish, Fr. Vincent Barzynski, C.R. In 1873, a lay society at Holy Trinity tried to hire a pastor of their own, rather than remain a mission offshoot of Fr. Barzynski's St. Stanislaus. This

Fr. Casimir Sztuczko, C.S.C.

Holy Trinity parish, late
19th century

Archbishop Francis Satolli,
Apostolic Delegate

prompted the bishop to padlock the parish, which remained closed for nearly two decades. Only the mediation of a papal representative, Archbishop Francis Satolli, in 1893 settled the Holy Trinity dispute. Nonetheless, a number of other Polish congregations eventually joined the schismatic Polish National Church, first organized in Scranton, Pennsylvania. Polish Nationals celebrated Mass in Polish and allowed lay congregations more authority than the Catholic hierarchy was willing to permit at this time.

As a result of these divisive ethnic disputes, and the city's explosive growth, Catholic Chicago in the late nineteenth and early twentieth centuries acquired a reputation as an ecclesiastical disaster area and a difficult jurisdiction to manage. Consequently, Roman authorities did not appoint native Chicago priests to govern the archdiocese. All but one of the nineteenth century bishops were foreign-born, and the first two archbishops of the twentieth century, Quigley and Mundelein, were New Yorkers. Not until 1997 did Rome finally appoint a native Chicagoan, Francis George, as Archbishop of Chicago.

Yet it's possible to over-emphasize the divisiveness of ethnicity in Catholic Chicago. Though each national parish and ethnic league cultivated its own culture and language, they all professed the same religious beliefs and remained devoted to the person and office of the Pope in Rome. Though they did not like it, the individual ethnic parishes all conceded legal title of their property to the Catholic Bishop of Chicago in his capacity as a corporation sole. They also shared a common devotional heritage. Popular devotions to Jesus, the Blessed Virgin, and the saints had proliferated throughout the Catholic world in the nineteenth century, and were cherished by all the ethnic leagues. Six parishes representing four different ethnic groups were named Immaculate Conception in the Chicago archdiocese by 1910. Similarly, six parishes were named Sacred Heart, each one founded by a different nationality.

The interior of the city's lone Belgian church contained statues of Jesus, Mary, and Joseph, and St. Anthony of Padua, as well as St. John Berchmans. The stained glass windows depicted St. Patrick and his famous shamrock, St. Joan of Arc as both a shepherd lass and a warrior saint, and St. Helena discovering the True Cross, along with numerous scenes from the Old and New Testaments. Ethnic divisions sometimes stretched Chicago's Catholic community to the breaking point, but it ultimately remained *catholic,* or universal, in its beliefs and practices.

Window from Assumption Church (Illinois St.) depicting Pope John XXIII and Chicago bishops as the Twelve Apostles

1916–1963

Putting the Church on the Map

T he Catholic Church in America came of age at the beginning of the twentieth century. In 1908 the Roman Congregation of the Propaganda declared that the United States was no longer a missionary territory, for it had developed its own clergy and religious and possessed sufficient financial resources to stand on its own. Immigrant groups such as the Irish, Germans, and French Canadians, who had been in America for some time, had grown more prosperous, counting many doctors, lawyers, and business executives among their membership. The Church was no longer exclusively poor or working-class. Yet, American Catholics still found themselves in an ambiguous, paradoxical sort of limbo – the largest single denomination in the United States but a suspect minority in a stridently Protestant country. Supremely confident in their dogmas and beliefs, American Catholics remained ill at ease socially.

In the years surrounding World War I, a new generation of bishops came to power in the most heavily Catholic areas of the United States. American-born but Roman-trained, these leaders aimed to instill self-confidence in their Catholic congregations and at the same time prove to other Americans that Catholics belonged in the United States. They were "consolidating bishops" who tried to tighten up the administration of their dioceses and tie them more closely to Rome. Yet they also sought to throw their weight around in American society, thus earning respect from non-Catholics.

George William Mundelein, who arrived in Chicago in 1916 and remained there until his death in 1939, was an outstanding example of this class of leader. Chicagoans were more confident and cocky than most American Catholics, yet they had experienced divisions and controversies and were still immigrant outsiders for the most part. Therefore, Mundelein's leadership aimed to overcome these lingering problems. In the homely phrase used by many of his contemporaries, Archbishop (later Cardinal) Mundelein put Chicago's Catholic Church on the map.

AMERICANIZATION

Archbishop Mundelein found the separate ethnic leagues in Chicago administratively untidy and unnecessarily expensive. Born in New York in 1872 and ordained for the Brooklyn diocese in 1895, he was a third-generation German-American and a confirmed Americanizer. In his first interview after he was appointed to the Chicago archdiocese, he effectively revoked the ethnic peace treaty that Archbishop Quigley had declared: "The people of the United States must be Americans or something else. They cannot serve two

Archbishop George William Mundelein assuming legal title as Catholic Bishop of Chicago (a corporation sole), in the presence of Judge John P. McGoorty, February 14, 1916

German harvest festival, with a patriotic/military theme, St. Henry's parish, c. 1919

masters." Too realistic to try and roll back his predecessors' actions by abolishing ethnic parishes, he did, however, decree a virtual moratorium on the establishment of new, non-English-speaking parishes. He also established a central school board to coordinate curriculum in the parish schools, and this newly-appointed board decreed that English must be the language of instruction for all subjects except catechism and reading.

Mundelein also tried to diversify the appointments of parish priests. In the summer of 1917, he assigned several newly ordained priests of Slavic background, including three Polish-Americans, to mixed territorial parishes. In response sixty-eight

World War I rally, St. Theodore's Parish

priests of the Polish Clergy Association, founded during his predecessor's administration, protested against these assignments as an attempt to "denationalize" the younger priests. Three years later, many Polish priests in Chicago signed a petition to the Vatican requesting Polish bishops and auxiliary bishops in a number of cities, including Chicago. Mundelein made certain that the Vatican ignored this petition and he steadfastly refused to name any Polish auxiliary bishops. However, he quietly reassigned the controversial young Polish priests to Polish parishes and abandoned any further attempts to diversify clerical assignments. Mundelein largely lost the battle with the Polish league. However, by encouraging the use of English and slowing down the proliferation of ethnic parishes, he began unifying and consolidating the Catholic community in Chicago.

Nearly all the American Catholic bishops, including Mundelein, gave heartfelt and unstinting support to the American war effort during World War I. Four days after the American declaration of war on Germany, at a meeting originally assembled for another purpose, Mundelein pledged unquestioning support of the war effort: "The moment the President of the United States affixed his signature to the resolutions of Congress, all differences of opinion ceased." Chicago's archbishop feared that anything less than all-out support would leave Catholics open to charges of disloyalty, and the savage treatment that socialists and other anti-war dissenters received indicates that his fears were not paranoid.

The long range goal of Mundelein's Americanism was the building of a unified religious denomination that would attain "separate but equal" status in the United States. The fighting words "separate but equal" nearly always carry a negative charge when used today. Taken from the 1896 Supreme Court decision *Plessy v. Ferguson* that ratified the practice of racial segregation in Southern states, this social doctrine has been widely discredited. As practiced in the United States, racial segregation generally turned out to be separate but decidedly *un*equal. Yet Catholics pursued a different version of this ideal that largely avoided the social stigma of racial segregation. Catholic leaders did not use the exact phrase "separate but equal"; rather they proclaimed their desire to make their community "fully Catholic *and* fully American." At the same time that African-Americans were suffering under a hypocritical and unjust regime of legalized discrimination, American Catholics in Chicago and elsewhere were building a more authentic version of a "separate but equal" community of Americans.

ABOVE: Album Cover, Cardinal's Cathedral Choristers, mid 1950s

RIGHT: Paulist Choir, Old St. Mary's, 1928

Msgr. Meter and his choir, late 1950s

THE ERA OF THE BOYS' CHOIRS

Sacred music has always formed an important part of Catholic worship. In 1903, Pope Pius X issued a document encouraging the use of Gregorian Chant in the Mass and urging parishes and dioceses to organize men's and boys' choirs. This ushered in the era of the boys' choirs, a distinct period in Catholic history that lasted until the Second Vatican Council.

In Chicago, Fr. William J. Finn, C.S.P., started the Paulist Choristers at Old St. Mary's parish in the South Loop. From 1928 until 1967, Fr. Eugene J. O'Malley, C.S.P., who had sung with the Choristers himself, directed the famous choir, drawing boys from all over the Archdiocese. Cardinal Francis George is one of many distinguished choral alumni. The Paulist Choristers sang at noon High Mass every Sunday at Old St. Mary's and conducted numerous concert tours across the nation. The Choristers disbanded after Fr. O'Malley's retirement in 1967.

The Cardinal's Cathedral Choristers, drawn from Quigley seminarians whose voices had not yet changed, sang the Pontifical High Mass every Sunday at Holy Name Cathedral. First organized in 1918 as the St. George Choral Society, the Choristers were renamed in 1931. They attained their greatest renown under the direction of Monsignor Charles Meter from 1941 to 1963. In the 1950s the Choristers recorded Christmas Carols from around the world under the title "Carols of the Nations." The Choristers were eventually disbanded in 1980.

The reforms of Vatican II, which introduced the vernacular Mass and encouraged more simple, congregational singing, brought an end to the era in which the Paulist and Cathedral Choristers flourished. The sounds of the boys' choirs have been replaced by a wide variety of sacred music, from guitar Masses to gospel choirs.

Archbishop George William
Mundelein, named a Cardinal in
Rome, 1924

GOING FIRST CLASS

Cardinal Mundelein earned respect for his institutionally separate religious group by building on a large scale and always "going first class," by exercising businesslike administration and political influence, and by trumpeting his American patriotism. Though Mundelein was an outsider from New York, he shrewdly and swiftly identified himself with his adopted city. Gifted with a remarkable memory for names and faces, he soon knew every priest and parish in the city as a ward boss knows the voters on his turf. Mundelein also won honors that reflected not only on himself and his Church but on his city as well.

In March of 1924, Pope Pius XI named both Mundelein and Archbishop Patrick Hayes of New York to the College of Cardinals. A cardinal's red hat is usually granted either as a personal recognition of outstanding achievement or as an automatic honor due to the importance of the bishop's city. New York had been the first American diocese to have a bishop named a cardinal, fifty years previously; and by the 1920s it was considered a foregone conclusion that whoever served there would receive this honor. Yet no American diocese west of the Atlantic seaboard had yet received a single cardinal, much less established itself as an automatic recipient of the honor. Upon his return from Rome in 1924, Cardinal Mundelein attributed most of the honor to his adopted city: "It has been remarked that I am the youngest member of the Sacred College, and yet this is not remarkable. Chicago is by far the youngest of the cities possessing a Cardinalatial seat. . . . It represents the coronation of a triumphant youth, a youthful church in a youthful city, on a youthful continent."

Two years later, Cardinal Mundelein brought the 28th International Eucharistic Congress to Chicago. First held in France in 1882, the bi-annual Eucharistic Congress had become a massive pilgrimage of priests, prelates, and lay people. This devotional gathering honoring Christ

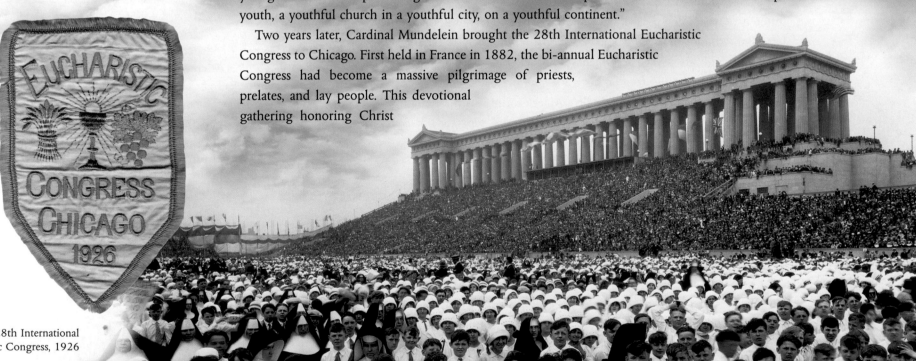

Banner from 28th International
Eucharistic Congress, 1926

Children's choir at
Eucharistic Congress, 1926

in the Blessed Sacrament had come to North America only once, to Montreal in 1910, and never to the United States; so Mundelein's ability to attract it to Chicago represented a considerable coup. A papal party of 49 cardinals captured the attention of the American press in 1926 from the moment they stepped off a ship in New York, through their triumphal progress on a specially painted red train from New York to Chicago, then throughout the Congress itself. About a million ordinary pilgrims joined the cardinals in Chicago from June 20th to the 24th.

Protestant reaction to the Eucharistic Congress varied with the distance from Chicago. In the rural Bible Belt, shock and dismay greeted the news of so much Romish display. Even in some large cities, Protestant reaction remained skeptical. One young Methodist minister in New York sourly noted that "the pomp of services, the exaltation of ecclesiastics may remove the thoughts of men from the humble Nazarene." Yet in Chicago, boosterism overcame nativism. The Chicago-based Protestant journal, *Christian Century*, remarked, a bit grudgingly: "One may criticize the taste of some of these things, as one may on aesthetic grounds criticize the orchestration of Salvation Army music, but . . . one must admit they are all highly effective." The Chicago daily newspapers were far more direct and effusive. The welcoming editorial in the *Chicago Tribune* best summed up the local attitude: "Chicago was chosen for the congress partly because the city is centrally located . . . but even more because the city is typically American. The tribute to the city is one which Chicagoans have not been slow to appreciate." To local civic boosters, the Eucharistic Congress was like the Olympic Games and a World's Fair all rolled into one.

Closing ceremonies of Eucharistic Congress, at St. Mary of the Lake Seminary, June 24, 1926

Solemn High Mass, Eucharistic Congress at Soldier Field, June 21, 1926, featuring the children's choir (the sea of white on the field)

The original St. Mary of the Lake
Seminary, c. 1850

AMERICAN ON THE OUTSIDE BUT ROMAN TO THE CORE

The Eucharistic Congress showed that Mundelein had assimilated his adopted city's motto, "Make no little plans." The seminary that he built for training Chicago priests illustrates this as well and provides an excellent example of his complete strategy for the archdiocese.

Chicago's very first bishop, William Quarter, had ambitiously established a school called the University of St. Mary of the Lake. Chartered by the Illinois legislature in 1844, it is the oldest institution of higher education in the state, older than the University of Illinois which was not organized until after the Civil War. In its early years, the University trained a number of priests for service in Chicago but it functioned more like a high school than a college by today's standards. It was always under-funded and frequently roiled by clerical factionalism. In 1866 the mentally unstable bishop, James Duggan, got into a terrible row with the school's long-time director, Fr. John McMullen, and abruptly closed St. Mary of the Lake.

When Mundelein arrived in Chicago, the archdiocese did not have a major seminary to provide philosophical and theological training for future priests. The bishop imported foreign-trained priests from Europe and sent native candidates to study in seminaries in various other cities of the United States. Ethnic considerations governed these decisions, like all others in the Catholic Church at that time. So, for example, most priestly candidates from German-American families were sent to St. Francis Seminary in heavily Germanic Milwaukee for their seminary studies. Polish students attended an exclusively Polish seminary in Orchard Lake, Michigan, or else Milwaukee's St. Francis Seminary where a Polish nationalist priest, Rev. Dominic Szopinski, taught them separate classes in Polish history and culture.

In 1920, Mundelein announced plans to remedy the lack of a Chicago-area seminary. He discovered that the charter for St. Mary of the Lake was still legally valid, so he had it reinstated. Then, with a $500,000 donation from lumber merchant Edward Hines as seed money, the archbishop built St. Mary of the Lake Seminary on a thousand-acre site in Lake County north of Chicago. In accord with his policy of going first class, he provided each seminary student with a private room and a bath and furnished the grounds with lavish accoutrements such as an Olympic-size swimming pool, a boathouse on the lake, ball fields and a private golf course. When the Lake County government challenged the tax exemption for this seminary property, Mundelein hired one of Chicago's leading law firms, Patterson, Kirkland, McCormick & Fleming (now known as Kirkland & Ellis), which fought successfully to retain this financial advantage. Mundelein thereafter

Birds-eye view of Immaculate Conception
Plaza at St. Mary of the Lake Seminary

Quigley Preparatory Seminary, c. 1925

retained the firm on a regular basis "as the watchdogs of my treasury and the defenders of my rights."

Manifesting his patriotism, Cardinal Mundelein instructed his architect to build the seminary buildings with early American, neo-colonial facades. Nevertheless, the interior style and functions of these buildings remained thoroughly Roman Catholic. Accordingly, the main chapel was modeled after a New England Congregational church in Old Lyme, Connecticut, but the interior was decorated in blue for the Blessed Virgin Mary. The main library recalled Thomas Jefferson's University of Virginia in architectural style, but the interior of the library was modeled on the Barberini Palace in Rome. American on the outside but Roman to the core, St. Mary of the Lake Seminary typified Mundelein's policy of building a "separate but equal" church. "It is almost symbolical," he stated on one occasion, "of the twin devotions of your heart, love of God and love of country."

By building a local seminary and not importing many foreign-born priests, Cardinal Mundelein built a corps of American-born but Roman-trained clergy, like himself. The seminary curriculum followed Roman seminary models and much of the philosophical and theological instruction was conducted in Latin. The best students from each class were sent to Rome for higher studies and for ordination in one of the ancient churches. At the same time, however, the seminary faculty tried to break down ethnic particularisms in the students, inculcating both American patriotism and a local *esprit de corps*, a dedication to the welfare of the Chicago Catholic Church as a whole, not just one ethnic group. As a result, by 1936, only 15% of the Chicago diocesan clergy were foreign-born, whereas a decade before Mundelein's arrival, over fifty percent had been foreigners. Not only were Mundelein's priests American-born, 75% of them were born in the Chicago area. By way of contrast, only 56% of the diocesan clergy in Mundelein's home diocese of Brooklyn were local products as late as 1945.

St. Mary of the Lake Seminary

Birds-eye view of St. Mary of the Lake Seminary, Mundelein, IL, c. 1934

Associated Catholic Charities of Chicago gathering,
April 1918

Catholic Charities Appeal, 1939

PARTICIPATION OF THE LAITY
IN THE APOSTOLATE OF THE HIERARCHY

George Mundelein did not put the church on the map singlehandedly, nor were the clergy the only significant actors in the drama. The Irish and Germans, and to some extent the newer immigrant groups, had produced many business executives and professionals who were eager to assume leadership roles in both church and state. In a letter sent to every parish at the end of his first year in Chicago, Archbishop Mundelein remarked: "Our greatest need today is a well-instructed, watchful, active Catholic laity. This is the day and the hour of the layman's apostolate." He didn't really mean it. Or rather, he did mean it but not in the same way we would understand such words today. The organization of Catholic Charities illustrates how Mundelein and other church leaders understood the role of the laity. They characterized it as Catholic Action, "the participation of the laity in the apostolate of the hierarchy."

On April 10, 1917 about 400 Chicago laymen [they were all men] attended a meeting at the LaSalle Hotel to discuss ways and means of reorganizing charitable work in the archdiocese and raising more money for charity. Cardinal Mundelein diverted their attention at this meeting by making an impassioned speech supporting the American war effort, but the lay leaders were not deterred from their charitable purpose. At the end of the year, in December 1917, they incorporated as the Associated Catholic Charities of Chicago. The roster of lay leaders who formed Catholic Charities reads like a 'Who's Who' of Catholic Chicago. Democratic political bosses Roger Sullivan, John P. Hopkins, and Robert Sweitzer wrote the constitution and by-laws of the group, and the board of directors included major business leaders such as the meatpacker Edward A. Cudahy and the lumber merchant Edward Hines. Though the board included a few Polish leaders, such as John F. Smulski and Julius Smietanka, and a smattering of German names, it was overwhelmingly Irish. The first president and long-time guiding light of the organization was a department store executive named Dennis F. Kelly.

The problem facing these charity leaders can be seen in the work of the St. Vincent de Paul societies. Most parishes sponsored such a society, whose main task was to seek out and aid needy families. However, the poorest parishes had both the neediest families and the least funds to help them with; so a new system was required to raise and distribute funds on a citywide basis. It was this task which the Associated Catholic Charities addressed with its first fundraising campaign in the spring of 1918. The parish pastors were asked to take up a Charities collection on Pentecost Sunday, and then volunteers from the local St. Vincent de Paul societies went door to door in each parish collecting even more money. Meanwhile, Dennis Kelly, his board of directors, and the archbishop himself solicited donations from corporations and wealthy individuals. The initial campaign, in 1918, raised $432,000 and the second year's efforts took in $509,000. These were significant amounts, considering the many demands and distractions of wartime; and the fundraisers prided themselves on keeping expenses down to less than 10% of the amounts collected. Nevertheless, they were privately disappointed, as they had hoped to raise about a million dollars per year.

There were severe limits to the effectiveness of lay fundraising in the Catholic Church at this time. Pastors were unlikely to pay much attention to demands from the lay executive board of Catholic Charities, and ethnic divisions afflicted charity work as it did everything else in the archdiocese. The leadership of Catholic Charities was unabashedly Irish so the Poles, Germans, and other ethnic leagues continued supporting their own institutions and ignored the Charities collection. Archbishop Mundelein, therefore, stepped in with his full episcopal authority and reorganized the still fledgling Charities organization. He relegated the lay president and board of directors to the task of fundraising in the business community, and took over the main charity appeal in the parishes himself. From 1920 until the late 1960s, the archdiocese imposed an assessment system of fundraising on the parish charity collection. Each parish was assigned a quota for charities, and if the Pentecost collection did not raise this much the pastor had to make up the balance out of ordinary parish funds. Compulsion worked where admonition had failed; the charity collection jumped to $639,000 in 1921 and reached $750,000 in 1924.

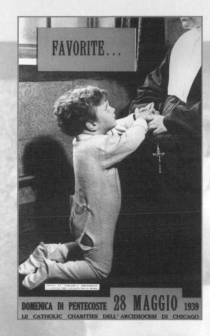

Once fundraising had been put in order, the organization of Catholic Charities fell into place. Mundelein appointed a full-time priest-director of charities, whose work overshadowed that of Dennis Kelly and the lay board of directors. The priest-director's main responsibility was to distribute welfare funds to the neediest parishes for the relief of poor families. The director also coordinated the work of pre-existing organizations, such as the various orphanages, although most of these remained separately incorporated and managed. Mundelein had initially been wary of association with non-Catholic agencies and thus refused any participation in Community Fund campaigns. The hardships of the Great Depression, however, changed his mind, and Catholic Charities has been a major beneficiary of the United Way campaign since the mid-1930s.

In practice, the Catholic Charities administration developed a pragmatic, flexible style that served the archdiocese well. Its work grew and grew until it eventually embraced over 100 different agencies and organizations offering relief and assistance to the needy. During the term of Mundelein's successor, Cardinal Stritch, the agency emphasized the needs of the aged, opening thirteen retirement homes. In addition, with a generous grant of over a million dollars from the Kennedy family of Massachusetts, the archdiocese and the Sisters of St. Francis opened the Lieutenant Joseph P. Kennedy, Jr., School for Exceptional Children in 1952. Catholic Charities also increased its efforts to assist the deaf and the blind. Indeed, as historian

Lt. Joseph P. Kennedy, Jr. School for Exceptional Children

Steven Avella has remarked, "Catholic Charities became a kind of safety net for any needs that slipped through the cracks of educational or parochial apostolates."

A priest-director remained in overall charge of the organization, but a lay executive director and many other specialized professionals soon took over the day-to-day work. Catholic Charities has been longer lived and more successful than any other project initiated by Cardinal Mundelein. The Cardinal himself and most of his contemporaries considered St. Mary of the Lake Seminary his greatest achievement, but the first rector of the seminary, Msgr. J. Gerald Kealy, disagreed. In an interview shortly before his death, Msgr. Kealy insisted that Catholic Charities was Cardinal Mundelein's greatest, though largely unsung, achievement. It accomplished just about everything it set out to do and it still pursues the work it was organized for: aiding the poor, the immigrants, and the homeless.

CATHOLIC ACTION

Though lay leaders took the initiative in organizing Catholic Charities, they were soon reduced to auxiliaries in the larger endeavor. Two other Catholic Action enterprises in the Chicago archdiocese owed their origins directly to clerical leadership: Bishop Sheil's Catholic Youth Organization and the "specialized Catholic Action" movements initiated by Msgr. Reynold Hillenbrand.

Auxiliary Bishop Bernard J. Sheil seemed made for Hollywood, a former baseball pitcher who organized youth boxing tourneys and earned a wide reputation as the "boys' bishop." The authorized, though possibly

Bishop Bernard J. Sheil and the CYO Boxing Tourney, 1950

apocryphal, story of the Catholic Youth Organization's genesis seems made to order for a Spencer Tracy movie. In the early 1920s, young Father Sheil drew the unpleasant duty of ministering to the county jail, occasionally walking young hardened criminals to their death in the electric chair. One day, so the story goes, Father Sheil whispered to the walls of the prison: "I will make you a promise and I will not forget. Someday I shall devote my life to this problem of youth." Sheil kept his promise by organizing the Catholic Youth Organization (CYO) in 1930. The CYO's signature activity was the annual boxing tourney. Sheil shrewdly judged that tough, problem kids, the kind who might end up at county jail, would not be drawn into an organization with ordinary sports or crafts

Catholic Women promote CYO Boxing Tourney

CYO day camp

activities, but that boxing would appeal to their street smarts.

Besides boxing, the CYO did initiate a full roster of youth activities including Boy and Girl Scout troops, baseball and basketball leagues, and summer day camps. Bishop Sheil also branched out into many other social action endeavors such as support for labor unions, community organizations, settlement houses, inter-racial forums, and adult education. Whenever anyone had a bright idea in the athletic or social welfare fields, they could usually get support from the CYO. Bishop Sheil took in strays as a matter of policy, both needy individuals and orphan organizations. His CYO grew into a veritable social work empire, untidily organized and shakily financed by contributions that Bishop Sheil elicited from wealthy individuals. If Catholic Charities was plodding, traditional, and dependable, the CYO was creative, unstable, and charismatic. Needy Chicagoans benefited from both.

One other approach to Catholic Action was developed by the scholarly second rector of St. Mary of the Lake Seminary, Msgr. Reynold J. Hillenbrand. Drawing on European examples, Hillenbrand instructed the seminarians and groups of lay people that he gathered around himself in the techniques of "specialized Catholic Action." In the specialized movements, small cells of Catholics organized themselves according to sex, age, and vocation; engaged in careful study of the papal social encyclicals; and attempted to apply Catholic social doctrines to the problems of everyday life. They employed a three-stage process of observation, analysis, and action, summed up in the three-word motto: 'See, Judge, and Act." The movements were specialized – Young Christian Students attempted to energize and transform the spirit of their schools; Young Christian Workers evangelized factory workers and promoted labor unions; and the Christian Family Movement sought to make married couples as holy and reform-minded as any priest or nun.

The full development of "specialized Catholic Action" in Chicago occurred after Cardinal Mundelein's death, during the administration of his successor Samuel Cardinal Stritch, in the 1940s and 1950s. Msgr. Hillenbrand formed a generation

Bishop Sheil presents boxing trophy to Cardinal Mundelein

TOP: Msgr. Reynold J. Hillenbrand, 2nd rector of St. Mary of the Lake Seminary

BOTTOM: Msgr. Hillenbrand conducting a liturgy workshop, 1964

Pat and Patti Crowley, founders of Christian Family Movement

of priests that was sensitive to Catholic social action and produced some outstanding leaders, such as Fathers John Egan, William Quinn, and Daniel Cantwell. Many lay persons, such as Edward Marciniak and the married couple Pat and Patti Crowley, followed Hillenbrand's guidance as well and pursued lifelong careers in social action. The summary comment of Fr. Andrew Greeley, in his short history of the American Catholic Church, still seems apt: "There began in the archdiocese of Chicago a series of experiments that would anticipate in many respects the spirit and teaching of the Vatican Council."

THE POLITICS OF RECOGNITION

In putting the Church on the map, Cardinal Mundelein was willing and able to throw his weight around politically. Catholic political influence at this time, however, was primarily defensive; episcopal statements on public policy issues remained very rare. The Church had many interests – a separate school system, tax exemptions, the welfare of its largely immigrant membership – to protect from political assaults. For example, the Cook County government had long subsidized Catholic orphanages and homes for abused women. The Sisters of the Good Shepherd had pioneered this form of public-private partnership in the nineteenth century when they gained tax support for their industrial school. The county courts sent orphans or juvenile delinquents, if they were known to be Catholic, to Catholic industrial schools and orphanages and provided a partial subsidy for their upkeep. The 1899 Juvenile Court Act ratified this arrangement, declaring that the court should place children "as far as practicable in the care and custody of some individual holding the same religious beliefs as the parents." In 1917 the Illinois legislature threatened to pass a bill that would ban such subsidies to Catholic orphanages from state funds. Archbishop Mundelein wrote to an Irish Catholic Republican named David Shananhan, who just happened to be speaker of the state House: "Will you kindly bury these bills in the waste basket or in a committee where they cannot be resurrected. . . . We want no

House of the Good Shepherd, late 19th century

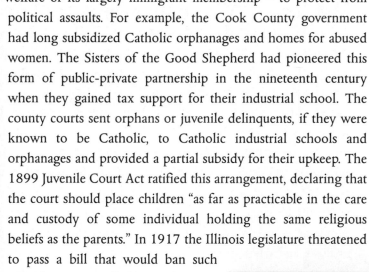

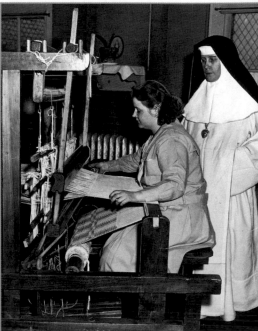

legislation on dependent children this session." Shanahan obliged.

Though Mundelein's emissary in Springfield during the 1917 battle had been a Republican, most Catholics voted Democratic and the Democratic party gradually asserted control of the city, county, state, and federal governments in the 1920s and 30s. Cardinal Mundelein forged especially

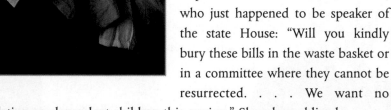

Learning to weave at the House of the Good Shepherd, 1939

Mayor Edward J. Kelly, standing behind Cardinal Mundelein

close ties with the local Democratic boss, Mayor Edward J. Kelly, and with President Franklin D. Roosevelt. During the Depression Mayor Kelly routinely allowed Bishop Sheil's Catholic Youth Organization to use Chicago park facilities free of charge for day camps and other recreational activities. President Roosevelt's welfare chief, Harry Hopkins, designated Catholic Charities as an official agency of government, authorized to dispense federal welfare funds to needy Catholics. In these and many other ways, church and state forged a private-public partnership.

Bishop Sheil and President Franklin D. Roosevelt at the dedication of the Outer Drive Bridge, October 5, 1937

Outdoor Benediction of the Blessed Sacrament, Madonna Center, 1952

During the winter months, the Mothers' Club sponsored a Bingo Night on February 14, the church ushers organized the St. Patrick's Day dance on March 17, and the Holy Name Society reflected at a day of recollection on Sunday, March 13. During the week of February 21, the eighth grade schoolchildren mounted a play entitled "The Maid of Lorraine," based on the life of St. Joan of Arc. The parish pastor, a former English professor at Quigley Preparatory Seminary, had written the play himself. Lent was observed with serious fasting by all adults, and Stations of the Cross services every Friday. Holy Week liturgical ceremonies were conducted according to the revised ritual introduced in 1956, but they were still spoken and sung in Latin.

An annual spring festival or bazaar had once been a mainstay of parish fundraising, but by 1960 it had dwindled in importance and was discontinued a year or two later. Increasingly, parish activities revolved around the school. On May 19, an Art Awards Night honored the best drawings by schoolchildren, and on May 26 the gym instructor put his star pupils through their paces at the annual Gym Show. The night before, on May 25, the Mothers' Club had organized a Sisters' Appreciation Party for the teachers in the school. The schoolchildren held the parishioners' attention as they crowned the statue of the Blessed Virgin on the First Sunday in May, Mary's month. As summer began, parish activities moved outside, with the parish picnic at Fullerton Woods in River Grove, on Sunday, June 26. The Holy Name Society had been sponsoring the annual picnic for a dozen years or so.

Towards the end of summer, the parish conducted a widely observed series of prayer services, the Forty Hours' Devotion. The forty hours commenced after the last Mass on Sunday August 21, then the Blessed Sacrament was exposed for adoration during the day and evening on Sunday, Monday and Tuesday. Each of the three evenings closed with a Holy Hour and Benediction of the Blessed Sacrament. As summer ended, the school year began, then another liturgical year commenced soon after.

Marian Year, Immaculate Heart of Mary School, 1954

The round of devotional and social activities at St. John Berchmans was typical of Catholic life in the middle of the twentieth century. Personal adoration of Jesus in the Blessed Sacrament and veneration of the Blessed Virgin Mary were two of the most popular devotions binding the diverse parish communities of Chicago together. The Eucharistic Congress of 1926 and the Marian Year ceremonies of 1954 had both filled Soldier Field to overflowing, but every

May Crowning, St. Vincent de Paul parish, 1950s

Fr. Boleslaus J. Kantowicz

LIFE IN A M.A.S.H. UNIT AND A BOOT CAMP

After the Japanese attacked Pearl Harbor on December 7, 1941, over 100 Chicago priests volunteered as military chaplains. At the height of World War II, in 1944, 67 Chicago priests were serving in the U.S. Army and 40 in the Navy. One of their number, Army chaplain James M. Liston, had died on February 7, 1943, when the ship transporting him to Europe was torpedoed and sunk. After the war, most of the chaplains returned to civilian life, but a few, such as Frs. Edward Saunders and Donald Kelly, U.S. Army and Navy, respectively, made the military a lifelong career.

Chicago priests returned to the colors when another war broke out in Korea. In 1951, 14 Chicago priests served in the U.S. Army, 6 in the Navy, and 5 in the Air Force. Two of their number, with the all-American names of Kelly and Kantowicz, can speak for those who served God and country.

Fr. Boleslaus J. Kantowicz, known as Boley to his classmates from the Mundelein class of 1940 and Fr. Ben to his family, was a veteran chaplain from World War II who returned to service when the Korean War broke out. But nothing in his previous experience had prepared him for life and death in a real-life M.A.S.H. unit. On October 8, 1951, he wrote to Cardinal Stritch:

"Am now stationed at 8063 M.A.S.H. 'MASH' stands for Mobile Army Surgical Hospital, a new army unit that provides immediate surgical assistance to the critically

Somewhere in the Pacific, June 1944

wounded behind the front lines. Its mobility and the skill of its surgical staff have saved countless lives. . . .

"Let no one try to tell you there is a stalemate here, for the mangled bodies of these men and the anguished minds of those who have not been wounded are ample testimony of the price of a so-called limited war. No war is worth the pain, misery, famine and destruction that have befallen this unfortunate land."

Back in the States, Fr. Donald F. Kelly (class of 1935) was serving as Senior Chaplain at the Naval Air Station in Alameda, California. In his "spare time" he volunteered his services at the nearby Coast Guard boot camp which trained 2500 men at a time but had no Catholic chaplain. Like Father Kantowicz, Fr. Kelly had volunteered for World War II but he never left the service.

On February 16, 1951 Fr. Donald Kelly wrote to Cardinal Stritch: "Many, many times, I long for the association of my Chicago classmates, and I ardently wish that I could lead the life of the average parish Priest in Chicago. . . . Your Eminence will be pleased to know that Chicago has a wonderful reputation, not only for its hospitality to servicemen, but for its particular brand of red-blooded Catholicism."

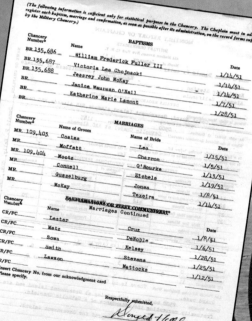

Fr. Donald F. Kelly

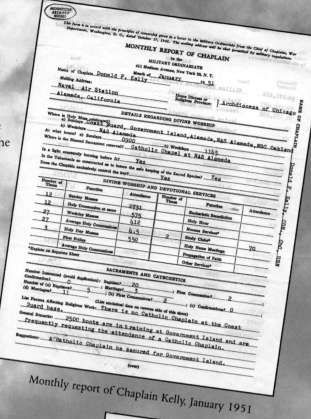

Monthly report of Chaplain Kelly, January 1951

51

year in nearly every parish the Forty Hours Devotion and the May Crowning brought these devotions down to the local, parish level. Dances, bingos, and other social events complemented devotional services. Many a Chicago Catholic congregation at mid-century adopted the slogan, "Live Your Parish."

TRAGEDY AND TRIUMPH

Parish life at mid-century, however, was not always idyllic and harmonious. Two tragedies — one ongoing and persistent, the other instantaneous and catastrophic — posed warnings for the future.

Chicago Catholics have always prided themselves on a close identification of parish and neighborhood. "What parish are you from?" remains a standard greeting when one Chicagoan meets another. This christening of neighborhoods as "sacred space" has assisted community-building efforts in parishes throughout the city, but it has also degenerated into battles over turf. Too often outsiders from a different ethnic or racial group were shunned rather than welcomed. In particular, when black Catholics tried to register as parishioners or enroll their children in school at all-white parishes they were usually told to go a black parish, even if it were miles away from their home. The flip side of "what parish are you from?" was "go back where you came from."

Throughout the first half of the twentieth century the Black Belt on Chicago's South Side grew and expanded into surrounding white neighborhoods, as African-American migrants from Mississippi, Alabama, and Louisiana came to Chicago looking for jobs and a better life. In 1910, 44,000 African-Americans comprised a mere 2% of Chicago's population; by 1960, their numbers had swelled to 813,000, 23% of all Chicagoans. The original black Catholic parish, St. Monica's/St. Elizabeth's was joined by two others, St. Anselm's and Corpus Christi, in the 1920s and 1930s. All three were

Fr. Daniel Cantwell

Holy Name Society institute at Our
Lady of Sorrows parish, 1951

Brothers and Sisters organize neighborhood cleanup, West Side

administered by missionary orders who focused their efforts on making conversions, with considerable success. As blacks attempted to move into other neighborhoods and parishes, they were usually met with hostility and often with violent resistance. Catholics could be found on both sides of the integration issue. Outspoken liberals, such as Fr. Daniel Cantwell of the Catholic Interracial Council, championed the rights of African-Americans to peacefully integrate into previously all-white communities; and a small number of diocesan priests, most notably Frs. Martin Farrell and Joseph Richards, began outreach programs in racially changing neighborhoods. Yet too often, Catholic priests and laity refused to welcome dark-skinned newcomers to their parishes. Cardinal Stritch, a Southerner by birth but a liberal by conviction, remained ambivalent and mostly silent on the issue.

A kind of guerrilla warfare developed on the South and West Sides of the city at the edges of the expanding black ghetto. On six occasions from 1946 to 1957, conflicts

Funeral for Sisters killed in Our Lady of Angels School fire, December 1958

between blacks and whites flared into outright race riots, most notably in the all-white suburb of Cicero in 1951 and at the Trumbull Park public housing development on the far South Side in 1953. As historian Steven Avella has noted, "All of them included significant participation by Catholic laity and, sometimes, the approval of Catholic clergy." Most of the Catholic laity simply voted with their feet and accelerated the already rapid move to the suburbs. Catholic parishes that had seemed like rock-solid anchors of white ethnic communities emptied out in a matter of months when it became obvious that neither legal maneuvers nor violence could stop black residents from moving in. The real tragedy of racial conflict in Chicago was the lack of vision, justice, and charity on the part of whites, including most Catholics. The more tangible, material problem posed by racial change was the abandonment of once thriving parishes by their white constituents. In the not too distant future, many inner city churches would resemble the "bare, ruined choirs" of a Shakespearean sonnet.

In one day of horror, unrelated to the racial issue, a single Catholic school building was reduced to ruins and scores of schoolchildren were killed or horribly burned. On December 1, 1958, a fire broke out in the school of Our Lady of Angels, a predominantly Italian parish on the West Side. More than one thousand four hundred children packed this overcrowded school, and many of them, trapped by the fire, desperately leaped from upstairs windows to injury or death below. Ninety-two children and three Sisters of Charity died in the tragedy. Archbishop Albert Meyer, who had arrived in Chicago just two weeks previously, and the Catholic schools superintendent, Msgr. William McManus who had been in office about a year, were reduced to shock and confusion as the authorities and the media began pointing

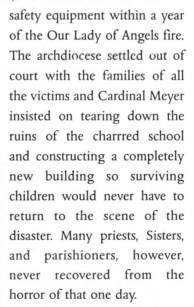

Senator John F. Kennedy and Cardinal Stritch at St. Patrick's Day dinner, 1956

fingers of blame for the disaster. In fact, like too many aging parish buildings, the school was a fire trap. The cause of the fire was never officially determined. Three and a half years later, a troubled youth admitted in a lie detector test that he had set the Our Lady of Angels fire, but he recanted his testimony in court and the case was dismissed by a judge in March 1962.

The Our Lady of Angels fire was the third most disastrous school fire in American history. It led to many new safety regulations, not just in Catholic schools, but in public buildings throughout the country. In Chicago, a January 1959 city ordinance required water sprinklers in school buildings of wood frame construction or two or more stories. It also mandated fire alarms wired directly to the Fire Department and monthly supervised fire drills. Nationwide at least 16,500 schools installed new fire safety equipment within a year of the Our Lady of Angels fire. The archdiocese settled out of court with the families of all the victims and Cardinal Meyer insisted on tearing down the ruins of the charred school and constructing a completely new building so surviving children would never have to return to the scene of the disaster. Many priests, Sisters, and parishioners, however, never recovered from the horror of that one day.

Cardinal Albert G. Meyer, Mayor Richard J. Daley, and President John F. Kennedy, at dedication of O'Hare Airport, March 1963

Racial change and white flight from the city exposed moral hypocrisy underneath the smugness of Chicago Catholicism at mid-century; and the near-abandonment of inner city parishes and the tragic school fire both highlighted a problem of aging and obsolescent buildings that would haunt the archdiocese later in the century. Furthermore, some observers criticized the archdiocese's handling of the Our Lady of Angels tragedy. Many years later, two journalists wrote a book about the fire that concluded: "When the fire shattered the aura of sanctity in which it held itself, the Church retreated to a defensive posture, responding the only way it knew how: it tore down the old school, replaced it with a new one, then acted as if the fire had never occurred." This judgment seems unduly harsh; nevertheless, most Chicago Catholics did move on from the disaster, remaining confident and proud.

Indeed, events seemed to be handing Catholics one triumph after another. In 1955 Richard J. Daley began his remarkable tenure as mayor of Chicago, which lasted through five terms in office. "Boss" Daley and his Democratic Party machine dominated Chicago politics until his death in 1976. Religious identity formed an important part of Daley's image as a devoted family man, rooted in the same parish and neighborhood where he grew up. He and his family worshiped at Nativity parish in heavily Catholic Bridgeport on Sundays, but he attended daily Mass at St. Peter's in the Loop, the Franciscan church a few steps from his City Hall office. In 1960, John F. Kennedy won office as President of the United States, the first and still the only Catholic ever elected to the top office in the nation. Mayor Daley's manipulation of the vote returns in Chicago was widely credited with ensuring Kennedy's narrow victory. In Rome, an elderly but visionary Pope John XXIII convoked an ecumenical council dedicated to *aggiornamento*, a renewal of the Church to enhance its mission in the modern world.

Daley and Kennedy, the Cardinal and the Pope, the chancery office and city hall; all seemed connected by webs of influence, as Chicago acquired a reputation as "a Catholic town." This statement was never literally true. At no time did Catholics form a majority of the city's population; yet their influence and attitude marked the city's landscape. Cardinal Mundelein had put Chicago Catholics on the map, and by midcentury the Catholic Church in Chicago could rearrange the map. When auto expressways sliced through the city in the late 1950s and early 1960s, the Cardinal and influential pastors convinced state and city officials to add at least four extra bends in order to spare Catholic churches from demolition. Chicago Catholics in the mid-twentieth century carried themselves with a self-confident swagger that verged on arrogance.

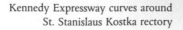

Kennedy Expressway curves around
St. Stanislaus Kostka rectory

3

1963–2006

Reaching Out, Speaking Out

Pope John Paul II reaching out to Chicago, 1979

A new era of Catholic history began at the time of the Second Vatican Council (1962–1965) when Pope John XXIII threw open the windows of the Church to let fresh air inside. Though the winds of change were invigorating, they also blew aside many familiar and beloved customs, thus unsettling numerous Catholics. The most recent period in Chicago Catholic history, therefore, has been marked by change and reform, but has also been filled with turmoil and confusion.

Besides the Second Vatican Council and the immense changes it brought in its wake, another event in the early 1960s marked a significant local turning point. On January 14, 1963, Cardinal Albert Meyer, the successor to Mundelein and Stritch, hosted the National Conference on Religion and Race at Chicago's Edgewater Beach Hotel. Co-hosting the conference, along with Meyer and the U.S. Catholic Bishops' Conference, were the National Council of Churches and the Synagogue Council of America. The Conference on Religion and Race marked a sea-change in Chicago Catholic attitudes. Just nine years previously, Cardinal Stritch had forbidden all Catholic participation in the General Assembly of the World Council of Churches that convened in Evanston, Illinois in August 1954. Now his successor was hosting and delivering the keynote speech to a conference of 657 delegates from all the major Protestant and Jewish denominations.

Cardinal Meyer's support for civil rights in 1963 represented a different kind of policy initiative. For the first time, a Chicago Catholic leader offered public policy leadership in an area where the Catholic Church possessed no significant self-interest. When Cardinal Mundelein spoke out in defense of the working class and labor unions in a memorable 1938 speech, he had been defending the Catholic population; but few black Americans were Catholic. Cardinal Meyer in 1963 was reaching out to other faith communities and speaking out forcefully on an issue of political morality, not interest group politics. Since then, Chicago Catholic bishops have been more outspoken than their predecessors on social and political issues. From 1963 on, therefore, Chicago Catholic leaders entered an outreach phase in which they joined with others and spoke out on controversial issues.

WE SHALL OVERCOME

The civil rights movement posed daunting challenges to the consciences of Catholics in Chicago. Led by black Protestant ministers and suffused with religious rhetoric and imagery, the attack on racial segregation in American society was a movement that no religious group could ignore. Cardinal Meyer highlighted the moral and religious dimension of the movement in his keynote address to the Conference on Religion and Race:

> The unresolved race question is indeed a pathological infection in our social and political economy . . . . It is also an obstacle to a right conscience before God. Our whole future as a nation and as a religious people may be determined by what we do about the race problem in the next few years.

National Conference on Religion and Race, January 1963: Seated, l. to r. Cardinal Albert G. Meyer, Dr. Benjamin E. Mays, Mayor Richard J. Daley; Standing, l. to r. Judge James B. Parsons, Lt. Gov. Samuel H. Shapiro

Albert Gregory Meyer was an unlikely and surprising champion of civil rights. A former seminary professor from Milwaukee, he had a cool, logical mind and a somewhat forbidding Germanic manner. Nothing in his background or experience had prepared him for the passion and turmoil of the civil rights movement. During his earlier career as a bishop and archbishop in Wisconsin he had studiously avoided involvement in "politics." Yet, he seemingly reasoned himself into a liberal frame of mind with a tidy scholastic syllogism. "All human beings are equal in the sight of God. Negroes are human beings. *Ergo,* Negroes are equal in the sight of God and must be treated equally. *Q.E.D.*"

Whether he actually reasoned this way or not, Cardinal Meyer acted as if he did. He took to heart a statement issued by the Catholic Bishops' Conference in November 1958 that "the heart of the race question is moral and religious. It concerns the rights of

Archbishop Albert Gregory Meyer arriving in Chicago in 1958

man and our attitude toward our fellow man. . . ." At a clergy conference in September 1960 he quietly but firmly instructed the priests not to fan the flames of racial hatred and to welcome black newcomers into their parishes. "We must do it, because the glory of Christ demands it." Admittedly, such admonitions had little effect in racially changing neighborhoods, as block-busting and white flight continued apace. Historian Steven Avella, who openly admires Meyer's leadership on racial issues, nevertheless concluded realistically: "Meyer's support provided a thrilling moment in Chicago Catholic history. . . but in the long run, the aim of the policy – that is, more stable neighborhoods and successfully integrated communities — failed. White Catholics simply moved out of the city into the suburbs."

More effectively, Cardinal Meyer began the task of integrating Catholic high schools. When Meyer arrived in the city, only a handful of Black Belt high schools had significant enrollments of African-American students. Fr. Martin Farrell of Holy Cross parish in Woodlawn convinced the Cardinal he should use his authority to compel the premier South Side high schools, such as Mt. Carmel and Mercy, to accept black students. In March 1960 the archdiocesan school board voted an official policy of racial integration, and Meyer backed this up with direct phone calls to recalcitrant principals. Farrell and other priests identified outstanding students in the black Catholic elementary schools and encouraged them to enroll in previously all-white Catholic high schools. At least 20 black students enrolled in each of the major South Side Catholic high schools in 1960; smaller numbers traveled great distances to welcoming North Side schools, such as Josephinum and St. Gregory's.

The Conference on Religion and Race marked the high point of Cardinal Meyer's principled campaign for racial justice. Like Catholic Charities many years before, the conference was the product of lay initiative. John McDermott, the director of the Chicago Catholic Interracial Conference, and Matthew Ahmann, who headed up the national umbrella group of Catholic Interracial Conferences,

Catholic Inter-racial Council of Chicago, John McDermott kneeling in center

presented the idea to Meyer in 1961. They envisioned an ecumenical gathering that would mark the 100th anniversary of the Emancipation Proclamation with a new dedication to racial equality. The Cardinal gave them the green light, and the landmark conference convened for four days of speeches and workshops in January 1963. Cardinal Meyer delivered the opening address and Rev. Martin Luther King, Jr. the final oration. The concluding session adopted an "Appeal to Conscience" that called for "a reign of justice in which voting rights and equal protection of the law will everywhere be enjoyed." Permanent, inter-racial, inter-religious organizations were established by the conference, at the national level and in ten target cities, including Chicago.

Chicago's host committee for the National Conference incorporated as the Chicago Conference on Religion and Race on May 16, 1963, with the Catholic archdiocese, the Protestant church federation, and the local synagogue council as the sponsoring members. Over the next few years it organized smaller conferences in the city and suburbs, brought together hundreds of inner-city black and suburban whites in family visits, and flooded the streets with clergy at times of racial tension in changing neighborhoods. It also lobbied Congress for passage of civil rights legislation.

Cardinal Meyer was absent from the city for long periods of time, attending the Vatican Council in Rome, and his tenure in Chicago was cut short by his untimely death in 1965. During his short time in Chicago, however, he put the Catholic Church on record in support of civil rights and racial integration. His successor, John Cardinal Cody, continued this rhetorical and symbolic support for civil rights; and many priests, nuns, and lay people played an active role in the growing civil rights movement.

In the mid-1960s the movement for racial justice in Chicago acquired a singular focus, the superintendent of the public schools, Benjamin J. Willis. Imperious and authoritarian, Willis resisted proposals to bus black students from their own neighborhoods to educationally superior schools in all-white neighborhoods. The temporary classrooms that piled up on the playgrounds of overcrowded ghetto schools were soon nicknamed "Willis Wagons." Al Raby, a black Chicago activist, once remarked that his life was simpler in the 1960s. He woke up each morning with one goal in mind, running Ben Willis out of town. When Rev. Martin Luther King came to Chicago in the summer of 1965 to encourage the city's civil rights leaders, he led a mass march of black and white supporters past the school board's headquarters in Chicago's Loop. King's "Willis Must Go" march of June, 1965 can be considered the lowest common denominator of the civil rights movement in Chicago. Anyone even vaguely supportive of the cause marched that day. These numbers, therefore, inevitably included many Catholics.

Though the marches against Willis were generally peaceful, a group of activists intentionally courted arrest, in the spirit of civil disobedience, by sitting down and blocking traffic at busy intersections. On a single day in June 1965, 3 priests, 6 nuns, and 14 Protestant ministers, all in clerical dress, were arrested. At this

Cardinal Meyer and Dr. Martin Luther King, Jr., at National Conference on Religion and Race, January 1963

time, Archbishop John Cody had been assigned to head the Chicago archdiocese but he had not yet arrived from his previous post in New Orleans. The vicar general and temporary administrator of the archdiocese, Bishop Cletus J. O'Donnell, issued a terse statement to the press supporting the right of individual priests to speak out as American citizens but affirming that they did not officially represent the position of the Catholic Church. Church authorities were deluged with a flood of angry mail from Catholics, outraged at photos of priests and nuns being dragged to jail. Some were classic cases of hate mail, but others raised an important issue that was never decisively settled in this turbulent era of reaching out and speaking out. Is a priest in a Roman collar or a Sister in her habit acting as an official representative of the Church?

Archbishop Cody had ordered the de-segregation of all Catholic schools in New Orleans and he had earned a national reputation for racial liberalism by excommunicating a white racist leader, Leander Perez. These actions may have positively influenced his appointment to the Archdiocese of Chicago. Shortly before he arrived in the city, the *Chicago Defender*, the city's premier black newspaper, welcomed the new archbishop, avowing "for the first time in its history, this diocese has a hard-fighting prelate. . . ." In any case, Cody continued strong Catholic support for civil rights in Chicago. He met privately with Martin Luther King on February 2, 1966, to discuss King's upcoming northern city campaign. At a July 10 mass rally in Soldier Field, he sent an auxiliary bishop, Aloysius Wycislo, to read a statement affirming that "your struggle and your sufferings will be mine until the last vestige of discrimination and injustice is blotted out here in Chicago and throughout America." One of Dr.

Sr. Rose Walter, M.M., Sr. M Raynold, B.V.M., Sr. M. Benet, O.S.B., Sr. M. Peter, S.S.N.D. marching in Selma, Alabama, March 12, 1965

John Cardinal Cody celebrates Black History Week, 1970s

OPPPOSITE LEFT: Cardinal Meyer and Msgr. Bergin in Rome for Vatican II

LEFT: Cardinal Meyer attending Vatican II

BELOW: Cardinal Meyer and Pope John XXIII

1961. When the council's first session opened in Rome on October 11, 1962, Meyer swiftly aligned himself with the progressive or liberal wing of the 2,450 bishops who gathered in Rome.

In four long and often tedious sessions the Second Vatican Council issued sixteen decrees, which varied in importance from earth-shaking to trivial. The Dogmatic Constitution on the Church [decreed on November 21, 1964] and the Pastoral Constitution on the Church in the Modern World [December 7, 1965] laid the doctrinal foundations for renewing the mission of the Church. Revising the topdown, hierarchical perspective, these theological statements affirmed the collegiality of the bishops and the priesthood of all believers, the People of God. In the Decree on Ecumenism [November 21, 1964] and the Declaration on the Relation of the Church to Non-Christian Religions [October 28, 1965], the Council Fathers reached out to other denominations and asked forgiveness of the Jewish people for the long history of oppression and discrimination. Perhaps the most noticeable decree of the council, from a practical point of view, was the very first one issued, the Constitution on the Liturgy [December 4, 1963]. Drawing on decades of liturgical experiments and reforms, the Council authorized the use of vernacular languages in the Mass and other sacramental celebrations.

Cardinal Meyer and Bishop O'Donnell returning from Vatican II, November 1964

Back in Chicago, Cardinal Meyer devoted his Lenten pastoral letter of 1964 to the ecumenical movement, urging local Catholics to treat all their fellow citizens with respect and justice. He also appointed a Liturgical Commission and convened a clergy conference in May, 1964 to instruct the priests in the renewed liturgy. Use of English in the administration of the Sacraments began in Chicago on September 14, 1964 and the Mass was first celebrated in English on November 29. Other alterations to customary routines followed later. For example, in 1970 the archdiocese authorized parishes to celebrate an "anticipated Sunday Mass" on Saturday afternoon or evening for the convenience of parishioners.

The American bishops made a singular contribution to the work of the Council by pushing forward the Decree on Religious Liberty. Latin American bishops still lived in societies where Catholicism was the dominant religion, and the European bishops had experienced a far more bitter and confrontational separation of church and state in their own countries. This left the Americans to make the case for religious liberty and toleration. Drawing on the theological work of the American Jesuit, John Courtney Murray, S.J., and encouraged by Pope John XXIII's encyclical *Pacem in Terris*, Cardinal Meyer took the lead. Meyer wrote directly to Pope Paul VI, who succeeded John XXIII in 1963, asserting that "the question of religious liberty is THE NUMBER ONE AND MORE IMPORTANT

QUESTION in the whole schema on Ecumenism." Meyer interceded with the Pope on two further occasions in 1964, when Council conservatives tried to bury the religious liberty decree in an unsympathetic committee and then tried to postpone a vote. The vote was actually deferred until the final session of the council, after Meyer's death in April 1965, but his strong advocacy had ensured that the decree would ultimately be approved.

Ordinary Catholics in America took religious liberty for granted, and they barely registered the Council debates on the subject. Lay people did not attend Cardinal Meyer's scripture conferences and they were not consulted on the changes decreed by the council. Most probably welcomed the use of English in the Mass and the more collegial attitudes of priests and bishops. Yet one seemingly minor

Holy Name Cathedral renovations, 1968

68

Holy Name Cathedral renovations, 1968

change symbolized a sense of unease that many lay Catholics experienced at the close of Vatican II. The Council Fathers drastically revised the Church's penitential practice of fasting. Catholics were no longer required to abstain from meat on Fridays throughout the year, and the Lenten fast was drastically reduced. The "fish on Friday" issue somehow epitomized all the changes that disturbed parishioners. If Catholics could now eat meat on Fridays, seemingly "anything goes."

Other practical changes in the day-to-day lives of Catholics followed the end of fish on Fridays. After the close of the Council at the end of 1965, parishes throughout the archdiocese remodeled their churches to fit the new style of liturgy. Ornate high altars were abandoned, or even ripped out, and priests celebrated Mass on simple tables, facing the congregation. Many statues and other devotional objects, such as vigil lights, were ripped out of churches and murals were whitewashed over. The whole fabric of sacred space that had eased the transition of immigrant Catholics in America was altered.

This highly visible transformation in the look of churches culminated with the renovation of Holy Name Cathedral in the opening years of Cardinal Cody's administration. Long in need of structural upgrading,

Women's liberation in the Church

the cathedral closed on the day after Easter, 1968, not to reopen again until Christmas Eve the following year. The church was completely gutted and the foundation rebuilt. A number of striking new artworks were put in place, most notably the massive crucifix suspended over the main altar and the immense bronze doors at the entrance to the cathedral. The old stained glass windows were replaced by highly abstract designs; and in lieu of statues, two metal sculptures were installed that almost looked as if they were smashed against the wall. A commemorative book on the history of Holy Name Cathedral concluded: "The renovation design faithfully reflected the liturgical changes instituted by Vatican II. . . . The building was stripped of most of its 19th century devotional pictures and statuary. . . . The final result was very different – back-to-basics and devoid of frills."

No more fish on Friday? Too bad! Cardinal Meyer on vacation

Some Catholics felt like the iconoclastic movement, the Protestant Reformation, and the invasion of the Vandals had hit the Catholic Church all at once. Others believed that the Council had not gone far enough and therefore took matters into their own hands. For example, many Catholics abandoned the regular reception of the Sacrament of Penance, even though nothing in the Council decrees had suggested this. Furthermore, most lay Catholics privately rejected the papal encyclical *Humanae Vitae* (1968) in which Pope Paul VI reaffirmed the traditional ban on artificial birth control. In fact, both reactions – that the Church had recklessly abandoned its traditions and that it had not gone far enough – had a similar cause – the bracing but unpredictable winds of change. When Pope John threw the church windows wide open, neither he nor anyone else knew what would fly in, or out.

DUE PROCESS IN THE CHURCH

In this volatile environment after the Second Vatican Council, reaching out and speaking out took many unusual and controversial forms. The Council Fathers had encouraged dioceses around the world to organize priests' councils or presbyteral senates to advise the local bishop and provide mechanisms for due process in disputes with authority. Archbishop Cody did not initially organize such a senate after his arrival in Chicago, so a group of mostly

Cross-section of racial and ethnic groups
prepare for permanent deaconate, 1970s

Ordination of permanent
deacons, May 21, 1977

PAN-AMERICAN PANORAMA

Though the permanent diaconate proved popular throughout the archdiocese, it held unusual importance for a relatively new group of Chicago Catholics, the Latinos. More than half of the first deacon class ordained in 1972 were of Hispanic origin, and a recent tally shows that between 20 and 25 percent of active deacons in the archdiocese bear Spanish surnames.

Ordination of Spanish-speaking permanent deacons, May 21, 1977

While the local Church had been wrestling with the changes of Vatican II, the face of the city had been literally changing. Not just African-Americans, but migrants from Latin America were transforming the population of the city; and unlike most black citizens, Latinos were nearly all Catholic by birth. Chicago is unusual in the variety of Latin-American nationalities that have settled within the city. Nearly 75 percent of all Latinos in North America reside in just five states: California, Texas, Florida, New York, and Illinois. Yet in the other major areas, one nationality predominates, such as Puerto Ricans in New York, Cubans in Miami, or Mexicans in California and Texas. Chicago, however, with its central location and wide variety of job opportunities, drew settlers from both Mexico and Puerto Rico (albeit at different times), as well as smaller numbers from Cuba, Central America, and South America.

Mexicans first came to the city about 1916, recruited to work on the railroads during World War I. They resembled the peasant immigrants from Europe who had preceded them, and indeed they settled side by side with Italians and Poles in areas of heavy industry. By 1930 Chicago's Mexican population numbered about 20,000, clustered in three different neighborhoods: the near West Side (next to the rail yards), Back of the Yards (by the meatpacking plants), and South Chicago (near the steel mills). Mexicans faced a threat that earlier immigrants escaped, the constant fear of deportation. Seemingly in 20-year cycles, the Immigration and Naturalization Service mounted sweeps for illegal immigrants. No other ethnic group has experienced the need to constantly justify its existence in America.

By the time Mexican Catholics arrived in Chicago, Cardinal Mundelein had begun to de-emphasize national parishes, but he was realistic enough to realize that the religious needs of the newcomers might best be served in their own churches. Following his recent actions in providing missionary priests for African-American parishes, Mundelein recruited a Spanish religious order, the Claretians, to care for the Mexicans. The Claretians established Our Lady of Guadualupe parish in South Chicago in 1925, and soon thereafter they devised an innovative way of financing their apostolate through the shrine of St. Jude that they established in the church. About the same time, Mundelein also gave the Claretians the old German church of St. Francis Assisi on the near West Side as a second Mexican national parish. A bit later, the Claretians extended their ministry to Back of the Yards with a mission outpost known as Immaculate Heart of Mary Vicariate. A decidedly second-class facility, Immaculate Heart looked like a garage with a church façade tacked onto it.

By the end of World War II, therefore, the archdiocese officially recognized two and one-half Mexican national parishes, a situation that was, in some ways, worse than no national parishes at all. As the community continued to grow, the few parishes fell short of meeting the Mexicans' religious needs. Yet when Mexican parents found their way to the nearest Catholic church to arrange a baptism or a wedding, an unsympathetic English-speaking pastor often told them to "go to the Mexican parish," even if it were miles away in a strange neighborhood. Mexican Catholics thus shared the experience of black Catholics – segregated out of sight and out of mind.

Puerto Rican migrants arrived thirty years later than the Mexicans, beginning after World War II. Chicago still offered industrial jobs, but many of the first Puerto Ricans were recruited by an employment agency for service as domestics and maintenance workers. By 1960, their numbers had reached 32,371 whereas Mexicans had increased to about 55,000. Not tied to the mills and the stockyards, Puerto Ricans settled in a more dispersed pattern than the Mexicans, who remained in the original three barrios and then spread further southwest into Pilsen and Little Village. Puerto Ricans, on the other hand, settled on the near North Side, in Uptown, in Woodlawn, and alongside the Mexicans on the West Side and in South Chicago.

For any number of reasons, the Catholic Church in Chicago had no intention of providing national parishes for Puerto Ricans. First of all, migrants from Puerto Rico were American citizens, not foreign nationals, so it might have seemed incongruous to provide them separate nationality parishes. Furthermore, the whole idea of national parishes had become increasingly exceptional throughout the twentieth century. After World War II, the Archdiocese was engaged in a tremendous building boom in the suburbs and the outer reaches of the city, so no resources were available for building more inner-city

Our Lady of Guadalupe Church

CYO Puerto Rican
Program, early 1950s

parishes. Yet the Puerto Ricans, like other Latinos, were indisputably Catholic, so they could not be neglected.

In fact, Bishop Sheil had been the first to notice and reach out to the Puerto Ricans right after the War. His private secretary, Monsignor Peter Meegan, took personal charge of an *ad hoc* spiritual and social ministry to Puerto Ricans, tendering welfare assistance and helping them find jobs. After Bishop Sheil resigned in 1954 and his CYO "empire" was dismantled, the Archdiocese attempted a new approach. As in so many areas, Catholic Charities took the lead. Cardinal Stritch asked Monsignor Vincent Cooke, director of Charities, to look into the needs of the Puerto Ricans, and he reported back with a series of memos, while immediately dispensing welfare aid to needy migrants. In a seminal recommendation on March 1, 1954, Msgr. Cooke suggested to the Cardinal: "We should devise a method of getting them integrated into our parochial and civil life. To bunch them in one parish with Spanish or Puerto Rican priests would hinder rather than hasten their amalgamation. They should be under the special care of thoroughly Americanized priests who speak their language and can gain their confidence." Cardinal Stritch and his successors consistently followed this plan in reaching out to Puerto Ricans and eventually to all Latinos in the archdiocese.

Mural at the offices of the Cardinal's
Committee for the Spanish-Speaking, 1960s

MISSION IN PANAMA

For nearly two decades, Chicago Catholics maintained a mission outpost in the Latin American nation of Panama. Responding to a call from Pope John XXIII for developed nations to devote ten percent of their resources and personnel to the Church in Latin America, Cardinal Albert Meyer struck an agreement with the Archdiocese of Panama City to establish an "experimental parish" in Panama. The first three Chicago priests, led by Fr. Leo Mahon, took up residence in Panama on March 1, 1963. San Miguelito, a sprawling geographical area on the outskirts of Panama City with a population of about 30,000 people, was completely unchurched previously. The purpose of the mission, besides providing church services to the people, was to experiment with new approaches to liturgy and evangelization suggested by the Second Vatican Council, and to serve as a training ground for North American priests interested in the Latino apostolate.

The Panama mission grew rapidly as several new parishes were established and the area grew in population to over 300,000 people by 1980. Eventually nine Chicago priests,

several priests from elsewhere in North America, and a number of Maryknoll Sisters, served in the mission. Five Panamanian men from the mission area were ordained priests and seven became permanent deacons.

The mission was controversial in several respects. There were conflicts between the North American priests and the local clergy, and the experimental nature of the ministry led some of the Panamanian bishops to question the North American priests' orthodoxy. Cardinal Meyer's successor, Cardinal John Cody, visited San Miguelito in both 1966 and 1968. Much to everyone's surprise, including his own, he was charmed by the people and fascinated by the experiment. Eventually, however, the continuing controversies and the heaviness of the financial burden spelled the end of the Panama mission. When the last Chicago priest was recalled in 1981, he was not replaced and the Archdiocese gradually phased out its financial support.

People of Panama

BELOW: Priests of the Panama Mission, with visitors in July 1966:
l. to r. Fr. John Keating, Fr. Leo Mahon, Fr. John Enright, Archbishop John Cody, Fr. James Murphy, Fr. John Greeley, Fr. Leo McTernan
BACKGROUND: Hillside in San Miguelito

gradually took over many parishes on the northwest and southwest sides by sheer force of numbers. As early as 1971 45 city parishes and eight more in the suburbs had a significant enough Hispanic presence to merit assignment of a priest who could speak Spanish. In many formerly European national parishes, Mass is now said in three languages on any Sunday – Polish [or Lithuanian, or Slovak, or Italian], Spanish, and English. The Spanish-speakers might come from a half dozen or more countries. The Chicago archdiocese forms a pan-American panorama.

The outreach to Hispanic Catholics did not always go smoothly, of course. Sometimes the first Spanish Mass in a parish was scheduled at an inconvenient time or conducted in the church basement, so the Spanish-speaking newcomers felt like second-class citizens. Yet Hispanic Catholics added new energy to the devotional life of the post-Vatican II church, with the sounds of mariachis and congas often ringing out at their liturgies. A re-enactment of the *Via Crucis* has transformed the streets of Pilsen into a pilgrimage route every Good Friday since 1977. Eight parishes in the formerly East European but now Mexican neighborhood sponsor the street procession, which begins at Providence of God church, snakes its way along Eighteenth Street, then culminates with a re-enactment of the Crucifixion in Harrison Park. Afterwards, the pilgrims conclude with a prayer service at St. Adalbert's church. Often the Cardinal joins the worshippers at the concluding ceremonies.

Karol Cardinal Wojtyla, Mayor Richard J. Daley, John Cardinal Cody, August 1976

The *Via Crucis* not only recalls the agonies of Jesus but focuses on the sufferings and injustices of this world as well. Each year the stations of the procession highlight persistent problems in the neighborhood, such as gang violence, alcoholism, unemployment, or transit cutbacks. Thus Hispanic Catholics bear witness to both their spirituality and their yearning for social justice, reaching out and speaking out as a new, powerful voice in Chicago.

BE NOT AFRAID

Latinos have not been the only Catholics in Chicago to celebrate their faith with striking public ceremonies. In the nineteenth and early twentieth centuries, Italian immigrants mounted elaborate street festivals on holydays and saints' days, and Irish Catholics flooded the streets of the South Side on days of First Communion or Confirmation. Polish Catholics sorrowfully mourned their dead in slow processions from the neighborhood funeral home to the local parish church where the Requiem Mass would be sung.

Chicago Catholics punctuated the twentieth century with city-wide religious celebrations that brought all Catholic groups together. Each generation cherished memories of these events that lasted a lifetime. In 1926 the Eucharistic Congress packed the newly built Soldier Field to overflowing with an estimated 150,000 worshippers at an outdoor Mass. On the Congress's last day, perhaps 600,000 made the 40-mile pilgrimage to St. Mary of the Lake Seminary in Mundelein, Illinois, braving a fierce downpour of rain during the closing ceremonies. Catholics filled Soldier Field once again in 1954 for commemoration of the Marian Year. Each of these celebrations manifested a defensiveness that reflected their times. The closing ceremonies of the Eucharistic Congress were held

Pope John Paul II with Cardinal Cody,
Rome, 1978

on private property in then sparsely populated Lake County, since previous Congresses in non-Catholic countries had prompted anti-Catholic demonstrations. The Marian Year Mass was hastily organized at the last minute in response to, and as competition for, a Protestant ceremony conducted by the World Council of Churches in Soldier Field a few months earlier. However, in 1979, in the new era of reaching out and speaking out, Chicagoans welcomed a visit from Pope John Paul II that not only energized their Catholic faith but brought the whole city together in celebration.

The College of Cardinals surprised the world in October 1978 by electing Cardinal Karol Wojtyla of Poland as the first non-Italian pope in over four centuries. Wojtyla had already visited Chicago on two separate occasions, in September 1969 and in August 1976. These earlier visits had been private tours by a little-known Polish bishop and were barely noted outside the Polish-American community. Cardinal Cody had not even been present in the city in 1969 to welcome Wojtyla. His reception as pope in 1979, however, was far grander.

In his first year as pope, John Paul II had already made historic visits to Mexico and to his native Poland. The nine triumphant days that the Pope spent in his homeland in June 1979 would serve as a catalyst for the overthrow of Communist rule in Eastern Europe and Russia. Everywhere John Paul II went he heartened his audience with the invocation "Be Not Afraid." In Poland, these boldly repeated words had the effect of a "psychological earthquake," in the words of Austrian Cardinal Franz Konig. The Polish state had systematically downplayed the role of the Catholic Church in Polish history. When Poles worldwide had celebrated their Millennium of Christianity in 1966, the Communist state banned a visit to Poland by Pope Paul VI and prevented the Polish Primate, Cardinal Stefan Wyszynski, from travelling to Rome. Poland's government played games with Wojtyla's schedule in 1979 as well, refusing his first choice of dates on the Feast of St. Stanislaus. Yet they dared not keep him out altogether, and the popular outpouring in June 1979 showed how Catholic Polish society remained. The peaceful organization of the crowds by Catholic organizers demonstrated that Poles could function as a civil society outside of state control, and provided a model of non-violent civil protest. A year later, Poles took these

Pope John Paul II greets crowds at
Five Holy Martyrs parish, October 5, 1979

lessons to heart and mounted the Solidarity movement. Though first suppressed by Communist authorities, a decade later Solidarity came to power in Poland's first post-Communist government.

Nothing in John Paul II's long pontificate quite topped his cataclysmic effect on Poland and Eastern Europe, but his first tour of America in autumn of 1979 was significant nonetheless. After three days in Ireland, the Pope visited six American cities from October 1 to October 7, addressing the United Nations General Assembly in New York and meeting with the President and members of Congress at the White House in Washington. The Chicago leg of the tour came at about the midpoint of the trip, and the Pope spent just 37 hours in the city, but his appearances left an indelible imprint.

Naturally the city's immense Polish population greeted the pontiff most warmly of all. They lined Milwaukee Avenue to cheer his motorcade from O'Hare on the evening of October 4th, and felt intense disappointment when his late arrival prevented a stop at the Copernicus Center on Lawrence

ABOVE: Pope John Paul II's motorcade to Grant Park, October 5, 1979

BELOW: Pope John Paul II addresses crowd at Quigley South, October 5, 1979

Visit to Chicago
of
HIS HOLINESS
POPE JOHN PAUL II

Mass at Grant Park, October 5, 1979

Mass at
Grant Park

3:00 p.m.
October 5, 1979

ALTAR
SEATING

Ticket for Grant Park Mass

Crowds at Grant Park Mass

Avenue. The next morning 17,500 members of Polish parishes who had secured much-coveted tickets attended Mass at Five Holy Martyrs parish on the southwest side.

Perhaps fifty thousand more packed the parking lots and surrounding yards to catch a glimpse of the first and only Polish pope. In traditional Polish fashion, they yelled *Sto lat*, may you live 100 years. The pontiff would come closer to realizing that wish than most suspected, eventually serving out the third longest tenure of any pope in history.

Yet John Paul II's mission was not just to Poles and Polish-Americans. Before the Five Holy Martyrs Mass, he had visited a predominantly Mexican parish in Pilsen and had specifically requested that his motorcade wind through African-American neighborhoods. After the Polish Mass, he spent the midday hours at Quigley Seminary South in substantive meetings with a delegation of American bishops. Crowds surrounded the seminary throughout these meetings, so the Pope made an unscheduled climb to the roof of the building to greet the well-wishers. Then at 3 PM Pope John Paul II celebrated a public Mass for all Chicagoans in the city's "front yard," Grant Park. Estimates of the crowd run from a half million to a million and a half worshipers and spectators, Catholic and non-Catholic alike. Every Chicagoan present that day cherishes a memory of peace and harmony in the crowd, remarking, for instance, that a black man offered to hold a white child on his shoulders so he could catch a better view of the pontiff.

The Pope captured exactly the right theme for this diverse gathering in one of America's most polyglot cities. He preached a homily on the unity of the American nation, the Catholic Church, and all of humanity. "Your ancestors came from many different countries," the Pope began. "The pattern repeats itself over and over: E pluribus unum, the many form a new unity. . . . This is America in her ideal and her resolution: 'one nation, under God, indivisible, with liberty and justice for all'." Then the Pope continued: "But there is another reality that I see when I look at you. . . . Coming together around the altar of sacrifice to break the Bread of the Holy Eucharist with the Successor of Peter, you testify to this even deeper reality: to your unity as members of the People of God." The Pope proclaimed that the Catholic Church was the People of God, not just the 370 bishops concelebrating with him that day; and he embraced all of Chicago and America, not just the Catholic Church. To all people of good will he left his indelible message, "Be Not Afraid."

Pope John Paul II approaches altar for Grant Park Mass

FORMER ORDINARIES

RT. REV. WILLIAM QUARTER: 1844–1848

RT. REV. JAMES O. VAN DE VELDE, SJ: 1848–1853

RT. REV. ANTHONY O'REGAN: 1854–1858

RT. REV. JAMES DUGGAN: 1859–1869

RT. REV. THOMAS FOLEY: 1869–1879 (Coadjutor Bishop and
Administrator)

MOST REV. PATRICK A. FEEHAN: 1880–1902

MOST REV. JAMES E. QUIGLEY: 1903–1915

HIS EMINENCE, GEORGE CARDINAL MUNDELEIN: 1915–1939

HIS EMINENCE, SAMUEL CARDINAL STRITCH: 1939–1958

HIS EMINENCE, ALBERT CARDINAL MEYER: 1958–1965

HIS EMINENCE, JOHN CARDINAL CODY: 1965–1982

HIS EMINENCE, JOSEPH CARDINAL BERNARDIN: 1982–1996

HIS EMINENCE, FRANCIS CARDINAL GEORGE: 1997–

AUXILIARY BISHOPS OF CHICAGO

MOST REV. ALEXANDER J. McGAVICK: 1898–1921

MOST REV. PETER J. MULDOON: 1901–1908

MOST REV. PAUL P. RHODE: 1908–1915

MOST REV. EDWARD F. HOBAN: 1921–1928

MOST REV. BERNARD J. SHEIL: 1928–1969

MOST REV. WILLIAM D. O'BRIEN: 1934–1962

MOST REV. WILLIAM E. COUSINS: 1948–1952)

MOST REV. RAYMOND P. HILLINGER: 1956–1971

MOST REV. ALOYSIUS J. WYCISLO: 1960–1968

MOST REV. CLETUS F. O'DONNELL: 1960–1967

MOST REV. JOHN L. MAY: 1967–1969

MOST REV. THOMAS J. GRADY: 1967–1974

MOST REV. WILLIAM E. McMANUS: 1967–1976

MOST REV. ALFRED L. ABRAMOWICZ: 1968–1995

MOST REV. MICHAEL R. DEMPSEY: 1968–1974

MOST REV. NEVIN W. HAYES, O.Carm.: 1971–1988

MOST REV. TIMOTHY J. LYNE: 1983–1995

MOST REV. JOHN G. VLAZNY: 1983–1987

MOST REV. PLACIDO RODRIGUEZ, C.M.F.: 1983–1994

MOST REV. WILTON D. GREGORY: 1983–1994

MOST REV. THAD J. JAKUBOWSKI: 1988–2003

MOST REV. JOHN R. GORMAN: 1988–2003

MOST REV. RAYMOND E. GOEDERT: 1991–2003

MOST REV. EDWIN M. CONWAY: 1995–2004

MOST REV. GERALD F. KICANAS: 1995–2001

MOST REV. GEORGE V. MURRY, S.J.: 1995–1999

MOST REV. JOHN R. MANZ: 1996–

MOST REV. JOSEPH N. PERRY: 1998–

MOST REV. JEROME E. LISTECKI: 2000–2005

MOST REV. FRANCIS J. KANE: 2003–

MOST REV. THOMAS J. PAPROCKI: 2003–

MOST REV. GUSTAVO GARCIA-SILLER, M.Sp.S.: 2003–

MOST REV. GEORGE J. RASSAS: 2006–

LOOKING FORWARD

On May 7, 1997, Francis George became the first native-born Chicagoan to serve as Archbishop of Chicago. He was born on January 16, 1937, and grew up in St. Pascal's parish on the northwest side. His older sister, Margaret Mary Cain, summed up his childhood for *The New World*: "At five years old, Francis knew he wanted to be a priest. That has never changed. He was the head altar boy at St. Pascal's, sang in the Paulist choir and was first in his class."

Midway through the eighth grade, Francis George was struck by a severe case of polio and was confined to St. Francis Hospital in Evanston for three months. Unable to attend Quigley Seminary because of his handicapped leg, he enrolled at St. Henry Seminary in downstate Belleville, then entered the Oblates of Mary Immaculate. He is, therefore, only the second Chicago bishop from a religious order, and the first who has overcome a significant physical handicap.

Ordained in 1963, Father George earned Masters and Doctorate degrees in both philosophy and theology, taught at five different seminaries or universities, and held office as provincial superior in the Midwest and as vicar general of his order in Rome from 1974 to 1986. Before coming to Chicago, he served as bishop of Yakima, Washington, and then archbishop of Portland, Oregon. Less than a year after his return to Chicago, he was named Cardinal on February 21, 1998.

Cardinal George took up several challenges outlined by Cardinal Bernardin in the year before his death. The first of these is evangelization. Cardinal George's first pastoral letter was entitled "On Becoming an Evangelizing Church," which reminded the faithful that the Church must go beyond providing services and call all people to conversion. The second challenge lies in passing on the faith to the next generation of Catholics. The Cardinal has spearheaded a renewal of catechetical programs and Catholic school curriculum. The third challenge is the preparation of ordained priests, permanent deacons, and lay ecclesial ministers. Seminary training and lay ministerial formation have been reviewed and renewed. In addition, priests and seminarians have been recruited from Poland, Mexico, Vietnam, the Philippines, and Africa in order to meet the needs of new immigrants. The face of the presbyterate matches the faces of Catholics in the pews.

Cardinal George has spoken out forcefully for racial justice and has continued to seek common ground with religious leaders of all faiths. Unfortunately, he has also had to deal with the aftermath of the priests' child abuse scandal, both in Chicago and at the national bishops' conference. While the sin of sexual abuse still manifests itself within the Catholic clergy and our society as a whole, the Cardinal continues to promote awareness and the need to confront this sin within our schools and parishes and to work toward the healing of victims.

The spiritual renewal of the Archdiocese, along with the strengthening of its mission, has brought many Catholics to adoration of the Blessed Sacrament, processions and public devotions. A Liturgical Institute with a national purpose has been established at the Seminary. The Archdiocese was consecrated to the Immaculate Conception of the Blessed Virgin Mary in 2004, and a new community of Poor Clares brings contemplative life to the southern part of the Archdiocese.

After the death of Pope John Paul II, Chicago's Cardinal participated in the conclave that chose Pope Benedict XVI. Cardinal George is looking confidently towards the future as a pastor and teacher. He enthusiastically supported the preparation of this history of the Archdiocese of Chicago, not out of any sense of nostalgia, but because he hopes to build on Chicago's legacy of faithful leadership in charting a course for the new century. The Cardinal's motto is "To Christ be Glory in the Church."

Cardinal Francis George, OMI, eighth Archbishop and sixth Cardinal of Chicago

BIBLIOGRAPHY

Prologue

Danckers, Ulrich, and Meredith, Jane. *Early Chicago*. 1999.

Dolan, Jay P. *The American Catholic Experience*. 1985.

Garraghan, Gilbert J. *The Catholic Church in Chicago, 1673–1871*. 1921

Hoy, Suellen. "Caring for Chicago's Women and Girls." *Journal of Urban History*. 1997.

Pierce, Bessie Louise. *A History of Chicago. Volume I, 1673–1848*. 1937.

Skerrett, Ellen; Kantowicz, Edward R.; and Avella, Steven. *Catholicism, Chicago Style*. 1993.

Walch, Timothy G. "Catholic Social Institutions and Urban Development." *Catholic Historical Review*. 1978.

Chapter 1

Burns, James A. *The Growth and Development of the Catholic School System in the United States*. 1912.

Cygan, Mary. "Ethnic Parish as Compromise: The Spheres of Clerical and Lay Authority in a Polish American Parish, 1911-1930." Cushwa Center Working Paper. 1983.

Ewens, Mary. "The Leadership of Nuns in Immigrant Catholicism," in *Women and Religion in America*, edited by Rosemary Radford Ruether. 1981.

Greene, Victor. *For God and Country: The Rise of Polish and Lithuanian Ethnic Consciousness in America*. 1975.

Hemesath, Sr. Caroline. *From Slave to Priest: A Biography of the Rev. Augustine Tolton (1854–1897)*. 1973.

Kantowicz, Edward R. "To Build the Catholic City." *Chicago History*. 1985.

Parot, Joseph J. *Polish Catholics in Chicago, 1850–1920*. 1981.

Rhodes, Helen Kathryn Marie. "An Historical Analysis of the Racial, Community and Religious Forces in the Establishment and Development of St. Monica's Parish Chicago 1890-1930." Doctorate of Education dissertation, Loyola University, 1993.

Sanders, James W. *The Education of an Urban Minority: Catholics in Chicago, 1833–1965*. 1977.

Shanabruch, Charles. *Chicago's Catholics: The Evolution of an American Identity*. 1981.

Skerrett, Ellen, et al. *Catholicism, Chicago Style*. 1993.

Chapter 2

Avella, Steven M. *This Confident Church: Catholic Leadership and Life in Chicago, 1940–1965*. 1992

Cowan, David, & Kuenster, John. *To Sleep With the Angels: The Story of a Fire*. 1996.

Greeley, Andrew M. *The Catholic Experience: An Interpretation of the Catholic Experience in America*. 1967.

Hoy, Suellen. "Caring for Chicago's Women and Girls: The Sisters of the Good Shepherd, 1859–1911." *Journal of Urban History*, 1997.

Hudson, Winthrop. *American Protestantism*. 1961.

Kantowicz, Edward R.
"Cardinal Mundelein of Chicago and the Shaping of Twentieth-Century American Catholicism." *Journal of American History*, 1981.
Corporation Sole: Cardinal Mundelein and Chicago Catholicism. 1983.
"To Build the Catholic City." *Chicago History*, 1985.

Skerrett, Ellen, et al. *Catholicism, Chicago Style*. 1993.

Chapter 3

Avella, Steven M. *This Confident Church: Catholic Leadership and Life in Chicago, 1940–1965.* 1992.

Bernardin, Joseph Cardinal. *Consistent Ethic of Life.* 1988.

Casuso, Jorge, & Camacho, Eduardo. "Latino Chicago," in *Ethnic Chicago*, ed. by Melvin G. Holli & Peter d'A. Jones. 1995.

Chicago Sun Times. *The Pope in America.* 1979.

Dahm, Charles. *Power and Authority in the Catholic Church: Cardinal Cody in Chicago.* 1981.

Garrow, David J. *Bearing the Cross: Martin Luther King, Jr. and the Southern Christian Leadership Conference.* 1986.

Holy Name Cathedral: 150 years, a Community of Diversity. 1997.

John Jay College of Criminal Justice. *The Nature and Scope of Sexual Abuse of Minors by Catholic Priests and Deacons in the United States, 1950-2002.* 2004.

Kantowicz, Edward R. "The Beginning and the End of an Era: George William Mundelein and John Patrick Cody in Chicago," in *Patterns of Episcopal Leadership*, ed. by Gerald P. Fogarty. 1989.

Kennedy, Eugene. *Bernardin: Life to the Full.* 1997.

Kerr, Louise Ano Nuevo. "Mexican Chicago," in *The Ethnic Frontier*, ed. by Melvin G. Holli & Peter d'A. Jones. 1977.

Kloehn, Steve. "Man of Indomitable Faith," and "In 37 Hours, Pope Charmed, Inspired City," in *Chicago Tribune*, April 3, 2005.

Kyle, Charles L. & Kantowicz, Edward R. *Kids First – Primero Los Ninos.* 1992.

National Review Board for the Protection of Children and Young People. *A Report on the Crisis in the Catholic Church in the United States.* 2004.

The Sixteen Documents of Vatican II. NCWC translation, no date.

Spilly, Alphonse P. *Selected Works of Joseph Cardinal Bernardin* (2 volumes). 2000.

Unsworth, Tim. *I Am Your Brother Joseph: Cardinal Bernardin in Chicago.* 1997.

Weigel, George. *Witness to Hope: The Biography of Pope John Paul II.* 1999.

The Archdiocese of
CHICAGO

CITY
PARISHES

136 windows in the Prudential Building
lighted to form a cross for Christmas, 1969

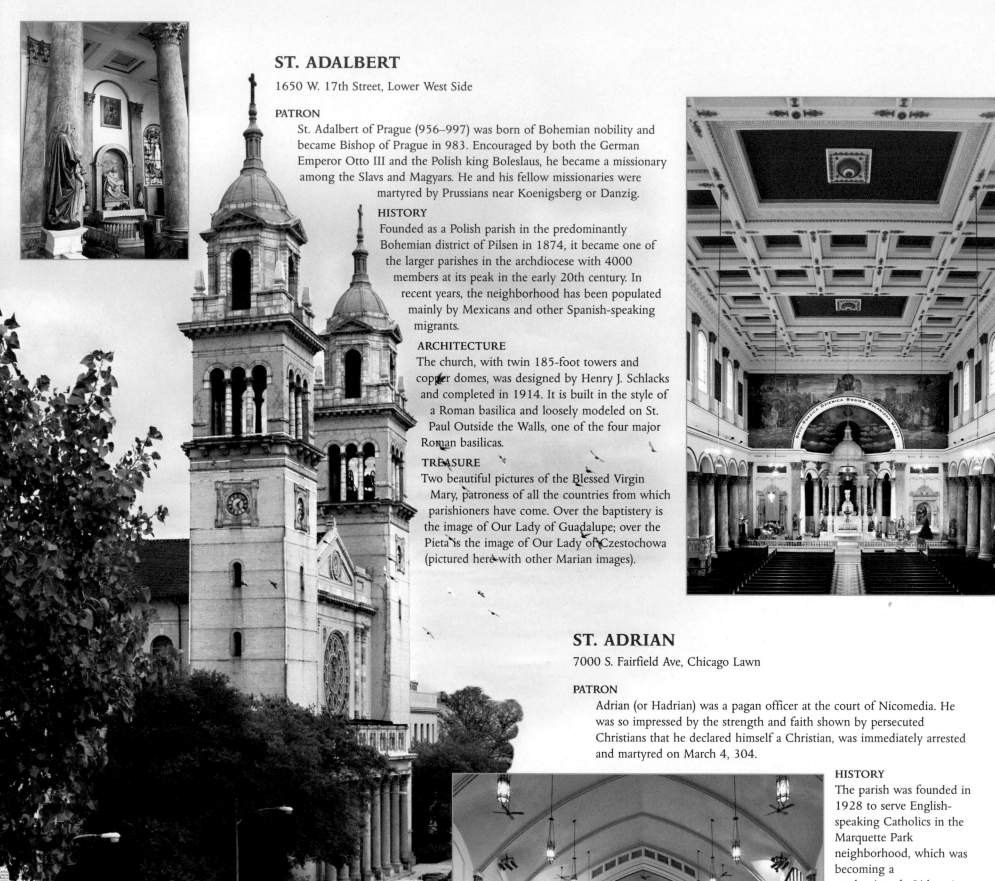

ST. ADALBERT

1650 W. 17th Street, Lower West Side

PATRON

St. Adalbert of Prague (956–997) was born of Bohemian nobility and became Bishop of Prague in 983. Encouraged by both the German Emperor Otto III and the Polish king Boleslaus, he became a missionary among the Slavs and Magyars. He and his fellow missionaries were martyred by Prussians near Koenigsberg or Danzig.

HISTORY

Founded as a Polish parish in the predominantly Bohemian district of Pilsen in 1874, it became one of the larger parishes in the archdiocese with 4000 members at its peak in the early 20th century. In recent years, the neighborhood has been populated mainly by Mexicans and other Spanish-speaking migrants.

ARCHITECTURE

The church, with twin 185-foot towers and copper domes, was designed by Henry J. Schlacks and completed in 1914. It is built in the style of a Roman basilica and loosely modeled on St. Paul Outside the Walls, one of the four major Roman basilicas.

TREASURE

Two beautiful pictures of the Blessed Virgin Mary, patroness of all the countries from which parishioners have come. Over the baptistery is the image of Our Lady of Guadalupe; over the Pieta is the image of Our Lady of Czestochowa (pictured here with other Marian images).

ST. ADRIAN

7000 S. Fairfield Ave, Chicago Lawn

PATRON

Adrian (or Hadrian) was a pagan officer at the court of Nicomedia. He was so impressed by the strength and faith shown by persecuted Christians that he declared himself a Christian, was immediately arrested and martyred on March 4, 304.

HISTORY

The parish was founded in 1928 to serve English-speaking Catholics in the Marquette Park neighborhood, which was becoming a predominantly Lithuanian district. Since the 1970s the parish and neighborhood have been predominantly Latino and

African-American. Mass is
celebrated in English and Spanish.
An annual potluck dinner helps
unite the parish.

ARCHITECTURE

The church, a modernized version
of Tudor Gothic, was designed by
the firm of Meyer & Cook and
completed in 1929.

TREASURE

An elegant, outdoor statue of
St. Adrian.

St. Adrian

ST. AGATHA

3147 W. Douglas Blvd., North Lawndale

PATRON

The only historical facts about St. Agatha are that she was born in
Sicily and died there as a martyr. Though she was venerated as a saint as
early as the sixth century, the dates of her life and death are unknown. In legends she is said
to have been tortured by fire and also had her breasts cut off, thus she is invoked against the
dangers of fire and diseases of the breast.

HISTORY

The parish was founded in 1893 to serve Irish families on the west side but never grew
too large since the surrounding Lawndale neighborhood became predominantly Jewish
in the 1920s. When African-Americans moved into the area in the 1960s, St. Agatha
pioneered a team ministry of three priests to evangelize the
newcomers. It has become the largest black Catholic parish on
the west side.

ARCHITECTURE

The modern church building was built in 1982
to replace a more elaborate Romanesque
church that could no longer be maintained. A
crucifix from its predecessor church now
stands on the reddish brown brick façade.

TREASURE

A small, elegant rose window, preserved from
the predecessor church.

ST. AGATHA CATHOLIC CHURCH
OUR LADY OF THE WESTSIDE SCHOOL

ST. AGNES OF BOHEMIA

2651 S. Central Park Ave., South Lawndale

PATRON
St. Agnes (1205–1282) was a Princess of Bohemia. Resisting a series of arranged marriages, she entered religious life and built a number of Franciscan convents, corresponding extensively with St. Clare of Assisi. Agnes spent 50 years in the cloister.

HISTORY
The parish was founded in 1904 to serve the growing Bohemian population in the area. Since the 1970s, the parish and neighborhood have been mainly Hispanic. The parish currently bills itself as the "largest Hispanic Catholic parish in the Midwest," with over 6,000 people attending nine Masses on Sundays.

ARCHITECTURE
The church was designed by Joseph B. Rezny and completed in 1926. It is Renaissance in style, with a single bell tower 100 feet tall.

TREASURE
The Perpetual Adoration Chapel "Prince of Peace."

ST. AILBE

9015 S. Harper Ave., Calumet Heights

PATRON
Though little is known for sure, St. Ailbe (died c. 541) was an evangelist throughout Ireland noted for his charity and his excellent preaching. The parish website suggests that Ailbe may have been "a mythical saint who takes on the likeness-image of the people who believe in him."

HISTORY

Founded as a mission of St. Laurence in 1889, St. Ailbe became a parish in 1892. Though the original parishioners were mainly Irish, the parish and neighborhood is now largely African-American.

ARCHITECTURE

The modern church building was constructed as a "temporary" church attached to the school in 1955 but has never been replaced. It was rededicated by Bishop George Murry, SJ in 1996.

TREASURE

Stained glass window of St. Ailbe, designed by David Csicsko. In keeping with the protean nature of the patron saint, Ailbe is depicted as a black man.

ALL SAINTS-ST. ANTHONY

518 W. 28th Place, Bridgeport

PATRON

All Saints commemorates all the saints in heaven, known and unknown, and calls to mind the doctrine of the Communion of Saints. St. Anthony of Padua (1195–1231) was a Franciscan friar, born in Lisbon, Portugal. He spent the latter part of his life in Italy and was called to teach theology at the University of Padua. A popular preacher in his own time, he has been a very popular saint among many ethnic groups and individuals. He is sometimes invoked as the patron saint of lost articles.

HISTORY

This parish was formed by the merger of All Saints, a formerly Irish parish, and St. Anthony, a formerly German parish, at the eastern edge of Bridgeport in 1968. All Saints was founded in 1875 at 25th Pl. and Wallace, St. Anthony in 1873 at 24th and Canal. In 1913 the Western Indiana Railroad, needing land to expand its tracks, agreed to build an entirely new parish complex at 28th Pl. and Wallace, in exchange for the property at 24th and Canal. The building of the Dan Ryan Expressway in the 1960s wiped out much of the territory of both parishes, prompting the merger.

ARCHITECTURE

The merged parish worships in the church of St. Anthony, built by Henry J. Schlacks in 1913 in Romanesque style. Church bells in the massive twin towers have recently been digitized.

TREASURE

F. X. Zettler stained glass windows and the mosaic of the vision of St. Anthony of Padua adorning the exterior above the main entrance were imported from Munich, Germany.

ST. ALOYSIUS

2300 W. LeMoyne St., Wicker Park

PATRON

Aloysius Gonzaga (1568–1591) was an Italian noble who signed away his legal claim to his family's lands and title to become a Jesuit novice. Tending plague victims in Rome in the outbreak of 1591, he contracted the disease and died at age 23. He is revered as a patron of youth.

HISTORY

Founded in 1884 as a German national parish, its first pastor, Msgr. Thiele worked with other Catholics to form a complex of institutions that included Josephinum Academy for girls and St. Elizabeth Hospital. From the 1950s on, the parish has included many Puerto Ricans and other Spanish-speaking parishioners. The current stewardship plan for the parish is called "Servants of God Transforming Lives and Communities."

ARCHITECTURE

The parishioners worshiped in a combination church-school building for many years until the modern church was built by the firm of Gaul and Voosen in 1965.

TREASURE

Stained glass windows.

ST. ALPHONSUS

1429 W. Wellington Ave., Lakeview

PATRON

Alphonsus Liguori (1696–1787) was a nobleman of Naples who first studied law, but then became a priest and preacher. He founded the Redemptorist religious order in 1732 and published numerous theological and devotional works.

HISTORY

Founded in 1882 as a German national parish, it was one of two North Side German parishes administered by the Redemptorist order (the other was St. Michael's). Besides the usual parochial school, the parish also built the Athenaeum in 1911 as a theater and community center for the neighborhood. Though the parish still celebrates one of the few German-language Masses in the archdiocese, it is now a very diverse community in a newly prosperous neighborhood. In 1999, the administration of the parish was transferred to diocesan priests.

ARCHITECTURE

Two teams of architects, Adam Boos and Josef Boettinghofer, and the St. Louis firm of Schrader & Conradi contributed designs for the massive Gothic church. The monumental front porch, or veranda, stands out as one of the most distinguishing features of the exterior. The church's roof and vaulted ceiling were destroyed by fire in 1950 but rebuilt the same year.

TREASURE

A massive Gothic marble reredos captures attention and draws all eyes to the sanctuary.

ST. AMBROSE

1012 E. 47th Street, Kenwood

PATRON

Ambrose (339–397) was a Roman noble and classical scholar who converted to Christianity and became bishop of Milan in 374. A noted preacher, scholar, and author of liturgical hymns, he stood firm against the Arian heresy and his preaching helped convert Saint Augustine of Hippo. The title "Honey Tongued Doctor" led to the use of a beehive and bees in his iconography, symbols which also indicate wisdom.

HISTORY

The parish was founded in 1904, primarily for Irish domestics who worked in this upper-class residential area populated mainly by Protestants. In the 1920s and 30s, many wealthy Irish-Americans, including Chicago mayor Edward J. Kelly, settled in the neighborhood. The area became African-American from the 1950s onwards.

ARCHITECTURE

The English Gothic church was designed by a parishioner, Zachary Taylor Davis, and completed in 1926.

TREASURE

The center window over the entrance depicts a Mass with uniformed military personnel of WWI in prayer, since the founding pastor was a chaplain in World War I.

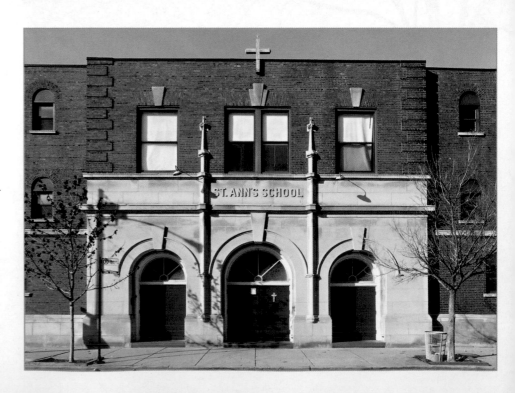

ST. ANDREW
3546 N. Paulina St., Lakeview

PATRON
Andrew (died c. 60) was one of the Twelve Apostles, a fisherman and the brother of Simon Peter. He preached in Asia Minor and Greece and possibly as far north as modern Russia (where he is revered as the national patron). He is said to have been crucified on an X-shaped cross, which has become his symbol and is also used as an emblem for Scotland on the Union Jack flag.

HISTORY
Founded in 1894, primarily for the Irish Catholics in a largely Protestant area of the city. Its most famous pastor was Auxiliary Bishop Bernard J. Sheil, the founder of the Catholic Youth Organization, who served the parish from 1935 to 1966. Sheil built a large gymnasium and recreation center that hosted numerous CYO events. The parish now anchors an ethnically diverse and increasingly prosperous neighborhood.

ARCHITECTURE
The Renaissance church building was designed by Egan and Prindville in 1913 and then enlarged from Joseph W. McCarthy's blueprints in 1932. It has two large stone campaniles on its façade, an impressive coffered ceiling, and one of the longest church naves in the city.

TREASURE
A wealth of stained glass windows of heroic size line both sides of the near 150-foot long nave, presenting excellent examples of the saints whose devotions were popular in the mid-twentieth century.

ST. ANN
1840 S. Leavitt St., Lower West Side

PATRON
Ann (or Anne) is traditionally revered as the mother of the Blessed Virgin Mary. Nothing certain is known of her life, though apocryphal sources give her name and that of her husband, St. Joachim. Devotion to Ann increased during the Middle Ages along with devotion to Mary.

HISTORY
Founded as a Polish parish in 1903 to relieve overcrowding at St. Adalbert's. The neighborhood and parish have become primarily Mexican in recent years.

St. Ann

ARCHITECTURE

The parish has used a combination church-school building, constructed in 1903.

TREASURE

The stained glass windows, especially that of St. Ann, mother of the Blessed Virgin and patron of the parish.

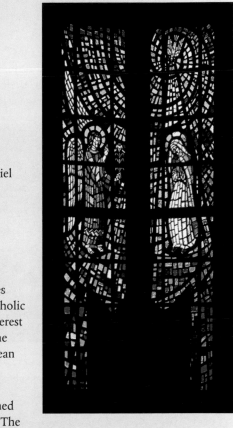

ANNUNCIATA

11128 S. Avenue G, East Side

PATRON

The annunciation to Mary by the angel Gabriel that she was to be the Mother of God. The Servite religious order chose the name to commemorate their church of Santissima Annunziata in Florence, Italy.

HISTORY

Founded in 1941 to serve a new subdivision along the Indiana-Illinois border. The Servites organized the parish on land donated by Catholic philanthropist Frank J. Lewis who had an interest in the real estate development of the area. The parishioners are of both Hispanic and European origin.

ARCHITECTURE

The modern, semi-circular church was designed by William Butorac and completed in 1971. The statue of the Pieta, on the east front lawn of church, was originally located at the entrance of Stonebridge, the Servite Priory in Lake Bluff IL.

TREASURE

The stained glass window at the back of the sanctuary depicts the Annunciation, and the other windows in the church depict the 7 Sorrows of Mary, a devotion unique to the Servite Order.

ST. ANSELM

6045 S. Michigan Ave., Washington Park

PATRON

Anselm of Canterbury (1033–1109) was born in Italy but moved to Normandy and became a Benedictine monk. After the Norman conquest of England, he was called to be Archbishop of Canterbury in 1093. He defended papal jurisdiction and the primacy of the spiritual over the temporal in the long-running investiture controversy.

HISTORY

Founded in 1909 for Irish-Catholics in a predominantly Protestant residential area. Under the pseudonym "St. Patrick's", St. Anselm's served as the model for Studs Lonigan's parish in the novels of James T. Farrell. The neighborhood became African-American in the 1920s and the parish was assigned to the missionary order, the Society of the Divine Word, in 1932. The Divine Word Fathers still administer the parish today.

ARCHITECTURE

Charles L. Wallace of Joliet designed the Romanesque church, completed in 1925.

TREASURE

A glorious rose window with the Risen Christ at the center.

ST. ANTHONY

11533 S. Prairie Ave., West Pullman

PATRON

St. Anthony of Padua (1195–1231) was a Franciscan friar, born in Lisbon, Portugal. He spent the latter part of his life in Italy and was called to teach theology at the University of Padua. A popular preacher in his own time, he has been a very popular saint among many ethnic groups, but particularly for the Italians.

HISTORY

Founded in 1903 as an Italian national parish. The Scalabrini Fathers, whose mission is to serve Italian immigrants, assumed administration of the parish in 1922. The parish has been predominantly Mexican since the 1970s and is currently administered by the Comboni Missionaries of the Heart of Jesus.

ARCHITECTURE

A church building with both Renaissance and modern influences was designed by Koerner and Farneti and completed in 1961. A huge statue of St. Anthony stands on the exterior, between two mosaics of Sts. Margaret and Bernadette; mosaics over the outer doors depict Bishop Scalabrini and St. Charles Borromeo.

TREASURE

The shrine of St. Anthony.

Assumption B.V.M.

ASSUMPTION B.V.M.

2434 S. California Ave., South Lawndale

PATRON

The assumption of the Blessed Virgin Mary into heaven upon her death.

HISTORY

Founded in 1903 as a Slovak national parish. It currently serves a Mexican-American congregation. The parish also is home to Kolbe House, the Catholic jail/prison ministry of the archdiocese. Mass and a picnic are celebrated outside on the adjacent boulevard in front of the church on the feasts of the Assumption and of St. Maximilian Kolbe.

ARCHITECTURE

A combination church-school building was constructed in 1914, followed by a rectory and a convent.

TREASURE

Shrine of Mary Assumed into Heaven in parish garden.

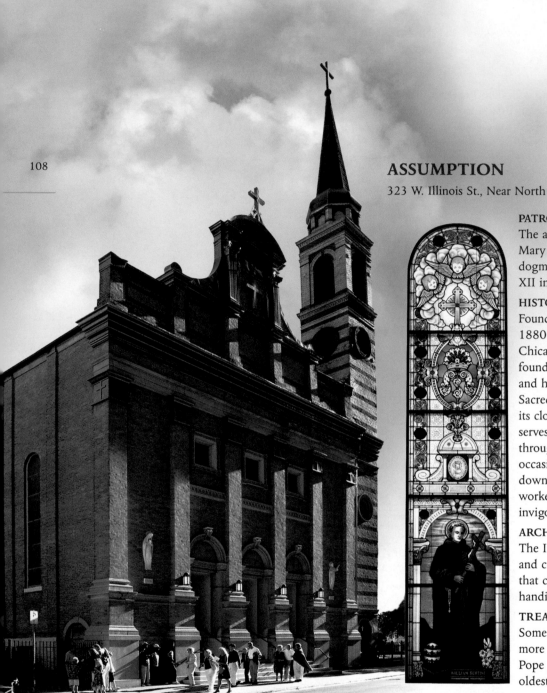

ASSUMPTION

323 W. Illinois St., Near North

PATRON

The assumption of the Blessed Virgin Mary into heaven was defined as a dogma of the Church by Pope Pius XII in 1950.

HISTORY

Founded by the Servite Fathers in 1880 as the first Italian parish in Chicago. St. Frances Xavier Cabrini founded the parish school in 1899, and her Missionary Sisters of the Sacred Heart staffed the school until its closing in 1945. The parish still serves Italians who come from throughout the area on special occasions, but is primarily a downtown church for nearby office workers and for the newly invigorated residential area of River North.

ARCHITECTURE

The Italian Renaissance church was designed by a parishioner, Giuseppe Beretta, and completed in 1886. A recent renovation preserved and enhanced the murals that cover the walls and ceiling and made the church accessible to the handicapped.

TREASURE

Some of the stained glass windows date from the church's founding but other more recent ones depict St. Frances Xavier Cabrini and post-Vatican II images of Pope John XXIII and Cardinal Meyer. The window pictured here is one of the oldest ones, depicting St. Philip Benizi, an early Servite superior.

ST. BARBARA

2867 S. Throop St., Bridgeport

PATRON

Barbara was a virgin martyr (died c. 235), but little is known of her life.

HISTORY

Founded in 1909 as a Polish parish to relieve overcrowding at St. Mary of Perpetual Help. Rev. Anthony Nawrocki, brother of St. Mary's pastor Stanislaus Nawrocki, was the first pastor, thus the founding of the parish was a "family affair" in both the literal and the figurative senses.

St. Barbara

ARCHITECTURE

The church, designed by the firm of Worthmann and Steinbach who built many of the city's Polish churches, was completed in 1914. In a high Renaissance style, it is one of the few octagonal houses of worship in the archdiocese. There are 25 stunning stained glass windows depicting the Gospel message and the lives of the saints.

TREASURE

A statue of St. Barbara.

ST. BARNABAS

10134 S. Longwood Dr., Beverly

PATRON

Barnabas (died c. 61), whose name means son of encouragement, was an early Jewish convert, coming to the faith soon after Pentecost. He is mentioned frequently in the Acts of the Apostles as a companion of Saint Paul. He died a martyr's death.

HISTORY

Founded in 1924 by Rev. Timothy Hurley for Irish Catholics in the heavily Protestant district of Beverly. The parishioners faced intense hostility at first, even enduring cross-burnings by the Ku Klux Klan. St. Barnabas became a prosperous, semi-suburban parish in the 1950s as many Catholics moved to the outskirts of the city.

ARCHITECTURE

The modern church, designed by McCarthy-Hundriesen &Associates and built in 1968 by Henry Brothers, is an enveloping amphitheater with interior walls of pale brick. It was one of the city's first churches built to the liturgical specifications of the Second Vatican Council.

TREASURE

A shrine honoring six saints of North and South America: Blessed Kateri Tekakwitha, St. Isaac Jogues, St. Katherine Drexel, St. Elizabeth Seton, St. Frances Cabrini, and St. Martin de Porres. They were painted by artist Meltem Aktas.

ST. BARTHOLOMEW

4949 W. Patterson Ave., Portage Park

PATRON

Bartholomew was one of the Twelves Apostles, sometimes also called Nathanael. Nothing is known for certain about his life or death, but he may have preached in Armenia and India, and tradition holds that he was flayed alive.

HISTORY

Founded in 1917 in a semi-suburban area of the northwest side, it has always had a congregation of many ethnic groups. Currently, the Latinos are the largest single number of parishioners, with Filipinos, Poles, Italians, Irish, and Germans also represented. The parish is proud of its bilingual (English/Spanish) celebrations, as well as its trilingual celebrations when Polish is added. St. Bartholomew is a thriving parish with an excellent grammar school.

ARCHITECTURE

The church was designed by Gerald A. Barry and completed in 1938. A brick and limestone colonial-style structure, the church consciously imitates the main chapel of St. Mary of the Lake Seminary. Both the seminary chapel and this church proclaim the compatibility of the Catholic Church with American ideals.

TREASURE

The crowned tabernacle depicting Christ the King.

ST. BASIL/VISITATION

843 W. Garfield Blvd., New City

PATRON

St. Basil (329–379) was born of a distinguished family in Caesarea, Asia Minor. His mother, father, and four of his nine siblings were canonized, including Saint Gregory of Nyssa. He became bishop of Caearea in 370. He founded monasteries and drew up rules for monks living in the desert and is considered the father of Eastern monastcism.

The Visitation honors the visit of the Blessed Virgin Mary to her cousin Elizabeth, mother of John the Baptist.

HISTORY

St. Basil (founded in 1904) and Visitation (founded 1886) were the two English-speaking parishes along Garfield Boulevard. Visitation was the larger of the two, one of the premier Irish parishes of the South Side. After a great deal of racial strife, the neighborhood became African-American in the 1960s. The two parishes dwindled in numbers and were consolidated, using the Visitation church building, in 1990.

ARCHITECTURE

The St. Basil church building, since torn down, was one of the few Byzantine style churches in the archdiocese. The Visitation church building, a Gothic structure designed by Martin Carr, was completed in 1899.

TREASURE

An outdoor shrine to Our Lady of Fatima.

ST. BEDE THE VENERABLE

8200 S. Kostner Ave., Ashburn

PATRON

Bede the Venerable (673–735) was a Benedictine monk of the monastery of Jarrow. He was a Scripture scholar, but is most noted for his Ecclesiastical History of England, completed in 731. Our knowledge of England before the 8th century is mainly the result of Bede's writing.

HISTORY

Founded in 1953 in an area of new post-war construction on the southwest side. The first Mass was celebrated in a former airplane hangar at 83rd and Cicero. Originally home to a high proportion of Chicago municipal employees of European descent, the community today houses an international community, including the original homeowners and their descendants, Hispanic, African-American, and Middle Eastern residents.

ARCHITECTURE

The first parish building is now a fieldhouse at a Chicago Park District property. The second church building now serves as the parish gymnasium. The permanent church was constructed in 1963, a modern design of Andrew Stoecker.

TREASURE

The most noted and remembered treasure of the parish is the Blessed Virgin Mary's grotto near the door of the education building, where it has been for many years. It served as the design for the souvenir shirt at the school's golden jubilee.

ST. BENEDICT

2215 W. Irving Park Rd., North Center

PATRON

Benedict of Nursia (480–547) was the twin brother of Saint Scholastica. He founded the monastery at Monte Cassino, where he wrote the Rule of his order. He is considered the father of Western monasticism.

HISTORY

Founded in 1902 as a German parish. Though remaining predominantly German, the parish also served other ethnic groups. In recent years the neighborhood has become revitalized.

ARCHITECTURE

The church, designed by Hermann J. Gaul and completed in 1918, is one of the most ornate Romanesque structures in the city.

TREASURE

The massive clock tower with six huge bells, imported from Germany.

ST. BENEDICT THE AFRICAN-EAST

340 W. 66th St., Englewood

PATRON

Benedict (1526–1589) was born of slave parents who had been taken from Africa to Sicily. Granted his freedom at age 18, he joined a group of Franciscan hermits near Palermo. His humility and cheerfulness set an example that helped reform his order. Though Benedict was not a Moor, the Italian phrase "il Moro" for "the Black" has often been added to his name.

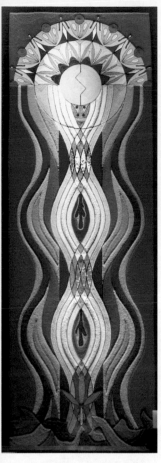

HISTORY

Since the Englewood neighborhood became entirely African-American in the 1960s, a number of parishes in the area dwindled in size. In 1989 St. Brendan, St. Bernard, Our Lady of Solace, St. Martin, St. Carthage, St. Justin Martyr, St. Raphael, and Sacred Heart were all consolidated into a new African-American parish. In 1995 the parish was split into East and West divisions.

ARCHITECTURE

A modern, circular church, with a distinctive bell tower.

TREASURE

Tapestry of Eucharistic community behind the altar.

St. Benedict the African-East

ST. BENEDICT THE AFRICAN-WEST

1818 W. 71st St.), West Englewood

PATRON

Benedict (1526–1589) was born of slave parents who had been taken from Africa to Sicily. Granted his freedom at age 18, he joined a group of Franciscan hermits near Palermo. His humility and cheerfulness set an example that helped reform his order. Though Benedict was not a Moor, the Italian phrase "il Moro" for "the Black" has often been added to his name.

HISTORY

Since the Englewood neighborhood became entirely African-American in the 1960s, a number of parishes in the area dwindled in size. In 1989 St. Brendan, St. Bernard, Our Lady of Solace, St. Martin, St. Carthage, St. Justin Martyr, St. Raphael, and Sacred Heart were all consolidated into a new African-American parish. In 1995 the parish was split into East and West divisions. The West parish is on the site of the former St. Justin Martyr parish.

ARCHITECTURE

A simple, stylish church with colorful drawings of Ethiopian crosses accenting white walls.

TREASURE

A Tao-type crucifix, showing crucified man of color surrounded by litany of historical and biblical African people.

ST. BONAVENTURE

1641 W. Diversey Pkwy., Lincoln Park

PATRON

Bonaventure (1221–1274) was born near Orvieto, Italy. He joined the Franciscan Order and studied theology and philosophy in Paris, where he was a contemporary of Saint Thomas Aquinas. A noted theological writer, he spoke in favor of reunion between Eastern and Western churches at the Council of Lyons.

HISTORY

Founded in 1911 as an English-speaking parish in a heavily German area. Though never a large parish, it has served a congregation of many different ethnic groups and the area has become newly prosperous in recent years.

ARCHITECTURE

A combination church-school building was designed in a Romanesque style by Joseph Molitor and completed in 1913. The parish never grew large enough to construct a full-scale, free-standing church, but the worship space in the combination building has been described as an intimate space, "simple, like a chapel in the city".

TREASURE

Statue of St. Gemma Galgani.

ST. BRIDE

7811 S. Coles Ave., South Shore

PATRON

Bride (453–523) is also known as St. Bridget of Ireland. Though little is known of her life, she is thought to have been born near Kildare where she later served as abbess of a convent. She is said to have been baptized by St. Patrick and helped to spread Christianity in Ireland.

HISTORY

Founded in 1893 as a mission of St. Kevin parish for Irish families in South Shore, it became a parish in 1900. It served a middle-class Irish neighborhood for much of the 20th century, and since the 1960s the area has been primarily middle-class African-American.

St. Bride

ARCHITECTURE

The church was built in a French Gothic style and completed in 1908.

TREASURE

The stained glass, from Munich-Chicago Studio, of Martha and Mary.

ST. BRONISLAVA

8708 S. Colfax Ave., South Chicago

PATRON

Bronislava (1200–1259) was a Polish nun of the Norbertine (Premonstratensian) Order. She was a cousin of Saint Hyacinth of Poland.

HISTORY

Founded as a Polish parish in 1928 to relieve overcrowding at Immaculate Conception, it was administered by a Polish order of Conventual Franciscans. The parish is now predominantly Latino, Polish-American, and African-American.

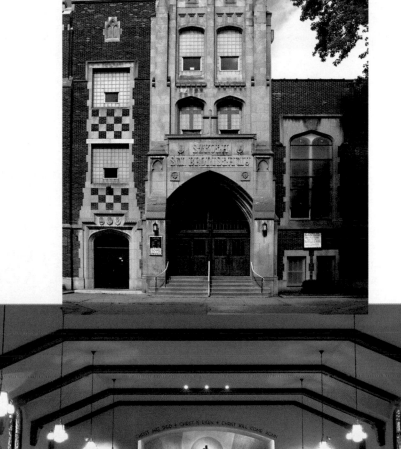

ARCHITECTURE

A combination church-school building, designed by Leo Strelka, was completed in 1929.

TREASURE

Fourteen beautiful stained glass windows from Munich, Germany, added in 1952, depict four Marian apparitions and a variety of other "favorite" saints.

ST. BRUNO

4751 S. Harding Ave., Archer Heights

PATRON

Bruno (1030–1101) founded the order of Carthusian monks. He was a priest-teacher in his own country of France and an advisor to Pope Urban II. A cheerful, active man, St. Bruno knew that God loves those who serve Him in joy.

HISTORY

Founded in 1925 as a Polish parish. The neighborhood and parish remained Polish through most of the 20th century, but the parish now welcomes many Latino families as well. Our Lady of the New Millennium statue has graced the parish twice and most recently the Papal Monstrance blessed by Pope John Paul II was used for Eucharistic Adoration on the Feast of St.Bruno, October 6, 2005.

ARCHITECTURE

A modern church, designed by John Fox, was completed in 1955. The small stained glass windows on the nave's upper walls are from the original church whose old bells still toll at Our Lady of the Snows shrine in Belleville. A Sacred Heart shrine was built on the rectory grounds in 1953, and in 1983 an outdoor shrine to Our Lady of Czestochowa was erected to mark the Polish heritage of the parish.

TREASURE

Stained glass triptych of St. Bruno.

ST. CAJETAN

2445 W. 112th St., Morgan Park

PATRON

Cajetan (1480–1547) was born at Vicenza and educated at Padua. In 1524 he formed the Congregation of Clerks Regular (Theatines) at Rome, with the mission of reviving the spirit and zeal of the clergy. Though not as well known as Ignatius Loyola and the Jesuits, Cajetan and the Theatines were major forces in the Counter-Reformation that reformed abuses and combated the Protestants.

HISTORY

Founded in 1927 on the far southwest side of the city. The neighborhood filled up after the Second World War. The population is predominantly Irish but includes many other nationalities as well.

ARCHITECTURE

The church was designed by the firm of Barry and Kay and completed in 1964.

TREASURE

A large stained glass triptych of Christ dominates the area above the entrance.

117

ST. CAMILLUS

5426 S. Lockwood Ave., Garfield Ridge

PATRON

Camillus of Lellis (1550–1614) was the son of a military officer who spent his youth as a soldier, fighting for the Venetians against the Turks. After suffering a leg injury he experienced a religious conversion, went to Rome, and founded the Congregation of the Servants of the Sick (the Camellians) in 1585.

HISTORY

Originally a mission of St. Joseph's in Summit, Illinois (called St. Florian Mission), it was organized as a Polish parish in 1921. The parish served the workers at nearby Midway Airport and during World War II a 2:30 AM Mass was celebrataed that proved so popular it was continued into the 1960s. The area filled up as a semi-suburban residential neighborhood after World War II. Though the parish remained predominantly Polish it has served many other nationalities as well.

ARCHITECTURE

A combination church-school building was completed in 1923 and has continued to be used up to the present. A new school, convent, and rectory were completed and dedicated in October, 1959.

TREASURE

Recently a picture of Divine Mercy was installed, and devotion has become very popular among the faithful. A procession with the statue of Our Lady of Fatima also attracts many of the local parishioners.

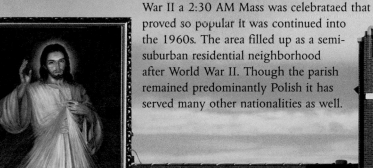

CHRIST THE KING

9235 S. Hamilton Ave., Beverly

PATRON

The Feast of Christ the King was instituted by Pope Pius XI in 1925 to proclaim the reign of Christ over all people, nations, and governments.

HISTORY

Founded in 1936 for the Irish Catholic families of a predominantly Protestant neighborhood. Beverly became a semi-suburban residential neighborhood after World War II, and this parish was the model used by priest-sociologist Andrew M. Greeley in his book The Church in the Suburbs.

ARCHITECTURE

The modern church, designed by John Jay Fox and Son in a fan-shaped design, was completed in 1955. A huge stained glass window of Christ the King dominates the entrance wall.

TREASURE

A hand-painted mural depicting events from Christ's life, using likenesses of parish priests and founding parishioners.

ST. CHRISTINA

11005 S. Homan Ave., Mount Greenwood

PATRON

Christina (died c. 250) was born to a wealthy pagan family, converted as a youth, and martyed near Lake Bolsena in Tuscany.

HISTORY

Founded in 1926 on the far southwest side of the city for English-speaking and Lithuanian Catholics. Lithuanians remained predominant among parishioners until the neighborhood filled in with many other nationalities after World War II.

St. Christina

ARCHITECTURE

A modern church was designed by Andrew G. Stoecker, a parishioner, and completed in 1956. The entire sanctuary and the vestibule are faced with marble.

TREASURE

A three-dimensional figure of Jesus the High Priest behind the main altar, is a replica of a statue in the retreat house at Mundelein Seminary.

ST. CLARE OF MONTEFALCO

5443 S. Washtenaw Ave.,
Gage Park

PATRON

Clare of Montefalco
(1268–1308) joined a community of Franciscan hermits that later was reorganized under the rule of St. Augustine. She was noted for devotion to the Passion of Christ.

HISTORY

First organized in 1909 as a mission by the Augustinian Fathers of St. Rita College, it became a parish in 1916. Though a territorial parish, open to all nationalities, it originally had a large number of Polish parishioners, and in recent years has become predominantly Hispanic. The Capuchin Franciscan Fathers have administered the parish since September 2002.

ARCHITECTURE

The church, a simplified Romanesque design in Lannan stone, was completed in 1955.

TREASURE

On either side of the nave vivid stained glass windows depict Augustinian saints such as Monica, Rita of Cascia, and, of course, the parish patron (pictured here).

ST. CLEMENT

642 W. Deming Pl., Lincoln Park

PATRON

Clement (died c. 101) was called the "first Apostolic Father". He served as third bishop of Rome from 92 until 101, when he was martyred in the Crimea. His "Letter to the Corinthians" reveals his extensive knowledge of Scripture, testifies to the life of primitive Christianity, and provides the earliest indication of the use of the Sanctus in liturgy.

HISTORY

Founded in 1905 as a German parish and designated a territorial parish in 1912, it continues to be an anchor of faith for people of "every race, language and way of life."

ARCHITECTURE

Early twentieth-century revival of Byzantine-Italian Romanesque tradition. The design by George D. Barnett was influenced by his larger Cathedral Basilica of St. Louis and by the church of Hagia Sophia in Constantinople. The church was completed in 1918, and the renovation in 1988 under Walker C. Johnson earned an International Design Award for Excellence.

TREASURE

The Sacred Triduum of Holy Week, culminating in the Baptism of catechumens, is celebrated each year at the font beneath a mural of the Tree of Life. This mural replicates the twelfth century mosaic in San Clemente and is the focal point of the unique Byzantine universe designed and created by priest-artist Gleb E. Werchovsky in 1930.

ST. CLOTILDE

8430 S. Calumet Ave., Chatham

PATRON

Clotilde (475–545) was the daughter of a Frankish king who married King Clovis of the Salian Franks. She led her husband to Christianity in 496, and after his death in 511 she retired to the city of Tours where she spent the rest of her life caring for the poor and the sick.

HISTORY

Founded in 1928 as a territorial (predominantly Irish) parish. The neighborhood became a middle class African-American community from the 1960s onwards, and many of the new parishioners came from St. Elizabeth, Corpus Christi, and St. Anselm, the original Black Catholic parishes of Chicago.

ARCHITECTURE
A combination church-school building, designed by Charles L. Wallace in Tudor Gothic style, was completed in 1930.

TREASURE
The original tabernacle over the altar.

ST. COLUMBA

13323 S. Greenbay Ave., Hegewisch

PATRON
Columba of Iona (521–597), also known as Columbkille, was of an Irish royal clan. He founded a number of monasteries in Ireland, then in 565 he organized the monastery on the remote island of Iona, off the coast of Scotland. He preached and evangelized throughout Ireland and Scotland, converting many.

HISTORY
Originally established as a mission in 1884, it became a parish in 1896. Though Hegewisch had been annexed to the city of Chicago in 1889, the area remained remote and isolated for many years. Despite the Irish name, the parish was always predominantly Polish and mainly working-class.

ARCHITECTURE
The modern church designed by Belli and Belli was completed in 1951.

TREASURE
Stained glass window of patron saint.

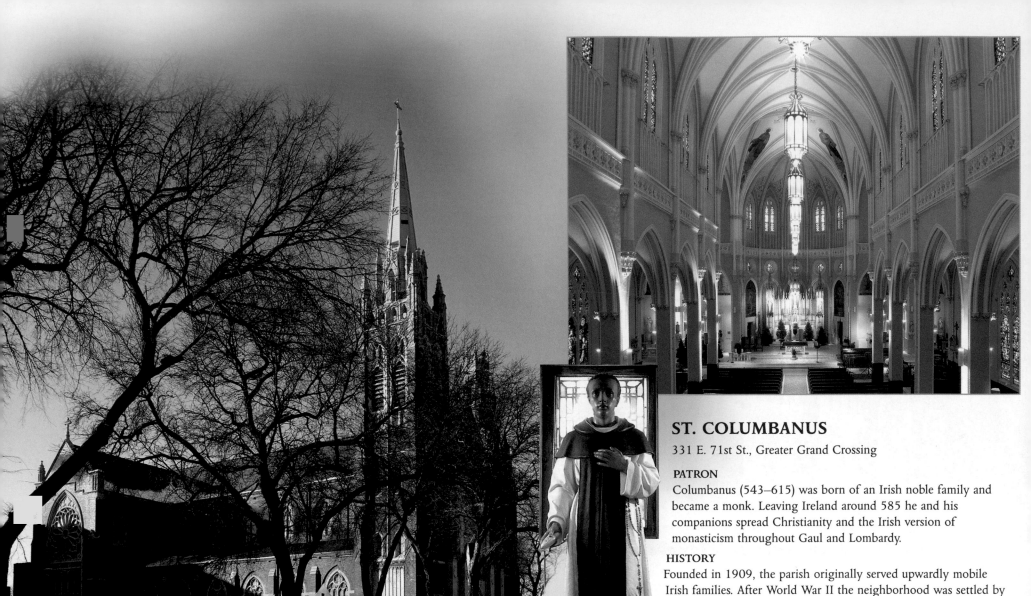

ST. COLUMBANUS

331 E. 71st St., Greater Grand Crossing

PATRON

Columbanus (543–615) was born of an Irish noble family and became a monk. Leaving Ireland around 585 he and his companions spread Christianity and the Irish version of monasticism throughout Gaul and Lombardy.

HISTORY

Founded in 1909, the parish originally served upwardly mobile Irish families. After World War II the neighborhood was settled by upwardly mobile, middle class African-Americans.

ARCHITECTURE

The church, designed by James Burns in an imposing Gothic style, was completed in 1925. The building was renovated in 2001 and an adoration chapel was installed in 2004.

TREASURE

The shrine of St. Martin de Porres, installed in 1977.

ST. CONSTANCE

5843 W. Strong St., Jefferson Park

PATRON

Constance (325–354) was the daughter of Roman Emperor Constantine. Having been cured of leprosy through the intercession of the virgin martyr, St. Agnes, she spent the rest of her life helping the sick.

HISTORY

Founded in 1916 as a Polish parish. Though it remains predominantly Polish, it also serves the English-speaking community.

ARCHITECTURE

The modern church, designed by A.J. Del Bianco and Richard Donatoni, was completed in 1970. A modern bell tower was installed in 1980. The altar, designed in 1981 by Jerzy Kenar, has a carved base depicting the tree of life. Kenar's other designs are the statues of the Blessed Mother, St. Joseph, the Holy Family, and St. Constance located inside the church and the figures of Jesus and Mary at the foot of the bell tower. The Divine Mercy chapel was renovated and dedicated to Pope John Paul II in 2005.

TREASURE

An icon of Our Lady of Czestochowa which was painted by Anna Maria Torwird and donated by Fr. Izidor Matuszewski, the General of the Pauline Fathers from Jasna Gora, Czestochowa, and blessed by the Primate of Poland, Joseph Cardinal Glemp.

St. Constance

ST. CORNELIUS

5205 N. Lieb Ave., Jefferson Park

PATRON

Cornelius (died c. 253) was elected Pope during a period of persecution when such an election meant a quick death sentence. The main achievement of his papacy was a policy of reconciliation with Christians who had lapsed from their beliefs due to fear of torture and death.

HISTORY

Founded in 1925 for English-speaking Catholics on the far northwest side of the city. The neighborhood filled in after World War II and the parish has served many different nationalities.

ARCHITECTURE

A modern brick, cruciform church, designed by Barry and Kay, was completed in 1965.

TREASURE

Mosaic with crucifix over the altar.

CORPUS CHRISTI

4920 S. King Dr., Grand Boulevard

PATRON
The Body and Blood of Christ in the Eucharist have been a special object of devotion for centuries and are commemorated with a feast two weeks after Pentecost.

HISTORY
Founded in 1901 for upwardly mobile Irish Catholics, the parish was all but abandoned in the 1920s when the neighborhood became African-American. From 1929 to 1932 the Franciscans used the parish buildings as a retreat center, but in 1932 they reopened the parish as a center of evangelization and community for African-Americans.

ARCHITECTURE
The church, designed by Joseph W. McCarthy in a Renaissance style, was completed in 1916. At the dedication of the church, Archbishop George Mundelein met Joe McCarthy for the first time and soon after adopted him as his own, semi-official architect. The twin towers of the church and the long colonnade connecting the school and rectory to the church form an exceptionally harmonious composition along the boulevard. Marble, gold, and precious stones adorn the original high altar.

TREASURE
Stained glass windows created by the F. X. Zettler Studio in Munich, Germany.

ST. DANIEL THE PROPHET

5330 S. Nashville Ave., Garfield Ridge

PATRON
The prophet Daniel was the hero and traditional author of the Old Testament book that bears his name. His name means "God is my judge." The most famous story from this book relates Daniel's miraculous salvation when thrown into a den of lions.

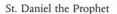
St. Daniel the Prophet

HISTORY

Founded in 1947. The first pastor, Matthew Mulligan, chose the name for the parish after his childhood hero, Msgr. Daniel Byrnes, who was pastor of his home parish of St. Agnes in Brighton Park. The parish has served a wide variety of ethnic groups in this middle-class area on the outskirts of the city, though Polish parishioners have generally predominated.

ARCHITECTURE

The church, designed by George S. Smith in a modernized English Gothic style, was completed in 1954.

TREASURE

Windows depicting St. Daniel the Prophet over the entrance to the church

ST. DENIS

8301 S. St. Louis Ave., Ashburn

PATRON

Denis (died c. 258) was an Italian missionary in Gaul who became the first bishop of Paris. He was beheaded at Montmartre (the mount of martyrs). He is venerated as the patron saint of France.

HISTORY

Founded in 1951 on the outskirts of the city. This semi-suburban neighborhood filled up in the 1950s and the parish has served a variety of different ethnic groups. It currently has parishioners of European, Latino, and African-American descent.

ARCHITECTURE

The modern church, a red brick edifice with a carillon tower, was designed by Barry and Kay and completed in 1964. The chancel is dominated by risen Christ on cross 25 feet high, made of multi-colored glass shards.

TREASURE

Artist Max Ingrand's 14 stained glass windows along either side of the nave rise from floor to ceiling, telling the story of the sacraments, creation, and fall and redemption of mankind.

ST. DOROTHY

450 E. 78th St., Greater Grand Crossing

PATRON

Dorothy (died c. 311) was a virgin martyr, executed during the persecution of Diocletian at Caesarea, Cappodocia in Asia Minor. Nothing certain is known of her life.

HISTORY

Founded in 1916 for English-speaking parishioners in a newly settled middle class area. The neighborhood became middle-class African-American in the 1950s. Since then this African-American parish recorded a number of "firsts," such as, the first to charter a railroad car for the March on Washington and the first to send a busload of parishioners to march with Martin Luther King in Selma, Alabama.

ARCHITECTURE

Charles L. Wallace of Joliet was commissioned in 1928 to erect a magnificent Gothic church, but because of the Depression and the founding of St. Clotilde parish which reduced the number of parishioners at St. Dorothy, the proposed cathedral ceiling was never built.

TREASURE

In 1991 eight stained glass windows were added depicting black saints from St. Monica to the Martyrs of Uganda.

ST. EDWARD

4350 W. Sunnyside Ave., Irving Park

PATRON

Edward the Confessor (1003–1066) was proclaimed King of England in 1042 at a time when there were invasions from without and powerful contenders from within. He was accessible to his subjects, generous to the poor, and had a reputation for visions and healings. Shortly after his death, his relative, William, the Norman victor of the Battle of Hastings, would become king.

HISTORY

Founded in 1899 by the Viatorian Fathers as a mission of St. Viator's, it became a parish in 1901. The parish served a variety of mostly second generation European ethnic groups. In recent years, the parish has also served parishioners from the Philippines, Latin America, India and other places.

St. Edward

ARCHITECTURE

A red brick church, designed by McCarthy, Smith and Eppig in a neo-Baroque style, was completed in 1940. The stained glass windows depict Scriptural scenes, the Joyful Mysteries of the Rosary, and a number of saints.

TREASURE

A marvelous rose window in the choir loft presents an array of musical instruments, such as, lutes, lyres, and keyboards.

ST. ELIZABETH

50 E. 41st St., Grand Boulevard.

PATRON

Elizabeth of Hungary (1207–1231), the daughter of the King of Hungary, was brought up in Thuringia and married the ruler of that principality. She bore three children and gave generously to the poor in her region. Her husband was killed on a Crusade, and Elizabeth's brother-in-law drove her from the court, where she died at an early age. This parish was named for her because the first frame church building was moved from a previous site to the location of the new parish on her feast day, November 19, 1881.

HISTORY

Founded in 1881 for Irish Catholics on the near South Side, St. Elizabeth's was located near the slowly expanding, segregated Black Belt. In 1924 the parish was merged with St. Monica's, the first African-American parish in the archdiocese, founded in 1889. Following the consolidation, St. Elizabeth was administered by the Society of the Divine Word, whose priests engaged in a mission of evangelization among African-Americans.

ARCHITECTURE

The original church burned in 1930, and the assembly hall was remodeled and used thereafter for worship services. In 1989 a modern church was dedicated by Cardinal Bernardin.

TREASURE

A glorious mural on the exterior depicts the history of the parish.

EPIPHANY

2524 S. Keeler Ave., South Lawndale

PATRON

Epiphany commemorates the visit of the Magi (or Three Kings) to the infant Jesus. The larger significance of the epiphany (which means manifestation or revelation) lies in the universality of Christ's redemption, intended for Gentiles as well as Jews.

HISTORY

Founded in 1901 for Irish and German immigrants. Cardinal Francis George's grandparents were among the early parishioners. The neighborhood and parish became predominantly Polish and Bohemian in the 1920s and then Mexican in the 1960s and 70s.

ARCHITECTURE

One of the last monumental Gothic churches built in Chicago, Epiphany was designed by Edward J. Schulte and completed in 1953. The interior walls were made of sandstone quarried by monks of St. Meinrad, Indiana.

TREASURE

Our Lady of Guadalupe tapestry, created by Esteban Lorenzo, woven from fragments of old vestments.

ST. ETHELREDA

8754 S. Paulina St., Auburn-Gresham

PATRON

Ethelreda (640–679), also known as Audrey, was a princess of East Anglia. Taking a vow of perpetual virginity, she became a nun and founded the Abbey of Ely where she lived an austere life.

HISTORY

Founded in 1926 for a predominantly Irish congregation. The neighborhood and parish became African-American in the 1970s.

ARCHITECTURE

The modern church was completed in 1953.

TREASURE

A statue of the patron saint stands by the Cross behind the altar.

St. Ethelreda

ST. EUGENE

7958 W. Foster Ave., Norwood Park

PATRON

Eugene I (died 657) was a Roman priest who had held various positions in the Church and was known for his charity and his sanctity. He was consecrated Pope in 654.

HISTORY

Founded in 1948 on the far northwest side, the parish was named for Eugenio Pacelli, who was then reigning as Pope Pius XII. The founding pastor was Fr. John M. Ryan. The parish has served a variety of European ethnic groups. The Sisters of Charity, BVM, staffed the school, but presently only one BVM Sister is teaching and the convent is now home to the Sisters of the Verbum Dei Missionary Fraternity.

ARCHITECTURE

The parish worshiped in a Quonset hut for 20 years, but a modern, circular church was designed by Frank Serpico and completed in 1969. The church has an unusual roof line which recalls the glass enclosure of the control tower at nearby O'Hare International Airport.

TREASURE

The parish patron, Pope St. Eugene I, is honored in a wall of stained glass in the vestibule.

ST. FELICITAS

1526 E. 84th St., Avalon Park

PATRON
Felicitas, also known as Felicity (died c.165) was a Christian widow, martyred in Rome during the persecution of emperor Marcus Aurelius. The story of her seven sons (also martyrs) is not documented and may be a pious legend.

HISTORY
Established as a mission in 1916, it became a parish in 1919 along with the nearby Our Lady of Peace parish. Originally Irish, the neighborhood and parish became African-American in the 1950s and 60s.

ARCHITECTURE
The church, designed by George S. Smith in a modernized Gothic style, was completed in 1955.

TREASURE
The shrine to St. Josephine Bakita, a former Sudanese slave.

ST. FERDINAND

5900 W. Barry Ave., Belmont-Cragin

PATRON
Ferdinand III (1199–1252) was king of Castile and Leon, and his reign definitively solidified the union of these two kingdoms, the forerunners of modern Spain. He reconquered much of southern Spain from the Moslems, converting the Great Mosque in Seville to a cathedral.

HISTORY
Founded in 1927 on the far northwest side. The parish has served a variety of different ethnic groups. Mass is celebrated in English, Polish, and Italian.

ARCHITECTURE

The modern church, designed by Barry and Kay, was completed in 1958.

TREASURE

The St. Ferdinand Statue and Garden, installed on the 75th anniversary of the parish in 2002.

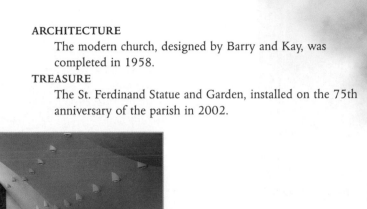

St. Ferdinand

FIVE HOLY MARTYRS

4327 S. Richmond St., Brighton Park

PATRON

The Five Holy Martyrs (died 1003) were the first canonized saints of Poland. Isaac and Matthew, two novices from Poland, and Benedict and John, two hermits from Italy living under the rule of St. Benedict, were requested by the King of Poland to begin a mission of evangelization. Christian, a Polish layman, joined them as their cook. They were martyred by local brigands.

HISTORY

Founded in 1908 as a Polish parish. The parish has remained Polish, due to a large immigration after the suppression of the Solidarity movement in Poland in the 1980s. Pope John Paul II celebrated a mass for the Poles of the archdiocese at this parish on October 5, 1979.

ARCHITECTURE

The church, designed in a Spanish mission style by Arthur Foster, was completed in 1920. Modern changes were added to the original church building in 1963 by architect John T. Schefke, nearly doubling the size of the church.

TREASURE

The papal chair and vestments from Pope John Paul II's visit.

ST. FLORIAN

13145 S. Houston Ave., Hegewisch

PATRON

Florian (died c. 304) was an officer in the Roman army stationed in what is now Austria. When ordered to execute a group of Christians during the persecutions of Diocletian, he refused, professed his own faith, and was martyred. Some of his relics were given to King Casimir of Poland and the bishop of Cracow, which led to Florian's patronage of Poland and Upper Austria. Since his Roman rank of centurion made him chief of a mobile fire brigade, he is honored as patron saint of firefighters.

HISTORY

Founded in 1905 as a Polish parish for the isolated industrial community of Hegewisch. While retaining a predominance of Polish-Americans, it has also welcomed the recent Hispanic influx into the neighborhood. The parish has the only Catholic school in the Hegewisch area. Mass is celebrated in English, Spanish, and Polish.

ARCHITECTURE

A three-story brick combination church/school building, designed by Bronislav Pstrong, was completed in 1927 and continues to serve the parish. The stained glass windows, the pipe organ, and the original church bell from 1905 were all restored for the parish's 100th anniversary.

TREASURE

The stained glass windows, in particular, the one entitled "Agony in the Garden."

ST. FRANCIS OF ASSISI

813 W. Roosevelt Rd., Near West Side

PATRON

Francis of Assisi (1181–1226) was the son of a wealthy cloth merchant. Captured during a war between Assisi and Perugia, he experienced a religious conversion and took the Gospels as the rule of his life, Jesus Christ as his literal example. He dressed in rough clothes, begged for his sustenance, and preached purity and peace. In 1212, he founded the Franciscan religious order and two years later Clare of Assisi became his spiritual student and founded the women's order of Franciscans.

HISTORY

Founded in 1853 as a German parish, but the parish and the neighborhood soon became very mixed ethnically. When Mexican-Americans first settled in Chicago during the First World War, they lived in the vicinity of St. Francis, so in 1925 the parish was entrusted to the Claretian religious order as a Mexican national parish. Construction of the University of Illinois campus displaced many parishioners and in 1994, the parish was merged with Holy Family. However, it reopened in 1996 after protests by the Mexican-American community.

ARCHITECTURE

After a 1904 fire seriously damaged the original church building, architect William J. Brinkmann rebuilt the church in a similar, Romanesque style.

TREASURE

One of the stained glass windows tells the history of the parish, including a threatening wrecking ball.

ST. FRANCIS OF ASSISI/
OUR LADY OF THE ANGELS

932 N. Kostner Ave., Humboldt Park

PATRON

Francis of Assisi (1181–1226) was the son of a wealthy cloth merchant. Captured during a war between Assisi and Perugia, he experienced a religious conversion and took the Gospels as the rule of his life, Jesus Christ as his literal example. Dressing in rough clothes and begging for his sustenance, he preached purity and peace. OUR LADY OF THE ANGELS: In 1635, on the feast of the Holy Angels, a poor woman of Costa Rica discovered a three-inch high statue of the Blessed Virgin carrying the Christ Child. A shrine was built on the site of the statue's discovery and became a place of pilgrimage.

HISTORY

Our Lady of Angels parish was founded in 1894 for English speaking (primarily Irish) Catholics, and in 1909 St. Francis of Assisi was organized within the same neighborhood as a Polish parish. St. Francis remained Polish for many years but Our Lady of Angels gradually acquired many Italian parishioners along with the Irish. In 1958 the school of Our Lady of Angels was devastated by a tragic fire that shocked the city and the nation. Ninety-two students and three Sisters died in the blaze. A new school building was constructed and stricter fire codes were adopted. Gradually the neighborhood became predominantly Latino. In 1990 the two parishes were merged, and services are now conducted in Polish, Spanish, and English.

ARCHITECTURE

The former St. Francis of Assisi parish church, was designed by Fox & Fox and completed in 1957. It is a modern design that recalls the Gothic churches of the past.

TREASURE

Stained glass windows based on the story of St. Francis and the Prayer of St. Francis.

ST. FRANCIS BORGIA

8033 W. Addison St., Dunning

PATRON

Francis Borgia (1510–1572) was born to the nobility, a great-grandson of Pope Alexander VI and the grandson of King Ferdinand of Aragon. After his wife died in 1546, he joined the Jesuits and became a notable preacher and eventually the General of the Order. His administrative and devotional reforms of the Order led to his informal title as "Second Founder of the Society of Jesus," after Ignatius Loyola.

HISTORY

Founded in 1949. The parish serves a congregation of many different European nationalities in a semi-suburban area on the outskirts of the city.

ARCHITECTURE

A modern, V-shaped church, designed by James R. Cronin & Associates, was completed in 1966. The sloping roof comes to a peak over the entrance, suggesting two hands folded in prayer. The Italian community of the parish recently donated the St. Padre Pio Plaza. Relics of the saint are displayed in a niche within the church.

TREASURE

A window above one entrance holds a large stained glass mural of the Holy Family donated by area schoolchildren.

ST. FRANCIS DE SALES

10201 S. Ewing Ave., East Side

PATRON

Francis de Sales (1567–1622) was born to a wealthy family in France and educated as a lawyer at the University of Padua. He entered the priesthood in 1593 and became noted for his preaching and service to the poor. He became bishop of Geneva, a heavily Calvinist center, in 1602. His books of spiritual direction have proven extremely influential, both in his own time and for centuries afterwards.

HISTORY

Founded in 1888 as a German parish. It gradually included German-speaking Luxemburgers and English-speaking Irish and Italian parishioners.

ARCHITECTURE

A combination church/school building was built in 1910 and rebuilt in 1927 after a devastating fire. Hand painted murals were installed in 1936; Conway Studios of Winona MN, installed heavy faceted glass and epoxy windows by artist Odell Prather during a 1971 renovation.

TREASURE

A shrine to Our Lady of Guadalupe.

ST. GABRIEL

4522 S. Wallace St., Canaryville

PATRON

Archangel Gabriel is one of three archangels mentioned by name in the Bible. He appeared to the Blessed Virgin Mary, informing her that she would give birth to Jesus.

HISTORY

Founded in 1880, in the Town of Lake, east of the Union Stock Yards. The neighborhood has always been known as Canaryville. Fr. Maurice Dorney, the founding pastor, served the parish for thirty-four years. He was known as the "King of the Yards," for his influence with both the meatpackers and the working people.

ARCHITECTURE

Father Dorney secured the services of the Burnham and Root architectural firm; and John A Root designed the church in a Romanesque style. The cornerstone of the church was laid in 1887 and the building was completed in 1888. Four stained glass windows are from Munich, Germany. The altars and communion rail were made by Daprato Studios, and the altars have shamrocks designed in the marble.

TREASURE

A chalice was presented by school children to Fr. Dorney for his 25th anniversary on January 27, 1899.

ST. GALL

5511 S. Sawyer Ave., Gage Park

PATRON

Gall (died c. 630) was an Irish monk who studied at Bangor with Saint Columbanus. He accompanied Columbanus on his missionary journeys on the continent of Europe. He was a pioneer of Christianity in Switzerland, where he lived and died as a hermit.

HISTORY

Organized in 1890 as a mission of St. Agnes in Brighton Park, it became a parish in 1899. Originally an Irish parish, it became heavily Polish in the first half of the twentieth century and then Latino in the latter half of the century.

ARCHITECTURE

The pie-shaped church building, designed by Pavlevic and Kovacevic and completed in 1958, was the first completely modern church structure in the archdiocese. Though the shape of the church was partly dictated by practical considerations, for it utilized the existing foundation of a basement chapel, the design anticipates the liturgical reforms of the Second Vatican Council.

TREASURE

Stained glass windows, designed by Radoslav Kovacevic, depict the Seven Sacraments.

ST. GENEVIEVE

4835 W. Altgeld Ave., Belmont Cragin

PATRON

Genevieve (422–500) is the patroness of Paris, France. She became a nun at age fifteen and was credited with inspiring the defense of the city from numerous invaders.

St. Genevieve

HISTORY

Founded as a mission of St. Sylvester in 1889, it became a parish in 1902. It served a mixed congregation of European origins until recent decades when it has become predominantly Latino. The parish conducts a school of evangelization, the Escuela San Andres, for the training of lay evangelists for Spanish-speaking people.

ARCHITECTURE

The modernized Romanesque church, designed by McCarthy, Smith & Eppig, was completed in 1941.

TREASURE

The altar contains a unique inlaid marble pelican, a traditional symbol of Jesus.

ST. GEORGE

9546 S. Ewing Ave., East Side

PATRON

St. George (died c. 303) was a soldier and martyr. That is all that's known for sure. Many legends have grown up about his life, most notably the story of how he killed a dragon. He is the patron of England.

HISTORY

Founded in 1903 as a Slovenian parish, but it served Croatian parishioners as well until the Croatians organized their own parish in 1914. The Slovenian Franciscans administered the parish for many years. Currently the parish and neighborhood is predominantly Latino.

ARCHITECTURE

The church building, designed by William J. Brinkmann in a Romanesque style, was completed in 1904.

TREASURE

Statue of St. George in armor graces center niche in altar.

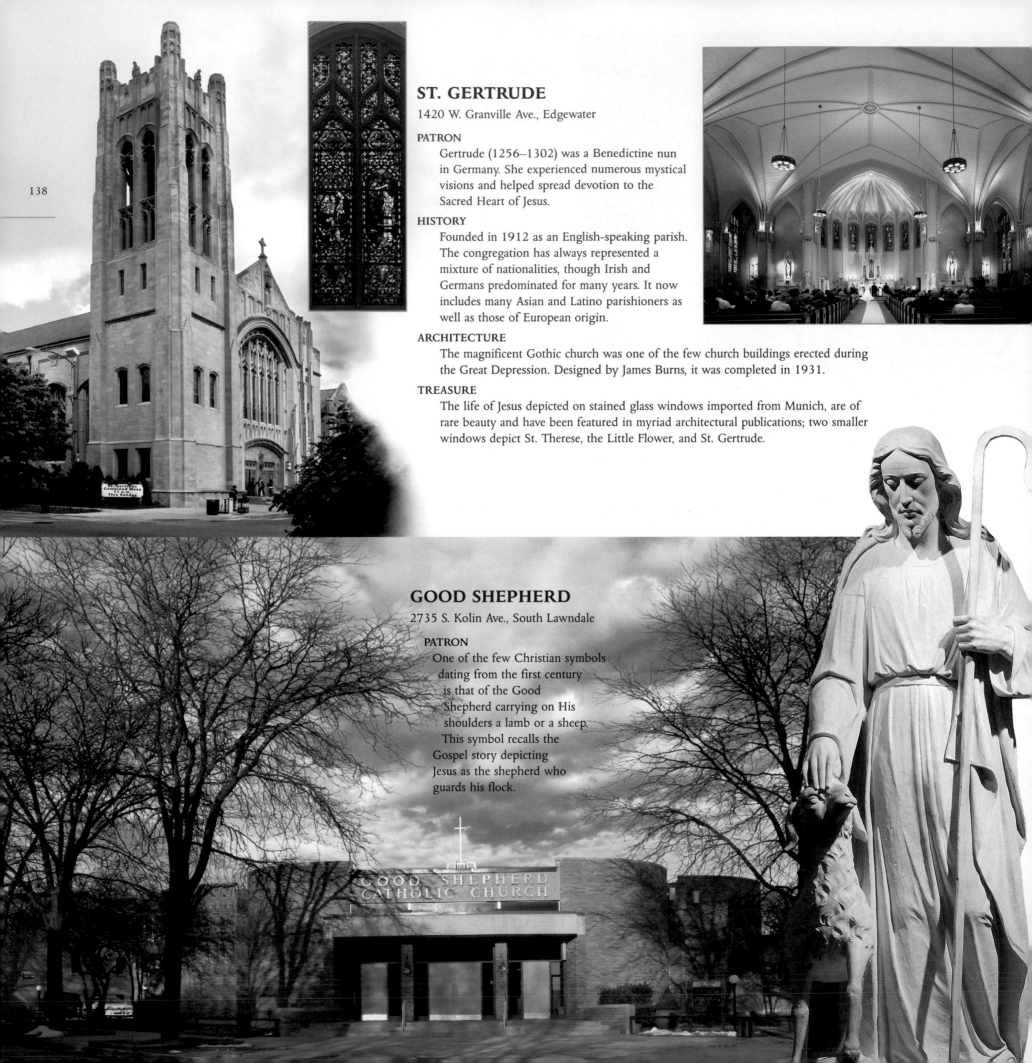

138

ST. GERTRUDE

1420 W. Granville Ave., Edgewater

PATRON

Gertrude (1256–1302) was a Benedictine nun in Germany. She experienced numerous mystical visions and helped spread devotion to the Sacred Heart of Jesus.

HISTORY

Founded in 1912 as an English-speaking parish. The congregation has always represented a mixture of nationalities, though Irish and Germans predominated for many years. It now includes many Asian and Latino parishioners as well as those of European origin.

ARCHITECTURE

The magnificent Gothic church was one of the few church buildings erected during the Great Depression. Designed by James Burns, it was completed in 1931.

TREASURE

The life of Jesus depicted on stained glass windows imported from Munich, are of rare beauty and have been featured in myriad architectural publications; two smaller windows depict St. Therese, the Little Flower, and St. Gertrude.

GOOD SHEPHERD

2735 S. Kolin Ave., South Lawndale

PATRON

One of the few Christian symbols dating from the first century is that of the Good Shepherd carrying on His shoulders a lamb or a sheep. This symbol recalls the Gospel story depicting Jesus as the shepherd who guards his flock.

Good Shepherd

HISTORY

Founded in 1907 as a Polish parish. The parish and neighborhood became predominantly Latino in the last decades of the twentieth century.

ARCHITECTURE

The modern church building, designed by Chester Tobolski, was completed in 1969.

TREASURE

A statue of Jesus, the Good Shepherd.

ST. GREGORY THE GREAT
5545 N. Paulina St., Edgewater

PATRON

Gregory the Great (540–604) was the son of a Roman senator. He became pope in 590. His two lasting legacies were the mission of evangelization he sent to England and his patronage and promotion of church music which later became known as Gregorian Chant.

HISTORY

Founded in 1904 as a German parish. After World War I, many Irish joined the parish and it has been an ethnically mixed, middle class parish ever since. Presently, there is a large Filipino population and the neighborhood is rapidly gentrifying.

ARCHITECTURE

The Norman Gothic church, designed by Comes, Perry, and McMullen of Pittsburgh, was completed in 1926. Cardinal Mundelein described the church as "a medieval gem in a modern setting." A fire struck the church on March 8, 2003, causing extensive smoke and water damage, but its wooden ceiling and many shrines survived the flames and the building has been restored to its original beauty.

TREASURE

The church is a repository of sacred artistic treasures, many produced by Old World artisans. The sanctuary holds an altar of sacrifice fashioned from the former Communion rail, a hand-carved filigree pulpit bearing images of the Four Evangelists, and a Holy Rood beam.

HOLY CROSS – IMMACULATE HEART OF MARY

4541 S. Wood St., New City

PATRON

Holy Cross: The Cross on which Christ died became an object of special respect and devotion in the early church, as evidenced by numerous references in the epistles of St. Paul. It became even more intense after the discovery of relics of the True Cross by St. Helena in the early 4th century.

Immaculate Heart of Mary: Devotion to Mary's Immaculate Heart became widespread after the Protestant Reformation, which downgraded the importance of Mary. St. John Eudes established a feast in honor of the Immaculate Heart in 1644 as the maternal feast of his congregation of priests, and this feast was extended to the rest of the Church in 1944 by Pope Pius XII.

HISTORY

Holy Cross was founded in 1904 as a Lithuanian parish and Immaculate Heart of Mary Vicariate was founded in 1947 as a mission church for Mexican-Americans. Both ministered to immigrant workers in the Union Stock Yards located nearby. After the stockyards closed in the 1970s, both parishes experienced hard times. In 1981 they were merged and the largely Mexican and Mexican-American congregation using both churches for worship and both parish plants for a wide variety of activities and services.

Immaculate Heart of Mary

ARCHITECTURE

The Baroque church, designed by Joseph Molitor, was completed in 1915. Its twin towers soar above the working-class houses and two-flats of the Back of the Yards neighborhood. The church's architecture helped ease the transition from Lithuanian to Mexican immigrant congregations, since both ethnic groups would have recalled similar Baroque churches in their home countries. Immaculate Heart of Mary was converted from a commercial building in the 1940s and its mission style recalls churches of Latin America.

TREASURE

The massive pipe organ in the main church.

HOLY FAMILY

1019 S. May St., Near West Side

PATRON

The Holy Family celebrates the lives of Jesus, Mary, and Joseph. This family unit is sometimes referred to as the "little Trinity," mirroring on earth the Holy Trinity of Father, Son, and Spirit.

HISTORY

The first Jesuit parish in the city, Holy Family was founded by Fr. Arnold Damen in 1857. By 1900, it was the largest English-speaking parish in the country. As the neighborhood changed in the 20th century, the congregation changed from Western European origins to Hispanic and African-American. By the late1960s, Holy Family was predominantly an African-American parish. When the existence of the parish was threatened at the end of the century, a vigorous fundraising campaign saved the church from extinction and restored its art and architecture. The church is currently owned by the Society of Jesus but staffed by archdiocesan priests.

Holy Family

ARCHITECTURE

The Victorian Gothic church, designed by Dillenburg and Zurcher, was constructed between 1857 and 1860. The second oldest church building in the city, Holy Family was saved by a providential wind shift during the Great Chicago Fire of 1871. In accord with a vow made by Fr. Damen, seven vigil lights burn perpetually in thanksgiving. John Van Osdel designed the belltower, which was completed in 1874 and was for a time the tallest structure in the city.

TREASURE

Recently a long-shuttered vault was opened and revealed a treasure trove of religious art. The vault contained chalices and monstrances from the 19th century; a set of gold vestments brought from Paris by Fr. Damen; and relics of St. Peter Claver and the North American Jesuit martyrs.

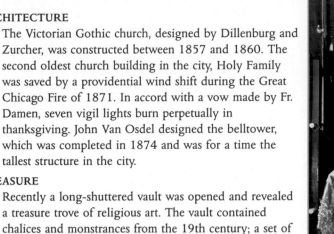

HOLY INNOCENTS

743 N. Armour St., West Town

PATRON

The Holy Innocents were the children of Judea, two years old or younger, slaughtered by King Herod in an attempt to kill the infant Christ, after he had learned of the Messiah's birth from the Magi.

HISTORY

Founded in 1905 as a Polish parish. It remained a Polish parish until 1975, when it was assigned territorial boundaries. The parish retains its strong identification with Polonia while welcoming Hispanics and Catholics of other ethnic groups. Although there has been much recent gentrification in the neighborhood, the parish continues to minister in English, Polish, and Spanish.

ARCHITECTURE

The church building, designed by Worthmann and Steinbach in a Romanesque style with many Byzantine flourishes, was completed in 1912. The interior was redesigned after a 1960 fire and recently restored for the parish centennial. Words of welcome are engraved in three languages over the triple entrance doors — Welcome, Witamy, Bienvenidos.

TREASURE

The Nativity window depicts the shepherds dressed in mountaineer garb of the Gorale of Southern Poland (where the original parishioners came from).

HOLY NAME CATHEDRAL

730 N. Wabash Ave., Near North Side

PATRON

The Holy Name of Jesus has been revered since the days of the early church. In his Epistle to the Philippians, St. Paul wrote: "That in the name of Jesus every knee should bow, of those that are in heaven, on earth, and under the earth."

HISTORY

St. Mary's, the first parish in the city, was the original cathedral of the diocese. Holy Name parish, north of the Chicago River, was founded in 1849 adjacent to the first St. Mary of the Lake Seminary. In the late 1850s and 1860s, the Chicago bishops used Holy Name church for services that drew large congregations. After the Chicago Fire of 1871 it was formally named the cathedral.

ARCHITECTURE

The Gothic cathedral, designed by Patrick C. Keely of Brooklyn, was completed in 1875 and has been renovated twice, in 1915 and 1968. The latter renovation removed most of the statues and other devotional objects and now represents a simplified aesthetic, according to the liturgical reforms of the Second Vatican Council. A dramatic Crucifix, depicting the glorified Christ on the Cross, dominates the sanctuary.

TREASURE

The five Cardinals' galeros (ceremonial hats) hanging from the ceiling.

HOLY NAME OF MARY

11159 S. Loomis St., Morgan Park

PATRON

Devotion to the Holy Name of Mary parallels devotion to the Holy Name of Jesus. Invocation of Mary's name is a form of prayer, asking the Blessed Virgin to intercede with her Son. This Marian devotion became especially strong after the Protestant Reformation, which downgraded the importance of Mary.

HISTORY

Holy Name of Mary was founded in 1940, the first parish explicitly organized for black Catholics, not handed down from an earlier ethnic group.

ARCHITECTURE

The modern church building, completed in 1970, was entirely planned and built by African-American artists. Raymond Broady was the architect and Bush Construction Co. the contractors. Carl W. Merschel, a professor at Olive-Harvey College, designed the interior.

TREASURE

The oval-shaped black Madonna statue, designed by African-American artist Frank Hayden.

Holy Name of Mary

HOLY ROSARY

351 E. 113th St., Roseland

PATRON

The Rosary, developed in the Middle Ages, consists of a series of meditations on the lives of Jesus and Mary conducted while reciting a formula of ten Hail Marys preceded by an Our Father and followed by a Glory Be. St. Dominic was the main proponent of this form of prayer. Fortunate outcomes at times of crisis in European history, such as the Battle of Lepanto against the Turks in 1571, were often attributed to praying the Rosary and thus popularized the devotion.

HISTORY

Founded in 1882. Holy Rosary parish served the Irish laborers employed at the "model town" of Pullman. Though many other ethnic groups also organized national parishes in Roseland, Holy Rosary remained the territorial parish for the area. Since the 1960s, the parish and neighborhood have been predominantly African-American.

ARCHITECTURE

The church building was designed by the same architect who planned and built the Town of Pullman, Solon S. Beman. The industrial magnate George Pullman insisted that his own architect design the church so that it would harmonize architecturally with his planned town. Designed in a Romanesque style, the church building was completed in 1890.

TREASURE

A stained glass window of Our Lady giving the Rosary to St. Dominic.

HOLY ROSARY

612 N. Western Ave., West Town

PATRON

The Rosary, developed in the Middle Ages, consists of a series of meditations on the lives of Jesus and Mary conducted while reciting a formula of ten Hail Marys preceded by an Our Father and followed by a Glory Be. St. Dominic was the main proponent of this form of prayer. Fortunate outcomes at times of crisis in European history, such as the Battle of Lepanto against the Turks in 1571, were often attributed to praying the Rosary and thus popularized the devotion.

HISTORY

Founded in 1904 as an Italian parish. The parish remained predominantly Italian but both Slovak and Irish parishes nearby were closed in the 1960s and 70s and their parishioners began attending Holy Rosary. The parish also has a large group of Latino parishioners. The parish and neighborhood are newly gentrified and prosperous.

ARCHITECTURE

The Italian Renaissance church building (architect unknown) was completed shortly after the parish's founding in 1904.

TREASURE

Oil paintings of the fifteen traditional mysteries of the rosary, and tapestries of the five new luminous mysteries.

ST. HYACINTH

3636 W. Wolfram St., Avondale

PATRON

Hyacinth of Cracow (1185–1257) was educated in Paris and Bologna. He became a Dominican friar in 1220 and brought the Dominican Order to Poland, then evangelized throughout Poland, Sweden, Norway, Denmark, Scotland, Russia, Turkey, and Greece. He is known as the Apostle of the North.

HISTORY

Founded in 1894 as a Polish parish. The Resurrectionist Order, from the city's first Polish parish, St. Stanislaus Kostka, organized this parish and still administer it today. Since the 1980s the parish has received a large number of new immigrants from Poland and is still one of the largest Polish parishes in the country. The church building was raised to basilica status by Pope John Paul II on November 30, 2003.

ARCHITECTURE

The Renaissance church building, designed by Worthmann and Steinbach, was completed in 1921. Its triple cupolas tower over the surrounding neighborhood.

TREASURE

Monumental murals and stained glass in the central dome of the church.

ST. IGNATIUS

6559 N. Glenwood Ave., Rogers Park

PATRON

Ignatius of Loyola (1491–1556) was a Spanish nobleman and a soldier. While wounded after a battle, he experienced a religious conversion. He founded the Society of Jesus (Jesuits) in 1534. The Jesuits became noted scholars, polemicists, and missionaries. In addition to the usual vows of poverty, chastity, and obedience, they took a special vow of loyalty to the Pope

HISTORY

Founded in 1906 by the Jesuits as an adjunct to Loyola University along the north lakeshore. It has remained an active middle-class parish, though the connection with the Jesuits was recently broken and the parish is now administered by diocesan priests. Latin American and African ethnic groups have joined with many of the original parishioners to form the current congregation.

ARCHITECTURE

The church building, designed by Henry J. Schlacks in imitation of the Gesu, the mother church of the Jesuits in Rome, was completed in 1917

TREASURE

The chapel, Our Lady Queen of the Angels, recently renovated.

IMMACULATE CONCEPTION

2745 W. 44th St., Brighton Park

PATRON

The Immaculate Conception is the dogma of faith stating that the Blessed Virgin was from the first instant of her conception, by a singular privilege and grace of God, preserved from all stain of original sin. Shortly after this dogma was defined by Pope Pius IX in 1854, Our Lady appeared to Bernadette Soubirous at Lourdes in 1858, describing herself as the Immaculate Conception. Devotion to Mary under this title became widespread thereafter.

HISTORY

Founded in 1914 as a Lithuanian parish. Always a working-class parish, it now includes many Latinos as well as Lithuanians.

ARCHITECTURE

The modern church building, designed by Belli and Belli, was completed in 1963. It has graceful sweeping lines that soften the severity of the modern design.

TREASURE

A large wooden "Lithuanian-styled" cross stands in front of the parish rectory. The Brighton Park Via Crucis (Way of the Cross) concludes its annual procession with the final scene in front of the church.

IMMACULATE CONCEPTION

2944 E. 88th St., South Chicago

PATRON

The Immaculate Conception is the dogma of faith stating that the Blessed Virgin was from the first instant of her conception, by a singular privilege and grace of God, preserved from all stain of original sin. Shortly after this dogma was defined by Pope Pius IX in 1854, Our Lady appeared to Bernadette Soubirous at Lourdes in 1858, describing herself as the Immaculate Conception. Devotion to Mary under this title became widespread thereafter.

HISTORY

Founded in 1882 as a Polish parish. Immaculate Conception was the original Polish parish in this working-class, steel mill district, but it was divided three times to form the Polish parishes of St. Michael,

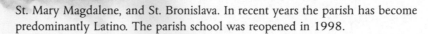

St. Mary Magdalene, and St. Bronislava. In recent years the parish has become predominantly Latino. The parish school was reopened in 1998.

ARCHITECTURE

The church building, designed by Martin A. Carr in a Renaissance style, was completed in 1899. It was restored in 2002, with new altars designed by Frank, Loshen, and McCreany of Washington, D.C., based on the original altars of 1899. In addition, a plaza was built to the north of the church and a handicap ramp was installed.

TREASURE

The statue of Mary, the Immaculate Conception, over the high altar.

IMMACULATE CONCEPTION

1431 N. North Park Ave., Near North Side

PATRON

The Immaculate Conception is the dogma of faith stating that the Blessed Virgin was from the first instant of her conception, by a singular privilege and grace of God, preserved from all stain of original sin. Shortly after this dogma was defined by Pope Pius IX in 1854, Our Lady appeared to Bernadette Soubirous at Lourdes in 1858, describing herself as the Immaculate Conception. Devotion to Mary under this title became widespread thereafter.

HISTORY

Founded in 1859, just five years after the definition of the dogma of the Immaculate Conception. The parish was organized to serve English-speaking Catholics who lived between Holy Name parish (now the cathedral) and the German parish of St. Michael. The neighborhood, close to downtown and to Lincoln Park, has undergone many changes over the last century and a half. Presently, the congregation includes upper-middle class condominium owners from Sandburg Village and public housing residents from Cabrini-Green. Immaculate Conception is sometimes called "the little church in the big city."

ARCHITECTURE

Parishioners worship in a simple, intimate church space on the lower level of the modern school building, completed in 1953. The former church was abandoned as structurally unsound in 1957.

TREASURE

The statue of Our Lady, formerly atop the bell tower of the old church, now stands on a pillar in a tree-lined walkway, welcoming people into the church and parish center.

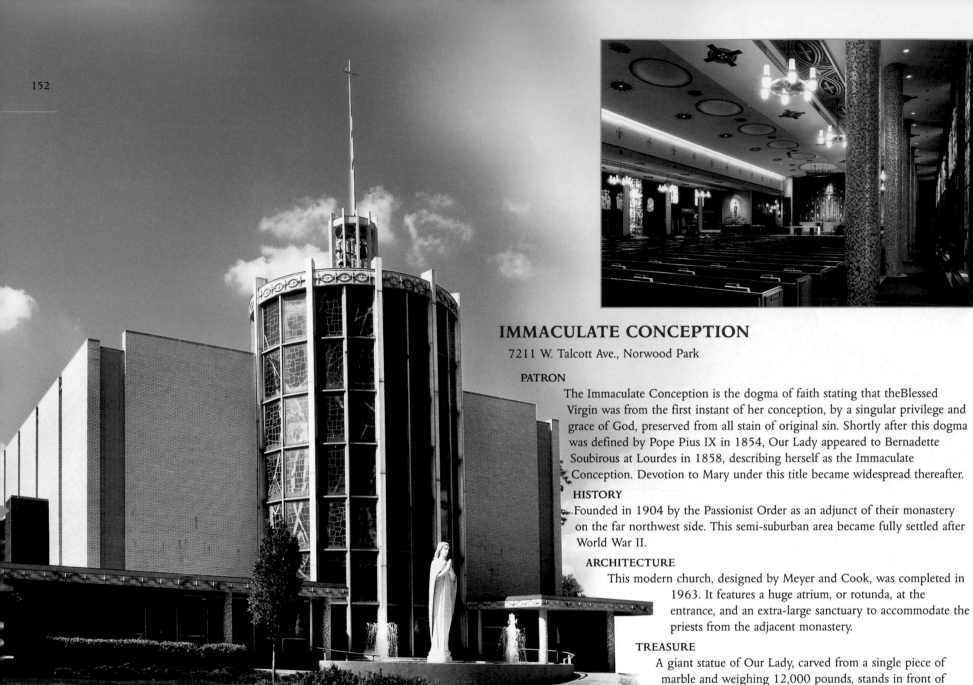

IMMACULATE CONCEPTION

7211 W. Talcott Ave., Norwood Park

PATRON

The Immaculate Conception is the dogma of faith stating that the Blessed Virgin was from the first instant of her conception, by a singular privilege and grace of God, preserved from all stain of original sin. Shortly after this dogma was defined by Pope Pius IX in 1854, Our Lady appeared to Bernadette Soubirous at Lourdes in 1858, describing herself as the Immaculate Conception. Devotion to Mary under this title became widespread thereafter.

HISTORY

Founded in 1904 by the Passionist Order as an adjunct of their monastery on the far northwest side. This semi-suburban area became fully settled after World War II.

ARCHITECTURE

This modern church, designed by Meyer and Cook, was completed in 1963. It features a huge atrium, or rotunda, at the entrance, and an extra-large sanctuary to accommodate the priests from the adjacent monastery.

TREASURE

A giant statue of Our Lady, carved from a single piece of marble and weighing 12,000 pounds, stands in front of church.

IMMACULATE HEART OF MARY

3817 N. Christiana Ave., Irving Park

PATRON

Devotion to Mary's Immaculate Heart became widespread after the Protestant Reformation, which downgraded the importance of Mary. St. John Eudes established a feast in honor of the Immaculate Heart in 1644 as the maternal feast of his congregation of priests, and this feast was extended to the rest of the Church in 1944 by Pope Pius XII.

HISTORY

Founded in 1912 as a Polish parish. Auxiliary Bishop Aloysius J. Wycislo, the second Polish priest named an auxiliary bishop for Chicago, served as pastor from 1959 to 1968. The parish now includes many different ethnic groups.

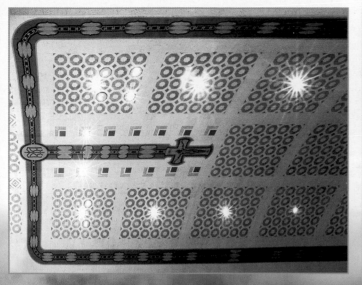

ARCHITECTURE
The modern church, designed by Pirola and Erbach, was completed in 1957.

TREASURE
A gigantic rosary painted on the ceiling.

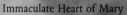
Immaculate Heart of Mary

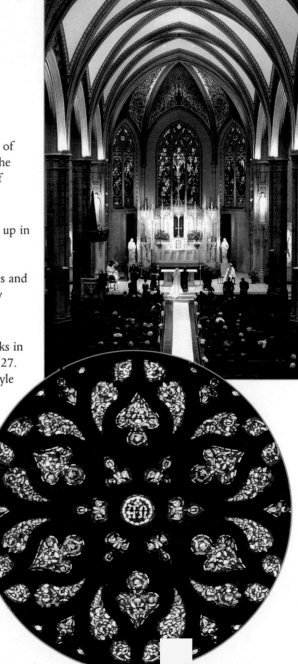

ST. ITA
1220 W. Catalpa Ave., Edgewater

PATRON
Ita (died c. 570) is the most popular female saint of Ireland after St. Brigid. A member of the Irish nobility, she founded a convent in County Limerick and lived a life of great austerity.

HISTORY
Founded in 1900. The first pastor, Fr. John Crowe, grew up in County Limerick not far from St. Ita's convent and thus named the parish after her. The north lakeshore neighborhood was, and still is, a district of large homes and elegant apartments. The parish now serves a culturally diverse congregation.

ARCHITECTURE
The church building, designed by Henry J. Schlacks in a French Gothic style, was completed in 1927. Cardinal Mundelein suggested this style to the architect, who accordingly carved a large "M" on the stone parapet.

TREASURE
Stained glass rose window on the east side of the church.

ST. JAMES

5730 W. Fullerton Ave., Belmont Cragin

PATRON

Two of the Twelve Apostles were named James. One, usually called James the Greater, was the son of Zebedee and the brother of John. He was the first Apostle to be martyred, in 44 AD. The other, usually called James the Less, was the son of Alphaeus. He became first bishop of Jerusalem and was martyred there about 62 AD.

HISTORY

Founded in 1914 as a Polish parish. It remained a predominantly Polish parish for most of its history but it now includes many Latino parishioners. Mass is celebrated in English, Polish, and Spanish.

ARCHITECTURE

The church, in a red-brick colonial style, was completed in 1968.

TREASURE

A mosaic of Our Lady of Czestochowa.

ST. JAMES

2907 S. Wabash Ave., Douglas

PATRON

James the Greater (died c. 44 AD), the son of Zebedee and Solome, the brother of John, was the first Apostle to be martyred. Tradition says that James spread the Gospel in Spain and that his body was translated there following his martyrdom in Jerusalem. James' tomb in Santiago de Compostela, Spain, has long been a major pilgrimage destination.

HISTORY

Old St. James, as it is often called, was founded in 1855 and is the mother church of South Side Irish parishes. Originally organized to serve workers in the railroad car works, it not only served the working-class but also the prosperous business class that built homes on the Near South Side. By the early 1900s African-Americans moving north during the Great Migration replaced the Irish. Today St. James is a diverse community of faith, where rich and poor, students and seniors, black and white, Asian and African worship together.

ARCHITECTURE

The church building, completed in 1880, was designed by the same architect who built Holy Name Cathedral, Patrick C. Keely of Brooklyn. The Joliet limestone of the façade and the Victorian Gothic style also recall the cathedral. The church was seriously damaged by a fire in 1972 but its Gothic fabric was saved, standing as a sign of stability in the neighborhood.

TREASURE

The 1891 Roosevelt organ.

St. James

ST. JANE DE CHANTAL

5252 S. Austin Ave., Garfield Ridge

PATRON

Jane Frances de Chantal (1572–1641) was born to the nobility of Burgundy, and married at age twenty to the Baron de Chantal. After having four children, she was left a widow in 1601. She became a spiritual disciple of St. Francis de Sales and in 1610 she founded the Order of the Visitation.

HISTORY

Founded in 1954 in a semi-suburban area on the far southwest side of the city. The neighborhood remains residential and is home to a wide variety of ethnic groups. Mass is celebrated in English and Polish.

ARCHITECTURE

The modern church, designed by Pavlevic and Kovacevic, was completed in 1964. The church is diamond-shaped with a serrated roof and striking modern bell tower.

TREASURE

Stations of the Cross, main altar, and mosaics in the church were designed by Sister Miriam Gordon, OP, the first principal of the school.

ST. JEROME

1709 W. Lunt Ave., Rogers Park

PATRON

Jerome (341–420) was a Roman lawyer who converted to Christianity in 365 and lived as a hermit in Syria. Pope Damasus I commissioned him to make a new translation of the Bible into Latin. The result of his 30 years of work was the Vulgate translation, which is still in use. He died in the Holy Land after living there again as a hermit.

HISTORY

Established in 1895 by Luxemburgers for the English-speaking Catholics of Rogers Park who previously attended either the German parish of St. Henry's or St. Mary's in Evanston. It now serves a multicultural community of people from North, Central, and South America; Europe; Asia; Africa; and the Caribbean and Pacific Islands.

ARCHITECTURE

Designed by Charles H. Prindeville in Italian Renaissance style, the church was completed in 1916 and enlarged in 1934, giving it one of the longest main aisles in Chicago. The interior is most impressive with 24 marble statues, mosaic pillars, heroic paintings, fresco and carved gold leaf ceiling.

TREASURE

Twenty stained glass windows portray scenes from the Bible as well as modern day life, including an American Soldier, Lady Liberty, and a 1934 window depicting Cardinal Mundelein.

ST. JEROME CROATIAN

2823 S. Princeton Ave., Bridgeport

PATRON

Jerome (c.341–420) was born in Dalmatia, a region of present-day Croatia. Pope St. Damasus I commissioned him to make a new translation of the Scriptures into Latin. The result of his 30 years of work was the Vulgate translation, still in use 1600 years later. St. Jerome is a Father and Doctor of the Church.

HISTORY

Founded in 1912 as a Croatian parish. It has been administered for its entire history by Croatian Franciscans and contiues to celebrate a Croatian language Mass each Sunday. Many parishioners are of Croatian or Italian descent.

ARCHITECTURE

The Romanesque church, designed in 1885 by Christian O. Hansen for a community of Swedish Lutherans, was purchased by St. Jerome's in 1922. A major renovation was recently completed.

TREASURE

A painting of the icon of Our Lady of Sinj. The original icon, in Sinj, Croatia, was credited with bringing a victory against the Ottomans on August 15, 1715. Every August 15, St. Jerome's parishioners carry Our Lady of Sinj up and down the neighborhood streets in a procession that is followed by a parish festival.

ST. JOACHIM
700 E. 91st St., Chatham

PATRON

Joachim was the husband of Saint Anne and the father of the Blessed Virgin Mary. Nothing is known of his life or death. Devotion to him increased in the Middle Ages along with the devotions to Mary and Anne

HISTORY

Founded in 1894 to serve Irish workers on the railroads. The parish remained largely Irish until the 1960s when the neighborhood became African-American.

ARCHITECTURE

The church building is the product of a 1933 remodeling of an older frame building. Architect George S. Smith designed a Romanesque brick structure which was built around the existing church.

TREASURE

A beautiful marble Baptismal font and pool greet worshipers when they enter the church.

ST. JOHN BERCHMANS

2517 W. Logan Blvd.,
Logan Square

PATRON

John Berchmans (1599–1621) was a Belgian Jesuit who died before ordination. He is a patron of youth and altar servers; and, like St. Therese of Lisieux, is revered as an example of how sainthood can be achieved in the course of an ordinary life.

HISTORY

Founded in 1905 as the first and only Belgian (Flemish-speaking) parish in Chicago, it was assigned territorial boundaries in 1916 and developed into a small, but diverse, parish with first a Polish and then later a Hispanic majority.

ARCHITECTURE

The church was designed by John F. Steinbach in Romanesque style and was completed in 1907. The adjoining rectory, convent, and school building, all designed in a similar style by the same architect, occupy a city block at the east end of Logan Blvd.

TREASURE

The Noah's Ark stained glass window in the east transept was designed by John J. Kinsella shortly before his death in 1923. It captures the morning sun brilliantly in the rainbow over the Ark.

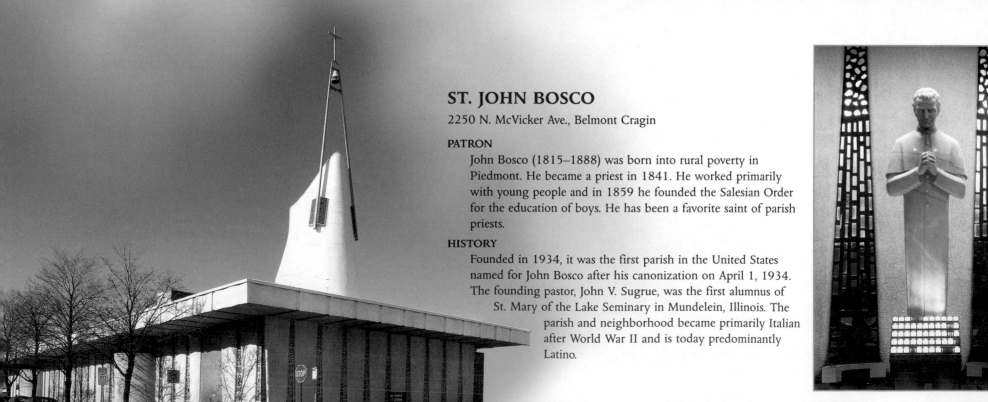

ST. JOHN BOSCO

2250 N. McVicker Ave., Belmont Cragin

PATRON

John Bosco (1815–1888) was born into rural poverty in Piedmont. He became a priest in 1841. He worked primarily with young people and in 1859 he founded the Salesian Order for the education of boys. He has been a favorite saint of parish priests.

HISTORY

Founded in 1934, it was the first parish in the United States named for John Bosco after his canonization on April 1, 1934. The founding pastor, John V. Sugrue, was the first alumnus of St. Mary of the Lake Seminary in Mundelein, Illinois. The parish and neighborhood became primarily Italian after World War II and is today predominantly Latino.

ARCHITECTURE

The modern church building, designed by Belli and Belli, was completed in 1965. It has a free-form bell tower which rises 100 feet over the rectangular structure.

TREASURE

John Bosco's statue in the same creamy Portuguese onyx as the altar.

ST. JOHN CANTIUS

825 N. Carpenter St., West Town

PATRON

John Cantius (1390–1473) was born in Kenty, a town in southern Poland. He studied at the University of Krakow, and became a priest and a professor of philosophy and theology. He is a patron of Poland, the city of Krakow, and the Jagiellonian University.

HISTORY

Founded in 1893 as a Polish parish by the Resurrectionist Order of priests. The parish retained its Polish character for many years, but construction of the Kennedy Expressway in the 1950s forced many parishioners to leave the neighborhood, and further decline of the inner city almost led to the parish's closure. A revival of the parish began in the late 1980s and today it is again thriving. The parish is presently administered by the Society of St. John Cantius, a new religious community of men that was founded at the parish in 1998.

ARCHITECTURE

The church building, designed by Adolphus Druiding, was completed in 1898. Like most of the larger Polish churches, it reflects the Baroque style that was so familiar to Polish immigrants.

TREASURE

The church interior is rich in sacred art and the parish has a rich program of sacred music, supported by five parish choirs. An unusual art treasure, however, is the poignant statue of the Holy Innocents in the vestibule.

ST. JOHN DE LA SALLE

10205 S. King Dr., Roseland

PATRON

John Baptist de la Salle (1651–1719) was born at Reims of a noble family, studied at St. Sulpice in Paris, and was ordained a priest in 1678. He founded the Brothers of the Christian Schools (Christian Brothers), who conduct schools for boys.

HISTORY

Founded in 1948 for English-speaking Catholics in the Rosemoor district at the northern end of Roseland. The parish and neighborhood became African-American in the 1960s and 70s.

ARCHITECTURE

A combination church/school building was completed in 1950.

TREASURE

The stained glass windows depict significant events in the life of Jesus.

ST. JOHN FISHER

10234 S. Washtenaw Ave., Beverly

PATRON

John Fisher (1469–1535) studied theology at Cambridge University and was ordained a priest in 1491. In 1504 he became both Chancellor of Cambridge and Bishop of Rochester. He was personal confessor for Queen Catherine of Aragon, first wife of King Henry VIII. When he rejected the king's claims as head of the Church of England, he was imprisoned for treason and executed on June 22, 1535. He is often paired with his contemporary, St. Thomas More, with whom he shares a feast day, June 22.

HISTORY

Founded in 1948. This southwest side area filled up with residences, including many bungalows, after World War II. The parish boundaries form a square mile, with the church at its center. It remains a vibrant parish with a school of 800 students. The Thanksgiving Day liturgy draws the entire commuity together, giving thanks to God through the Mass and the music of parish choirs.

ARCHITECTURE

The modern church, designed by John L. Bartolomeo, was completed in 1956. The sanctuary crucifix was designed by a parishioner, Klemens Kwapizewski. The stained glass windows, designed by Gabriel Loire, reflect Old and New Testament stories of sacrifice.

TREASURE

A mural of St. John Fisher.

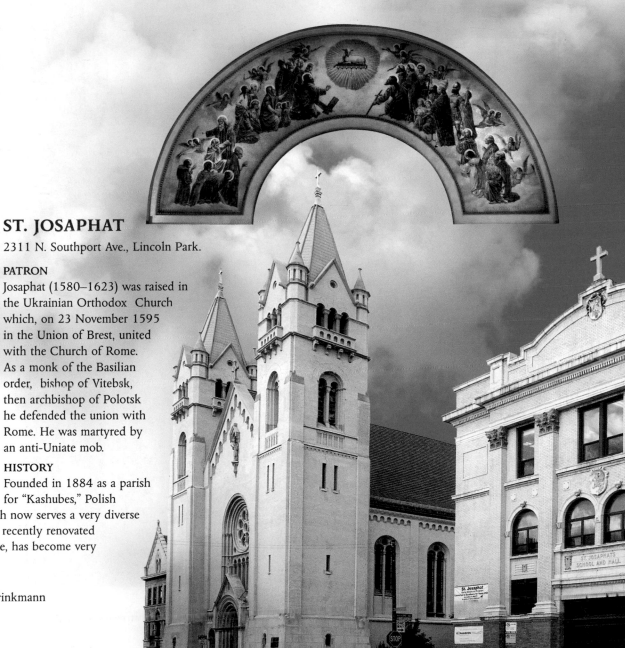

ST. JOSAPHAT

2311 N. Southport Ave., Lincoln Park.

PATRON

Josaphat (1580–1623) was raised in the Ukrainian Orthodox Church which, on 23 November 1595 in the Union of Brest, united with the Church of Rome. As a monk of the Basilian order, bishop of Vitebsk, then archbishop of Polotsk he defended the union with Rome. He was martyred by an anti-Uniate mob.

HISTORY

Founded in 1884 as a parish for "Kashubes," Polish immigrants from the German-occupied region of Poland. The parish now serves a very diverse congregation in a newly prosperous, gentrified neighborhood. The recently renovated church, with its excellent music program and traditional architecture, has become very popular for weddings, with over 65 weddings each year.

ARCHITECTURE

The church was designed in the Romanesque style by William J. Brinkmann and completed in 1902.

TREASURE

Impressive mural over the arch of the sanctuary.

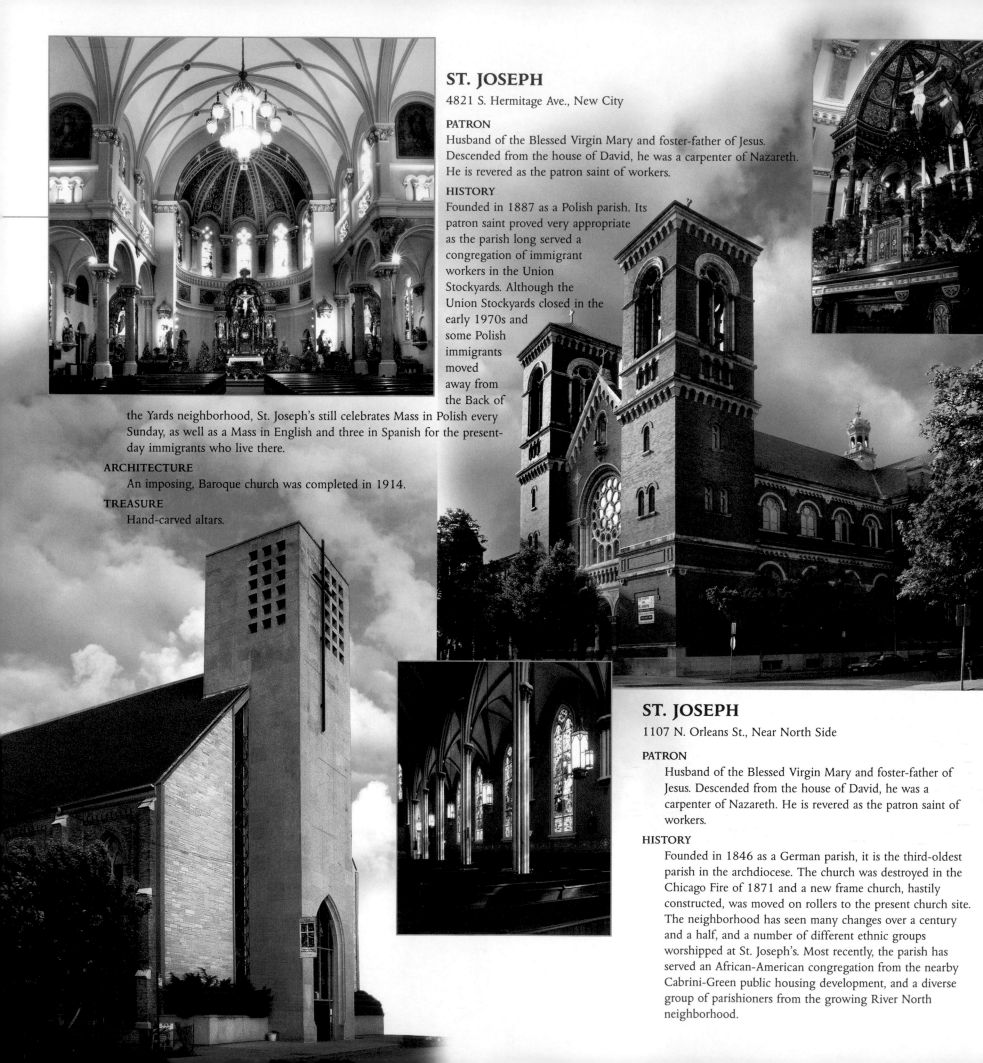

ST. JOSEPH

4821 S. Hermitage Ave., New City

PATRON

Husband of the Blessed Virgin Mary and foster-father of Jesus. Descended from the house of David, he was a carpenter of Nazareth. He is revered as the patron saint of workers.

HISTORY

Founded in 1887 as a Polish parish. Its patron saint proved very appropriate as the parish long served a congregation of immigrant workers in the Union Stockyards. Although the Union Stockyards closed in the early 1970s and some Polish immigrants moved away from the Back of the Yards neighborhood, St. Joseph's still celebrates Mass in Polish every Sunday, as well as a Mass in English and three in Spanish for the present-day immigrants who live there.

ARCHITECTURE

An imposing, Baroque church was completed in 1914.

TREASURE

Hand-carved altars.

ST. JOSEPH

1107 N. Orleans St., Near North Side

PATRON

Husband of the Blessed Virgin Mary and foster-father of Jesus. Descended from the house of David, he was a carpenter of Nazareth. He is revered as the patron saint of workers.

HISTORY

Founded in 1846 as a German parish, it is the third-oldest parish in the archdiocese. The church was destroyed in the Chicago Fire of 1871 and a new frame church, hastily constructed, was moved on rollers to the present church site. The neighborhood has seen many changes over a century and a half, and a number of different ethnic groups worshipped at St. Joseph's. Most recently, the parish has served an African-American congregation from the nearby Cabrini-Green public housing development, and a diverse group of parishioners from the growing River North neighborhood.

St. Joseph

ARCHITECTURE

The Gothic brick church was completed in 1878, replacing the frame structure erected after the Chicago Fire. The façade and bell towers have been rebuilt and modernized.

TREASURE

Stained glass windows

ST. JULIANA

7200 N. Osceola Ave., Edison Park

PATRON

Juliana Falconieri (1270–1341) was born in Florence and entered the recently founded Servite Order at an early age. Though not the first woman admitted to this Order, she is considered its female foundress since she wrote the rule for the Order.

HISTORY

Founded in 1927 for English-speaking Catholics in the farthest northwest side neighborhood of Chicago. The semi-suburban residential area filled up after World War II. The parishioners are of many different European ethnic backgrounds.

ARCHITECTURE

The modern church, designed by Fox & Fox, was completed in 1964. Its angular bell tower and aluminum cross rise nearly 100 feet above the ground.

TREASURE

The focal point behind the black marble altar is a "tree of life" symbolizing the Cross of Christ.

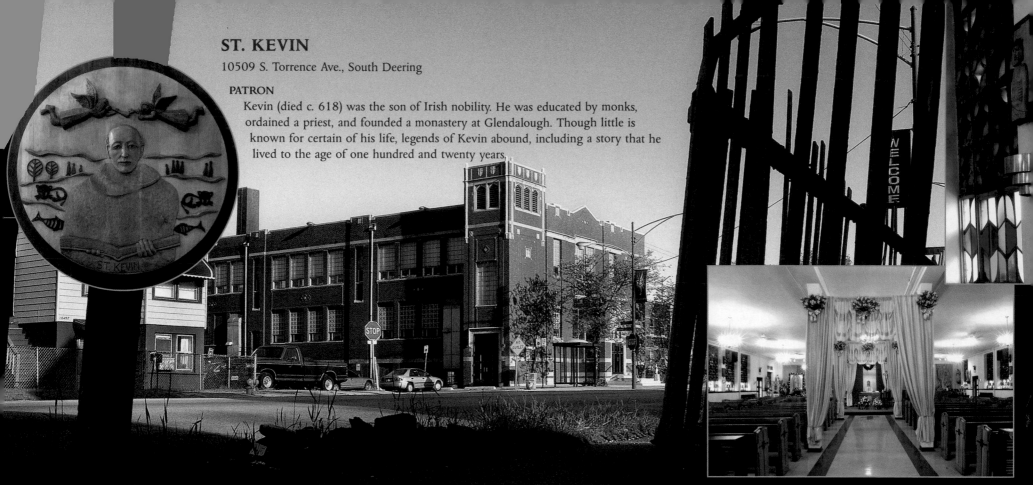

ST. KEVIN

10509 S. Torrence Ave., South Deering

PATRON

Kevin (died c. 618) was the son of Irish nobility. He was educated by monks, ordained a priest, and founded a monastery at Glendalough. Though little is known for certain of his life, legends of Kevin abound, including a story that he lived to the age of one hundred and twenty years.

HISTORY

Founded in 1884 for a working class community near the first steel mill in the "Irondale" district. The parish remained a predominantly Irish, working-class community until the mid-twentieth century. It now serves a diverse congregation of European, Latino, and African-Americans origins.

ARCHITECTURE

The combination church/school building, completed in 1926, continues to serve the parish.

TREASURE

Carved wooden art work by Jerzy Kenar and mosaics by Jean Morman Unsworth.

ST. KILIAN

8725 S. May St., Auburn-Gresham

PATRON

Kilian (640–689) was a son of Irish nobility, who became a priest and a monk. He set out with eleven companions as a missionary to Germany, where he was martyred.

HISTORY

Founded in 1905. The parish originally served an Irish and German congregation in a semi-suburban neighborhood on the far southwest side. The parish and neighborhood became predominantly African-American in the 1960s.

ARCHITECTURE

The church, designed in a simplified Renaissance style by McCarthy, Smith and Eppig, was completed in 1937. There are beautiful inlaid wood designs throughout the church.

TREASURE
Celtic designs, stenciled on the walls
with gold leaf, capture candlelight
like shimmering foil.

St. Kilian

ST. LADISLAUS

5345 W. Roscoe St., Portage Park

PATRON
Ladislaus (1040–1095) was a king of Hungary, who annexed
Dalmatia and Croatia to his kingdom. Known for his
enlightened government, devotion to his
people and to the Church, he was chosen
commander-in-chief of the First
Crusade, but died before the
expedition left.

HISTORY
Founded as a Polish parish in
1914 in a still rural area. The
parish remained Polish as
the neighborhood filled
up after World War II.
Today the parish
includes English,
Spanish, and Polish
speaking parishioners.

ARCHITECTURE
The Romanesque
church, designed
by Leo Strelka,
was completed
in 1955.

TREASURE
The rose
window.

SANTA LUCIA-SANTA MARIA INCORONATA

3022 S. Wells St., Armour Square

PATRON

Lucia, or Lucy (died. c. 304), was a virgin martyr of Sicily. She is the patron saint of those suffering from diseases of the eye, and a monthly blessing and anointing of the eyes are held in the parish.
Santa Maria Incoronata honors the Queenship of the Blessed Virgin Mary.

HISTORY

Santa Maria Incoronata was founded as a mission for Italian immigrants in 1897 then became an Italian parish in 1901, staffed by the Scalabrini Fathers. As the neighborhood became overwhelmingly Chinese in the decades between the world wars, a mission church for Italians, named Santa Lucia, was opened at 30th and Wells. In 1963 the church building of Santa Maria Incoronata was given over to St. Therese Chinese mission and the parish was consolidated with Santa Lucia at the latter's site.

ARCHITECTURE

A combination church/school building, designed by Ray Basso in 1961 at the Santa Lucia site, serves the consolidated parish. It has been renovated and made handicapped accessible.

TREASURE

A relic of Santa Lucia in the church.

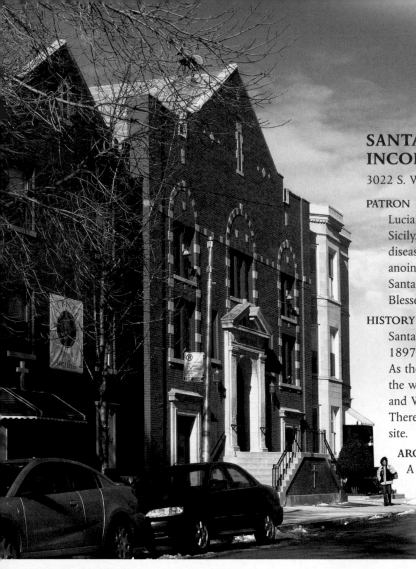

ST. MALACHY

2251 W. Washington Blvd., Near West Side

PATRON

Malachy (1094–1148) was the son of a teacher. He became a priest and championed the liturgical and disciplinary reforms of Pope Gregory VII. He was named successively abbot at Bangor, bishop of Connor, and Archbishop of Armagh. He helped St. Bernard of Clairvaux establish Cistercian monasteries in Ireland.

HISTORY

Founded in 1882 for the West Side Irish. As the neighborhood became more transient in the early 20th century, Fr. James Callaghan attempted to make St. Malachy's an actors' and actresses' church, like the famous St. Malachy's Actor's Chapel in New York, but Chicago's theater

St. Malachy

industry was never large enough to support it. The neighborhood became largely African-American by World War II and public housing demolished most of the private residences after the war. St. Malachy's now is the oldest black parish on the West Side.

ARCHITECTURE

The original parish church was demolished when Western Avenue was widened in the late 1920s. The present church, designed by Edward T. P. Graham in a Renaissance style, was completed in 1930.

TREASURE

The original hand carved pulpit is still used, and a wood-carved granary door from Africa now serves as the base of the altar.

ST. MARGARET MARY

2324 W. Chase Ave., West Ridge

PATRON

Margaret Mary Alacoque (1647–1690) became a nun of the Visitation Order at Paray-le-Monial in France. From 1672 to 1675 she received a series of visions from Our Lord encouraging devotion to His Sacred Heart. Through her influence, this devotion became widespread.

HISTORY

Founded in 1921 on the far north side of the city by Irish Catholics moving west from St. Jerome's parish and by Luxemburger Catholics, many of whom owned truck farms and nurseries in the area. The parish and neighborhood have remained a middle-class, residential area. Over the years, the parish population has greatly diversified and now includes Filipino, Indian, African, and Hispanic Catholics, who have found a welcome home in the parish.

ARCHITECTURE

The church, designed by Joseph W. McCarthy in a California Mission style, was completed in 1938. Modeled on the Santa Barbara mission, the church appealed to Cardinal George Mundelein as a nearly perfect embodiment of his ideals — simple, utilitarian, and inexpensive to build, but with impeccable Catholic and American symbolism.

TREASURE

Stained glass window depicting a soldier and a sailor, since the founding pastor was a World War I chaplain.

ST. MARGARET OF SCOTLAND

9837 S. Throop St., Washington Heights

PATRON

Margaret (1046–1093), the granddaughter of King Edmund Ironside of England, was born in Hungary while her family was in exile due to the Danish invasion of England. After returning to England, she fled again from the Norman Conquest of 1066 and took refuge at the court of King Malcolm III of Scotland, whom she married in 1070. Margaret founded abbeys and used her position to work for justice and improved conditions for the poor.

HISTORY

Established in 1874 as a mission church, served from the Academy of Our Lady. It became a parish in 1893, served originally by the Benedictine Fathers; and the early parishioners were mainly Irish and German. The neighborhood became predominantly African-American in the 1960s and 70s. The parish church and school serve both black and white parishioners worshipping in peace.

ARCHITECTURE

The church, designed in a Tudor Gothic style by Charles L. Wallace of Joliet, was completed in 1928. A painting of the Last Supper, installed in 1977, depicts Jesus and the Apostles as African men.

TREASURE

The Stations of the Cross were produced by Sister Stanisia, a School Sister of Notre Dame in 1927, with parishioners as models.

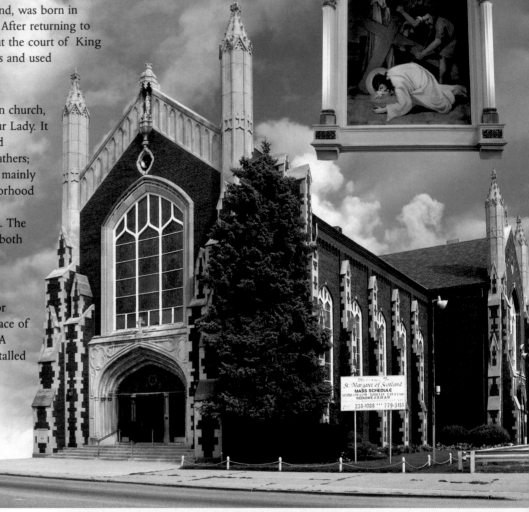

SANTA MARIA ADDOLORATA

528 N. Ada St., West Town

PATRON

Santa Maria Addolorata venerates the Blessed Virgin Mary as the Sorrowful Mother, who endured Seven Sorrows, namely: the prophecy of Simeon, the flight into Egypt, the loss of the Child Jesus for three days in the Temple, meeting Jesus as he carried the Cross to Calvary, the Crucifixion, the removal of Jesus from the Cross, and Jesus' burial in the tomb.

HISTORY

Founded in 1903 as an Italian parish. The parish has been administered since 1905 by the Scalabrini Fathers, whose special work is the care of Italian immigrants. The construction of the Kennedy Expressway destroyed most of the Italian neighborhood. The parish is now predominantly Latino, but the area is newly prosperous and gentrifying.

ARCHITECTURE

The modern church, designed by Joseph Bagnuolo, was completed in 1960.

TREASURE

Devotions to Our Lady of Sorrows, La Virgen de Guadalupe (pictured here), and Madre de la Divina Providencia.

Santa Maria Addolorata

ST. MARK

1048 N. Campbell Ave., West Town

PATRON

Mark (died c. 74) was an early disciple who traveled with Peter, Paul, and Barnabas. One of the four evangelists, he wrote the earliest of the Gospel accounts of Jesus' life and death. He was martyred, perhaps at Alexandria. His relics are buried at Venice, where he is the patron saint.

HISTORY

Founded in 1894 for the Irish of the near northwest side. The parish became predominantly Polish in the first half of the 20th century and then Latino (mainly Puerto Rican), since the 1960s.

ARCHITECTURE

The modern church, designed by Barry & Kay, was completed in 1960.

TREASURE

The faceted glass sidewalls, designed by Gabriel Loire of Chartres, France.

ST. MARTIN DE PORRES

5112 W. Washington St., Austin

PATRON

Martin de Porres (1579–1639), the illegitimate son of a Spanish nobleman and a young freed black slave, grew up in poverty. He became a servant in a Dominican priory and so impressed the friars with his care of the sick, that they dropped the stipulation that "no black person may be received to the holy habit or profession of our order" and Martin took vows as a Dominican brother. Established an orphanage and children's hospital for the poor children of the slums.

HISTORY

Founded in 1988 by the consolidation of St. Mel/Holy Ghost, Resurrection, and St. Thomas Aquinas parishes.

ARCHITECTURE

The church building, the former St. Thomas Aquinas parish church, was designed in a Tudor Gothic style by Karl M. Vitzthum in 1925.

TREASURE

The stained glass windows.

ST. MARY

1500 S. Michigan Ave., Near South Side

PATRON

The Blessed Virgin Mary, wife of St. Joseph, Mother of Jesus. The parish was dedicated to St. Mary of the Assumption, commemorating the assumption of Mary into heaven after her death.

HISTORY

Founded in 1833, "Old St. Mary's" is the oldest parish in the city, predating even the establishment of the diocese. It has been located at six different places near the center of the city. It was the first cathedral for the diocese, but all its buildings were destroyed in the Chicago Fire of 1871, and after rebuilding, the bishop's seat was transferred to Holy Name church north of the Chicago River. The Paulist Fathers took over St. Mary's in 1903, administering it as a "downtown church" for office workers. The South Loop has recently developed a new residential area and the parish moved into a new building in 2002.

St Mary

ARCHITECTURE

The modern church, designed by Prisco, Serena and Sturm, was dedicated on July 21, 2002.

TREASURE

Statue of Our Lady of the Assumption and the crucifix behind the altar were both transferred from the previous church building.

ST. MARY OF THE ANGELS

1850 N. Hermitage Ave., Logan Square

PATRON

The Blessed Virgin has been revered as Our Lady of the Angels or the Queen of Angels at least since the 13th century. Many miracles have been attributed to images of Our Lady of Angels, both in Europe and Latin America.

HISTORY

Founded in 1899 as a Polish parish. The Resurrectionist Order, from Chicago's first Polish parish, St. Stanislaus Kostka, organized St. Mary's as the Polish neighborhood expanded northwards at the turn of the century. It remained a Polish parish until the 1970s when many Latinos joined the congregation. In 1989 the parish was threatened with closure but a vigorous fundraising drive led by present and former parishioners saved it. Priests from Opus Dei replaced the Resurrectionists in administering the parish. The surrounding Bucktown district is now newly prosperous and gentrified.

ARCHITECTURE

The church, one of the finest examples of Roman Renaissance architecture in the United States, was designed by Worthmann and Steinbach and completed in 1920. Fr. Francis Gordon, the pastor at the time, reportedly hoped to be named an auxiliary bishop for the Poles of Chicago so he built the church to cathedral proportions.

TREASURE

The massive dome, surrounded by numerous angels.

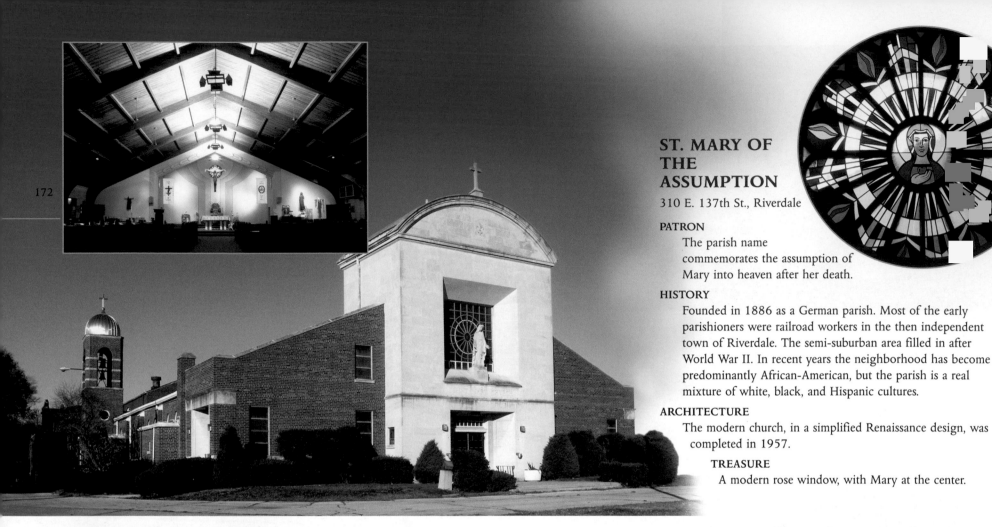

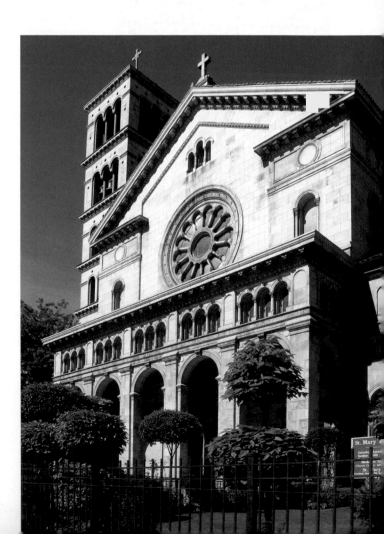

ST. MARY OF THE ASSUMPTION

310 E. 137th St., Riverdale

PATRON

The parish name commemorates the assumption of Mary into heaven after her death.

HISTORY

Founded in 1886 as a German parish. Most of the early parishioners were railroad workers in the then independent town of Riverdale. The semi-suburban area filled in after World War II. In recent years the neighborhood has become predominantly African-American, but the parish is a real mixture of white, black, and Hispanic cultures.

ARCHITECTURE

The modern church, in a simplified Renaissance design, was completed in 1957.

TREASURE

A modern rose window, with Mary at the center.

ST. MARY OF THE LAKE

4200 N. Sheridan Rd., Uptown

PATRON

St. Mary of the Lake is a title of the Blessed Virgin Mary especially dear to Chicagoans. The major seminary of the archdiocese, first founded near Holy Name Cathedral in the 1840s, then reconstituted in Mundelein, Illinois in the 1920s was named St. Mary of the Lake. This parish, near the Lake Michigan lakeshore on the North Side, adopted the title as well.

HISTORY

Founded in 1901. The neighborhood was originally a fashionable "North Shore" residential district but has undergone many changes over the past century. Presently the parish is one of the city's most diverse and cosmopolitan, serving European-Americans, Latin-Americans, Africans, and Asians. Though the neighborhood is newly gentrifying and prosperous, the poor remain a constant reality in Uptown and at St. Mary's.

ARCHITECTURE

The church, designed by Henry J. Schlacks and completed in 1917, is one of the finest examples of Italian Renaissance architecture in the city. The architect loosely modeled the building on Rome's St. Paul's Outside the Walls. The free-standing

St. Mary of the Lake

campanile is similar to St. Pudentiana's in Rome. A Last Judgment mural extends high over the entire apse of the building.

TREASURE

An icon by Joseph Malham, "Theotokos of the Lake," is located at the northwest corner of the church building.

ST. MARY MAGDALENE

8426 S. Marquette Ave., South Chicago

PATRON

Friend and disciple of Jesus. Traditionally identified as a "fallen woman" or reformed prostitute, Mary Magdalene is simply identified in the Gospels as the woman out of whom Jesus drove seven devils. She stood by the Cross as Jesus died, anointed his dead body, and was one of the first to whom the Risen Christ appeared.

HISTORY

Founded in 1910 as a Polish parish. It remained a parish for Polish steelworkers and their families until the mills shut down in the 1970s and 80s. The parish and neighborhood are now predominantly Latino and African-American. Mass is offered in English and Spanish.

ARCHITECTURE

The church building was completed in 1954 in a modernized Romanesque style.

TREASURE

A sweeping mural of the Crucifixion, painted by John Mallin, fills the dome behind the altar.

ST. MARY OF PERPETUAL HELP

1039 W. 32nd St., Bridgeport

PATRON

The miraculous image of Our Lady of Perpetual Help in its present form comes from a 13th century Greek icon. Tradition maintains that St. Luke was the original artist.

HISTORY

Founded in 1882 as a Polish parish. It remained a parish for Polish workers in the Union Stockyards until the Yards closed in the early 1970s. In recent years the neighborhood has seen a growth in new housing and an influx of new residents of many ethnic backgrounds and cultures.

ARCHITECTURE

The church, designed by Henry Engelbert in a Romanesque-Byzantine style, was completed in 1889. The central dome towers 137 feet over the neighborhood. Since 1999, the church has undergone extensive restoration of the original structure, the interior decoration executed by John Mallin in 1961, and the 1928 Austin organ. A time capsule from June 1, 1895 was recently opened revealing precious historical documents.

TREASURE

A new mosaic of Our Lady of Perpetual Help by the Soprani Studios of Rome.

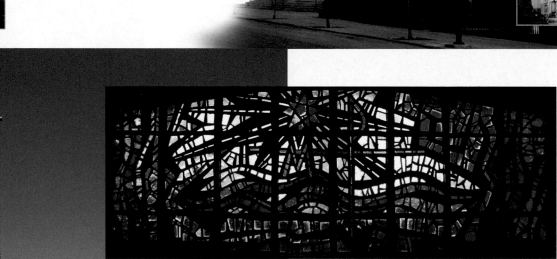

ST. MARY, STAR OF THE SEA

6435 S. Kilbourn Ave., West Lawn

PATRON

It's not immediately evident why this title of the Blessed Virgin Mary usually invoked by sailors would be adopted by this very landlocked parish. However, a parish tradition claims that the founding pastor, Fr. Joseph H. McGuire, named the parish after a holy card he carried in his breviary for many years.

St. Mary Star of the Sea

HISTORY

Founded in 1948. This parish and neighborhood, established in the post-World War II building boom, has a diverse congregation of various European ethnic origins, with a growing Hispanic community.

ARCHITECTURE

The modern church was completed in 1954, with an addition designed by James R. Cronin and Associates added in 1961.

TREASURE

A dramatic window above and across the entrance depicts a mighty starburst over rolling waves.

ST. MARY OF THE WOODS

7033 N. Moselle Ave., (south side of Hiawatha facing Moselle), Edgebrook

PATRON

The founding pastor, Daniel B. O'Rourke, wished that his new parish be dedicated to the Blessed Virgin Mary, and he chose this particular title to commemorate the wooded character of the neighborhood.

HISTORY

Founded in 1952. This pleasantly wooded, semi-suburban area on the far northwest side of the city, is heavily Catholic. The parishioners come from a variety of European ethnic origins and include many professionals and city workers.

ARCHITECTURE

The modern church, designed by Gaul & Voosen, was completed in 1953. Michael F. Gaul and John C. Voosen, partners in the architectural firm, were also parishioners of St. Mary's.

TREASURE

Several stained glass windows, designed by Max Ingrand, depict various apparitions of the Blessed Virgin, each set within a forest motif. The altars and Stations of the Cross continue this sense with their leafy engravings. All this beauty directs your senses to a lovely crystal piece etched with the corpus and cross that hangs above the altar. Transparent and stunning in its simplicity, the crystal cross is the highest and most prominent of St. Mary of the Woods treasures.

MATERNITY B.V.M.

3635 W. North Ave., Humboldt Park

PATRON

The name of the parish commemorates the motherhood of the Blessed Virgin Mary. The title "Mother of God" was solemnly ratified by the Council of Ephesus, 431 AD, affirming that her Son, Jesus Christ, was truly both God and Man.

HISTORY

The parish was founded in 1904 as a mission of St. Genevieve and became a parish in 1909. The parish served a variety of different ethnic groups over the years and is now predominantly Hispanic. Mass is celebrated in English and Spanish. The combination church/school building, designed by William F. Gubbins, was completed in 1911.

TREASURE

Statue of Mary in courtyard.

ST. MATTHIAS

2310 W. Ainslie Ave., Lincoln Square

PATRON

Matthias (died c. 80 AD) was chosen an Apostle to replace the traitor Judas Iscariot. He preached the Gospel for more than 30 years in Judea, Cappadocia, Egypt and Ethiopia. He died a martyr at Colchis in Asia Minor.

HISTORY

Founded in 1887 as a German parish in what was still a farming district outside the city. Though the parish remained German for decades, it eventually became a very diverse, middle-class parish. The neighborhood is now newly prosperous and gentrified.

ARCHITECTURE

The church, designed by Hermann J. Gaul in a red brick Romanesque style, was completed in 1915.

St. Matthias

TREASURE

Devotional shrines to Our Lady of
Guadalupe, Mother of Perpetual Help, Our
Lady of Penafrancia and to the Divine
Mercy.

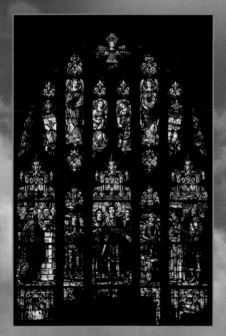

ST. MAURICE

3615 S. Hoyne Ave., McKinley Park

PATRON

Maurice (died c. 287) was a Roman officer in a legion of
Christian soldiers during the reign of Emperor Maximian. His
legion, as many as 6600 men, was massacred en masse when
they refused to participate in pagan sacrifices prior to battle.

HISTORY

Founded in 1890 as a German parish. The German character
of the parish diminished after World War I, so St. Maurice
became a territorial parish for the neighborhood of McKinley
Park, which had a heavily Polish predominance. The parish
now is primarily Latino.

ARCHITECTURE

The Gothic church, designed by McCarthy, Smith and Eppig,
was completed in 1936

TREASURE

Stained glass windows, with decorative stone tracery, depict
Bible scenes and saints, including St. Maurice.

ST. MICHAEL

1633 N. Cleveland Ave., Lincoln Park

PATRON

Michael, whose name means "Who is like God?," is one of the three archangels mentioned in the Bible. He led the army of God against Lucifer and the rebel angels and is thus usually depicted in warrior garb.

HISTORY

Founded in 1852 as a German parish. Though not the oldest German parish, it is essentially the mother church of the North side German community. The parish has been administered by the Redemptorist Order of priests since 1860. The neighborhood has gone through many changes in a century and a half and is now a very prosperous, gentrified residential district.

ARCHITECTURE

The church, designed in a Romanesque style by August Wallbaum, was completed in 1869. Though gutted by the Chicago Fire of 1871, it was rebuilt shortly thereafter. The Baroque high altar, made completely of wood, and statuary, which includes 87 angels, are among the most ornate and impressive in the archdiocese. The altar carving depicting Leonardo da Vinci's "Last Supper," purchased from the Columbian Exposition (1893), is made out of a single slab of wood.

TREASURE

Shrine to Our Mother of Perpetual Help.

ST. MICHAEL

8237 S. South Shore Dr., South Chicago

PATRON

Michael, whose name means "Who is like to God?", is one of the three archangels mentioned in the Bible. He led the army of God against Lucifer and the rebel angels and is thus usually depicted in warrior garb.

HISTORY

Founded in 1892 as a Polish parish. Bishop Paul Rhode, the first Polish auxiliary bishop in Chicago, served as pastor from 1897 until he was named bishop of Green Bay in 1915. The parish continued to serve Polish steelworkers until the steel mills closed in the 1970s and 80s. The parish and neighborhood are now predominantly Latino.

178

ARCHITECTURE

The church, designed in a Gothic style by William J. Brinkmann, was completed in 1909. U.S. Steel donated the steel for the structure since 90% of the parishioners worked at the mills.

TREASURE

The main altar is made of butternut and oak, with a statue of Michael the Archangel defeating Lucifer.

St. Michael

ST. MICHAEL THE ARCHANGEL

4821 S. Damen Ave., New City

PATRON

Michael, whose name means "Who is like to God?", is one of the three archangels mentioned in the Bible. He led the army of God against Lucifer and the rebel angels and is thus usually depicted in warrior garb.

HISTORY

Founded in 1898, the first Slovak parish in Chicago. Several orders of Benedictine priests administered the parish for most of its history. The parish continued to serve the families of Slovak workers in the Union Stockyards until the yards closed in the early 1970s. The parish and neighborhood are now predominantly Latino.

ARCHITECTURE

The combination church/school building was completed in 1909.

TREASURE

A statue of St. Michael the Archangel vanquishing Lucifer.

ST. MONICA

5136 N. Nottingham Ave., Norwood Park

PATRON

Monica (332–387) was the mother of Saint Augustine, who attributed to her most of the credit for his conversion to Christianity. Born in North Africa, a Christian from birth, she was given in marriage to a bad-tempered, adulterous pagan named Patricius. She prayed constantly for the conversion of her husband (who converted on his death bed), and of her son (who converted after a wild youth).

HISTORY

Founded in 1948. This semi-suburban residential area on the far northwest side of the city filled up in the post World War II boom years. The parishioners come from a diverse group of European ethnic origins.

ARCHITECTURE

The modern church, designed by John Voosen, was completed in 1988. It was the first completely wheelchair-accessible church in the archdiocese.

TREASURE

The 9 by 7 foot sanctuary crucifix, "Croce Santa Monica" reminiscent of a medieval masterwork, was created by local husband and wife artists Joseph Ramirez and Meltem Aktas.

NATIVITY B.V.M

6812 S. Washtenaw Ave., Chicago Lawn

PATRON

The name of the parish refers to the birth of the Blessed Virgin Mary and it recalls a famous shrine to Our Lady of Siluva in Lithuania.

HISTORY

Founded in 1927 as a Lithuanian parish. It has remained heavily Lithuanian to this day, with two Masses celebrated in Lithuanian every Sunday.

Nativity B.V.M.

ARCHITECTURE

The church, designed by John Mulokas, was completed in 1957. The architect combined Lithuanian folk elements with a Baroque design to create a distinctively Lithuanian look.

TREASURE

The mural over the altar and the stained glass windows commemorate many titles of the Blessed Virgin Mary.

NATIVITY OF OUR LORD

653 W. 37th St., Bridgeport

PATRON

The parish name commemorates the birth of Jesus Christ on Christmas Day. The name was chosen since the first Masses for the congregation were celebrated in a stable on the grounds of the Union Stockyards.

HISTORY

Founded in 1868 to serve the Irish of Bridgeport. The parish has been closely connected with the Irish politicians who lived in this neighborhood, especially the two Mayors Daley. In recent years, parishioners of Polish, Lithuanian, Italian, and Mexican descent have joined the Irish in the congregation.

ARCHITECTURE

The church, designed in a Romanesque style by Patrick C. Keeley of Brooklyn, the same architect who built Holy Name Cathedral, was completed in 1885.

TREASURE

Joyful Mysteries of the Rosary encircling the chancel were painted in oil by Cook County jail prisoners.

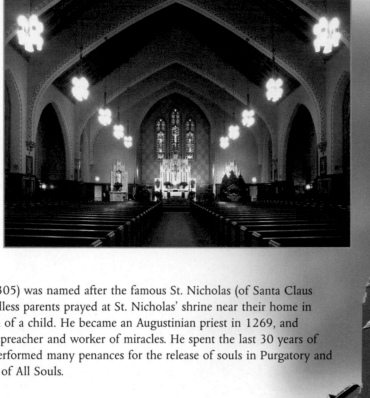

ST. NICHOLAS OF TOLENTINE

3721 W. 62nd St., West Lawn

PATRON

Nicholas of Tolentine (1245–1305) was named after the famous St. Nicholas (of Santa Claus fame) because his formerly childless parents prayed at St. Nicholas' shrine near their home in Italy and were granted the birth of a child. He became an Augustinian priest in 1269, and earned a reputation as a tireless preacher and worker of miracles. He spent the last 30 years of his life in Tolentino, Italy. He performed many penances for the release of souls in Purgatory and has been proclaimed the patron of All Souls.

HISTORY

Founded in 1909 as a mission of St. Rita's, it became a parish in 1916. The neighborhood filled up after World War II with families of Irish and European descent, and the parish presently ministers in the midst of a primarily Latino community.

ARCHITECTURE

The church was designed in an English Gothic style by Arthur E. Foster in 1924. As the community grew, the upper church was completed, according to the plans of Gerald A. Barry, in 1939.

TREASURE

The beautiful stained glass windows in the upper church, which tell the story of Salvation History.

Notre Dame de Chicago

NOTRE DAME DE CHICAGO

1335 W. Harrison St., Near West Side

PATRON

The parish is dedicated to the Blessed Virgin Mary under the French title of Our Lady of Chicago.

HISTORY

The parish was founded in its present location in 1864 but it is actually a continuation of an earlier French parish named St. Louis. The French Canadian population of Illinois was centered in rural Kankakee county, but a number of French Canadians also settled in Chicago. By the early 20th century, there were not enough French-speaking Catholics on the West Side to support Notre Dame, so in 1918 Cardinal Mundelein handed over the parish to a Canadian religious order, the Blessed Sacrament Fathers, to conduct a shrine of perpetual adoration in the church building. In recent years, as the neighborhood has become gentrified around the University of Illinois at Chicago campus, diocesan priests now administer Notre Dame as a residential parish.

ARCHITECTURE

The church, designed by Gregoire Vigeant in the style of the Romanesque Revival, with a neoclassical interior, was completed in 1892. It is one of the few octagonal, central plan churches in the city. The church is listed on the National Register of Historic Places.

TREASURE

The mural depicting salvation history inside the restored dome that supports a bronze statue of Our Lady.

OUR LADY OF FATIMA

2751 W. 38th Pl., Brighton Park

PATRON

The parish name commemorates the apparitions of the Blessed Virgin Mary to three shepherd children of Fatima, Portugal, between May 13 and October 13, 1917. Our Lady of Fatima asked the children to pray the Rosary for world peace, and devotion to her was widespread during the twentieth century.

HISTORY

The parish is the result of a consolidation, in 1991, of St. Agnes and Sts. Joseph and Anne. St. Agnes, founded in 1878, was predominantly Irish, while Sts. Joseph and Anne was founded in 1889 by French Canadians. The parish today has a large Hispanic community.

ARCHITECTURE

The church building is the former Ss. Joseph and Anne parish church. Designed in a French Provincial Gothic style by LaPointe and Hickok, it was completed in 1892. The parish was originally named St. Joseph, but a shrine of St. Anne was added in 1900 and became a place of pilgrimage on St. Anne's feast day, July 26. Though the parish name has changed again, St. Anne's shrine remains a popular place of devotion.

TREASURE

The reliquary in the shrine holds the largest relic of St. Anne in the United States, a gift of the shrine in Apt, France. Crutches hang on the wall as a testimony to the miraculous cures effected by intercession of the saint.

OUR LADY GATE OF HEAVEN

2338 E. 99th St., South Deering

PATRON

The parish name refers to the invocation in the litany of the Blessed Virgin which names her as the *porta coeli* or *janua coeli*, that is, the gate of heaven. This title of the Blessed Virgin commemorates her power as an intercessor with her son, Jesus Christ, who is the Savior of humankind, the Way, the Truth and the Life. Mary, the Mother of God, therefore, is the gate to the Way.

HISTORY

Founded in 1947. The developer of the Jeffrey Manor housing subdivision donated the land for the parish as an anchor of his development. In the 1960s and 70s, the parish and neighborhood became predominantly African-American, but it has retained the middle class character that was stamped upon it in the post World War II boom.

ARCHITECTURE

A combination church/school building was completed in 1953.

TREASURE

The Baptismal font, where the children, the real treasures of the parish, become members of the Church.

OUR LADY OF GOOD COUNSEL

3528 S. Hermitage Ave., McKinley Park

PATRON

Our Lady of Good Counsel refers to an icon of the Blessed Virgin discovered in a small town south of Rome in 1467. Devotion to the Blessed Virgin Mary under this title has been widespread ever since.

HISTORY

Founded in 1901 for the Irish in this industrial area of the South Side. It replaced an earlier French parish, St. Jean Baptiste de Bridgeport, which had been founded in 1882 but abandoned in 1900. After World War II, many German and Polish Catholics also began attending the parish. In recent years the parish and neighborhood have become predominantly Latino.

ARCHITECTURE

The three-story combination church/school building was completed in 1902. The church occupies the second floor, with a parish hall below and the youth center above.

TREASURE

The original stained glass windows, which are over 100 years old.

Our Lady of Good Counsel

OUR LADY OF GRACE

2455 N. Hamlin Ave., Logan Square

PATRON

The parish name refers to a miraculous image of the Blessed Virgin Mary in Ipswich, England, which was a site of popular devotion in the Middle Ages. The image was destroyed by order of King Henry VIII during the Protestant Reformation. The title probably comes from the prayer in which Our Lady is invoked in the words, "Hail Mary, full of grace."

HISTORY

Founded in 1909. The parish congregation has always been diverse, but it changed along with the neighborhood from Irish, to Polish, to Latino predominance. Its most famous pastor, Msgr. Victor Primeau, who built the present church, was French Canadian.

ARCHITECTURE

The church was built during the Depression, during the pastorate of Msgr. Victor Primeau, and completed in 1935. Msgr. Primeau requested the architects, McCarthy, Smith & Eppig, to construct the church in an octagonal shape, similar to Notre Dame de Chicago, the French church where he had previously served.

TREASURE

Stained glass window with Cardinal Mundelein and Msgr. Victor Primeau.

OUR LADY OF GUADALUPE

3200 E. 91st St., South Chicago

PATRON

The parish name refers to an apparition of Our Lady to St. Juan Diego, an Indian peasant in Spanish colonial Mexico, in 1531. The image of the Blessed Virgin, surrounded by roses, was miraculously imprinted on Juan Diego's cloak and has been an object of widespread devotion in Mexico ever since. Our Lady of Guadualupe has been declared the patron saint of all the Americas.

HISTORY

Founded in 1923 as the first Mexican parish in the city. Mexican-Americans began immigrating to Chicago during World War I and first settled in the steel mill district of South Chicago. The parish has been administered by the Spanish Claretian Order of priests for its entire history. An early pastor, Fr. James Tort, established a shrine of St. Jude in the parish in 1929 and it became a nationwide object of devotion and a sturdy financial support for the ministry of the parish. The parish and neighborhood have remained Latino.

ARCHITECTURE

The church building, designed by James Burns, was completed in 1928.

TREASURE

The marble altar with statue of St. Jude Thaddeus, now the National Shrine of St. Jude, holds several major relics used in blessings.

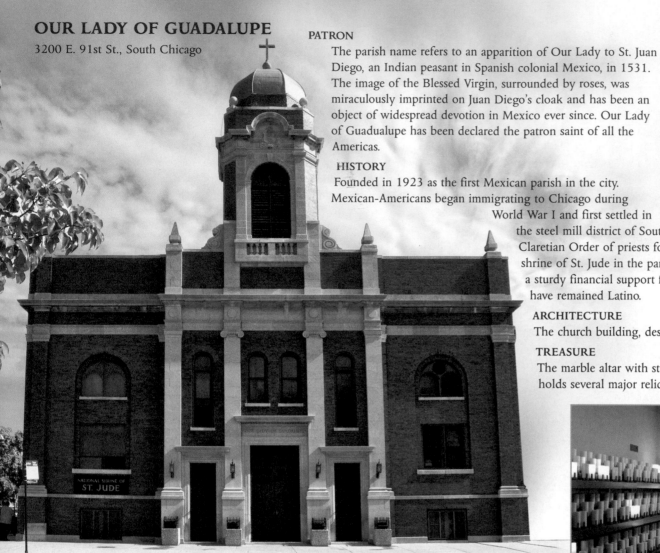

OUR LADY OF LOURDES

4640 N. Ashland Ave., Uptown

PATRON

The parish name commemorates the appearance of Our Lady to Saint Bernadette Soubirous at Lourdes, France in 1858. The shrine at Lourdes has been immensely popular as a place of pilgrimage and devotion ever since, and the grotto where Our Lady appeared has been widely reproduced in churches and churchyards.

HISTORY

Founded in 1892. Originally an Irish parish, it has become very diverse over the years with families from over twenty different ethnic backgrounds. The parish is now predominantly Latino, but the neighborhood is newly prosperous and gentrifying.

ARCHITECTURE

The church, designed in a Spanish Renaissance style by Worthmann and Steinbach, was completed in 1916. When Ashland Avenue was widened in 1928 and 1929, the church was literally moved across the street and turned halfway around to face Leland Avenue. The church was then cut in two, with a 30 foot extension inserted, increasing capacity by 300 people. The stained glass windows, depicting the life of the Blessed Virgin Mary, have been recently restored

TREASURE

The 24-hour adoration chapel (the grotto) was designed as a replica of the original cave in Lourdes, France, and is a jewel box of stained glass and statuary.

Our Lady of Lourdes

OUR LADY OF MERCY

4432 N. Troy St., Albany Park

PATRON

The parish name commemorates an appearance of Our Lady in 13th century Spain, in which Mary carried two bags of coins to ransom Christians imprisoned by the Moors. This apparition is also referred to as Our Lady of Ransom. The feast day is September 24.

HISTORY

Founded in 1911 to serve Catholics living near the terminus of the Ravenswood L line. Always a diverse parish, with Irish, Polish, Italian, and German founding families, the parish is now 70% Latino (Mexican, Guatemalan, Ecuadorian, Puerto Rican), and 25% Filipino. In addition, the neighborhood includes people from Korea, Syria, and India. Urban gentrification has recently arrived in the neighborhood as well.

ARCHITECTURE

The church, designed by Barry & Kay, was constructed in two sections, from 1958 to 1961. The façade is a modernized Renaissance design graced by twin towers clad in stainless steel. A statue of Our Lady sits atop a golden dome which is placed above the main altar. The altar's baldachino has black marble columns modeled after Bernini's in St. Peter's.

TREASURE

The golden dome.

OUR LADY, MOTHER OF THE CHURCH

8747 W. Lawrence Ave., O'Hare

PATRON
After the Second Vatican Council, in 1967, Pope Paul VI dedicated the world to Our Lady, Mother of the Church.

HISTORY
Founded in 1966 in a new residential area just east of O'Hare Airport. It was the first parish founded by Cardinal Cody in Chicago and possibly the first parish anywhere named for Our Lady, Mother of the Church, after Pope Paul VI's dedication of the world to Mary under that title. The parish serves a congregation of diverse European ethnic origins.

ARCHITECTURE
The modern church was designed by Meyer & Cook in 1968, and was renovated in 1987 according to the plans of John Voosen. A further renovation, by Serena Sturm Architects, was completed in 2004.

TREASURE
Three stained glass windows, depicting the Sacraments of initiation, were designed and installed by artist Robert Harmon as a background to the sanctuary.

OUR LADY OF MOUNT CARMEL

690 W. Belmont Ave., Lakeview

PATRON
The parish name commemorates the apparition of Our Lady to the founder of the Carmelite Order, St. Simon Stock, in 1251. During this apparition, Our Lady gave St. Simon the scapular, two pieces of cloth to be worn under ordinary clothing in devotion to Mary.

HISTORY
Founded in 1886. Originally Irish, the parish and neighborhood have been home to many different ethnic groups. The area has become newly prosperous and gentrified in recent years. Mass is celebrated in English and Spanish.

ARCHITECTURE
The church, designed by Egan & Prindeville in an English Gothic style, was completed in 1913.

TREASURE
The restored E. M. Skinner pipe organ is used in worship services and during performances by the William Ferris Chorale, which makes this church its home.

Our Lady of Mount Carmel

OUR LADY OF PEACE

7851 S. Jeffery Blvd., South Shore

PATRON

Our Lady has been venerated as a peacemaker, or Queen of Peace, since the middle ages in Western Europe and more recently in Latin America. During World War I, Pope Benedict XV added the title Queen of Peace to the litany of the Blessed Virgin.

HISTORY

The parish was founded in 1919, by a former World War I army chaplain, Fr. Edward F. Rice, and dedicated under the new title of Our Lady of Peace. It originally served a predominantly Irish congregation, but in the 1970s the parish and neighborhood became African-American.

ARCHITECTURE

The cornerstone of the church was laid in 1924, but the church was not completed until 1935. It was designed in an Italian Renaissance style by McCarthy, Smith & Eppig, with a magnificent free-standing campanile.

TREASURE

The stained glass window of Our Lady of Peace.

OUR LADY OF THE SNOWS

4806 S. Laramie Ave., Garfield Ridge

PATRON

A miraculous August snowfall on one of the seven hills
of Rome in the 3rd century was judged to be a sign of
where to build the great basilica of St. Mary Major
whose nickname became "Our Lady of the Snows".

HISTORY

Founded in 1959 on the far southwest side of the city near Midway Airport. Though the
area was largely settled by descendants of European immigrants, the parish had African-American
parishioners from the beginning since it included the LeClaire Courts public housing development.

ARCHITECTURE

The modern building, designed by Kefer and Cronin in 1960, was originally planned as a
temporary church, but was completely renovated in 1986.

TREASURE

Eucharistic chapel has wall of stained glass by Potente Studios of Kenosha WI.

OUR LADY OF SORROWS

3121 W. Jackson Blvd., East Garfield Park

PATRON

The parish name commemorates the Blessed Virgin Mary as the
Sorrowful Mother, who endured Seven Sorrows, namely: the prophecy
of Simeon, the flight into Egypt, the loss of the Child Jesus for three
days in the temple, meeting Jesus as he carried the Cross to Calvary,
the Crucifixion, the removal of Jesus from the Cross, and Jesus' burial
in the tomb.

HISTORY

Founded in 1874. It has been administered by the Servite Order of
priests for its entire history. The parish served an Irish and Italian

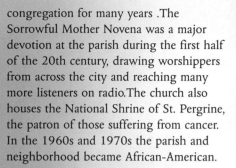

congregation for many years .The Sorrowful Mother Novena was a major devotion at the parish during the first half of the 20th century, drawing worshippers from across the city and reaching many more listeners on radio.The church also houses the National Shrine of St. Pergrine, the patron of those suffering from cancer. In the 1960s and 1970s the parish and neighborhood became African-American.

ARCHITECTURE

The church, designed in an Italian Renaissance style by Henry Engelbert, John F. Pope, and William Brinkmann , was begun in 1892 but not completed until 1902. It was declared a basilica by the Vatican in 1956.

TREASURE

The shrine altar of the Seven Holy Founders.

Our Lady of the Sorrows

OUR LADY OF TEPEYAC

2226 S. Whipple St., South Lawndale

PATRON

Tepeyac was the name of the hill in Mexico where Our Lady of Guadalupe appeared to St. Juan Diego in 1531. The parish name, therefore, is an alternate title for Our Lady of Guadalupe, patron saint both of Mexico and of all the Americas.

HISTORY

Founded in 1990 as a merger of St. Casimir, a formerly Polish parish, and St. Ludmilla, a formerly Bohemian parish. The new parish, predominantly Mexican-American, uses the buildings of the former St. Casimir's.

ARCHITECTURE

The church, built in 1917, is a central plan, octagonal structure with a great dome over the crossing.

TREASURE

The original main altar.

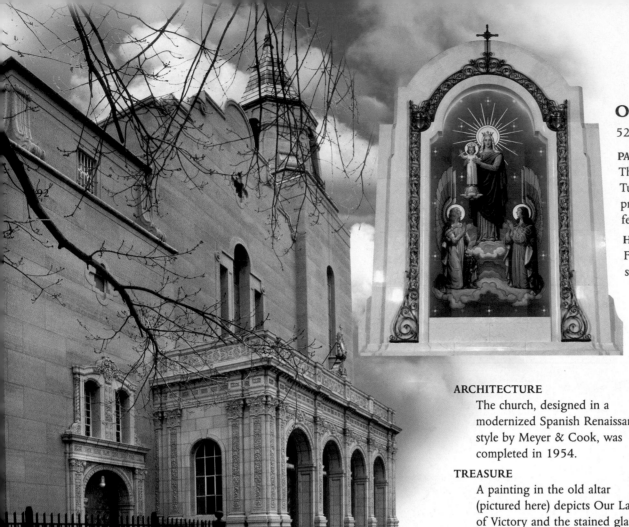

OUR LADY OF VICTORY

5212 W. Agatite Ave., Portage Park

PATRON
The parish name commemorates the victory of Christian forces over the Turks at the Battle of Lepanto in 1571. Believing that Christians praying the Rosary had secured the victory, Pope Pius V introduced the feast of Our Lady of Victory in 1572.

HISTORY
Founded in 1906 on the far northwest side of Chicago. The parish has served a diverse congregation of various European ethnic origins.

ARCHITECTURE
The church, designed in a modernized Spanish Renaissance style by Meyer & Cook, was completed in 1954.

TREASURE
A painting in the old altar (pictured here) depicts Our Lady of Victory and the stained glass window at the opposite end of the church, over the choir loft, shows Christ the King of Victory.

ST. PANCRATIUS

4025 S. Sacramento Ave., Brighton Park

PATRON
Pancratius, or Pancras, (died c. 304) was a Roman martyr, of whose life nothing is known for sure. His relics were sent from Rome to England as part of the evangelization of that country, so he is especially venerated in the British Isles.

HISTORY
Founded in 1924 as a Polish parish. The area has remained a community of working-class immigrants and their descendants. Though many

St. Pancratius

parishioners are still Polish, there is also a large Latino group. Masses are celebrated in English, Spanish, and Polish.

ARCHITECTURE

The church, designed in a modernized Romanesque style by Emil Mastandrea and George Uitti from the architectural firm of Thomas Higgins, was completed in 1960.

TREASURE

Cherubs holding sanctuary lamps are from the previous church.

ST. PASCAL

3935 N. Melvina Ave., Portage Park

PATRON

Pascal Baylon (1540–1592) was a Spanish peasant who worked as a shepherd from ages 7 to 24. He became a Franciscan lay brother, often serving as cook or doorkeeper. His charity to the poor and afflicted, his unfailing courtesy and humility, and his devotion to the Eucharist were remarkable.

HISTORY

Founded in 1914. The parishioners have always come from a wide variety of European ethnic origins. The parish has inspired several religious vocations, including Francis Cardinal George, who grew up in St. Pascal's and attended the parish school.

ARCHITECTURE

The church, completed in 1930, was designed by B. J. Hutton and Raymond Gregori in a Spanish-Moorish style to honor the patron of the parish. The exterior has many Art Deco features, reflecting a style that was current at the time of construction.

TREASURE

There is carved repetition of pelicans (symbol of the Eucharist), eagles, peacocks, and angels of all sizes inside and outside of the cross.

ST. PATRICK

718 W. Adams,, Near West Side

PATRON

Patrick (387–461) was kidnapped from England and shipped to Ireland as a slave. After escaping, he studied in monasteries on the continent of Europe then returned to Ireland as a missionary. In 33 years he effectively converted the country to Christianity. He is the patron saint of Ireland.

HISTORY

"Old St. Patrick's" was founded in 1846 to serve the Irish Catholics west of the Chicago River's south branch. It was the second parish established in Chicago. The Chicago Fire started nearby but only sideswiped the church, which is the oldest surviving church building in the city. A thriving working-class parish for many years, it became a "downtown church" serving office workers in the Loop during the twentieth century. In recent years the parish has undergone a revival as new urban residents have moved in and the parish has also drawn a large congregation from around the city.

ARCHITECTURE

The Romanesque church, designed by Asher Carter and Augustus Bauer, was completed in 1856, The bell towers, one in a Western and the other in an Eastern style to symbolize the universality of the Church, were added in 1885. Between 1912 and 1922, artist Thomas A. O'Shaughnessy transformed the interior with highly original Celtic designs. The church has recently been restored, renovated, and returned to its early twentieth century artistic glory.

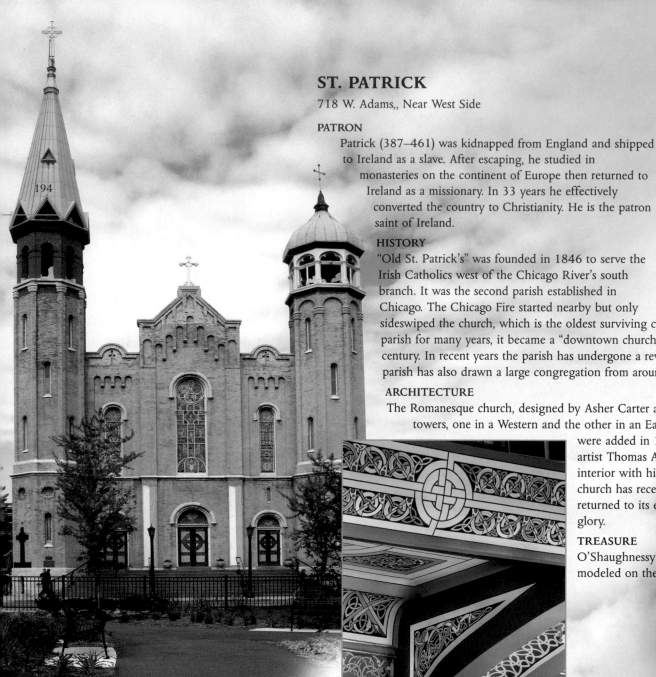

TREASURE

O'Shaughnessy"s Celtic stencilwork, modeled on the Book of Kells.

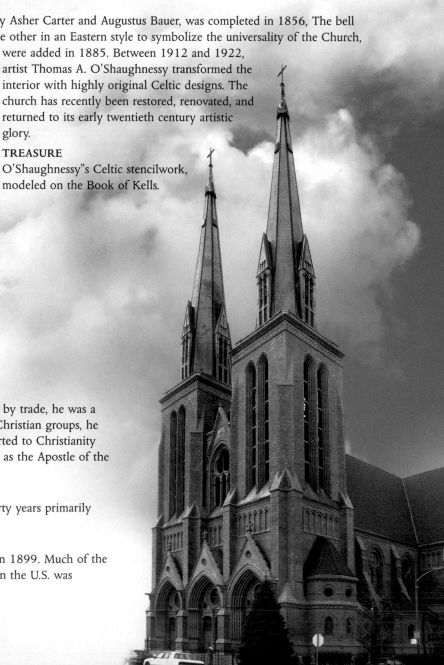

ST. PAUL

2127 W. 22nd Pl., Lower West Side

PATRON

Paul the Apostle (died c. 65), a Jew of Tarsus, was originally named Saul. A tentmaker by trade, he was a devout Pharisee who persecuted Christians. On his way to Damascus to harass other Christian groups, he had a conversion experience when knocked to the ground and struck blind. He converted to Christianity and became such an effective preacher throughout the Roman world that he is known as the Apostle of the Gentiles. He was martyred in Rome.

HISTORY

Founded in 1876 as a German parish. Later it became multicultural and in the last thirty years primarily Mexican. Mass is celebrated in English and Spanish.

ARCHITECTURE

The church, designed by Henry J. Schlacks in a German Gothic style, was completed in 1899. Much of the craft work was performed by parishioners. This first brick Gothic church constructed in the U.S. was

described by Ripley's Believe It or Not as "the church built without a nail." The church towers soar 245 feet above the neighborhood.

TREASURE

2500 square feet of mosaics, designed in Venice, with pieces of glass no more than ½ inch square, embellish the arches and walls.

St. Paul

ST. PETER

110 W. Madison St., Loop

PATRON

Peter (died c. 64) was one of the Twelve Apostles. Originally named Simon, he and his brother Andrew were fishermen, called by Jesus to follow Him. Jesus renamed him Peter, which means Rock, and designated him as the foundation or head of the early Church. Peter thus was the first Pope and was martyred in Rome.

HISTORY

Founded in 1846 as one of the first two German parishes (along with St. Joseph's). The church at Clark and Polk Streets survived the Chicago Fire. Franciscan Friars were entrusted with the administration of the parish in 1875; and Franciscans continue to minister at St. Peter's Church today. The current church was built in 1953 and is located in the heart of Chicago's Loop where it is easily accessible to the thousands of people who live in, work in, or visit downtown Chicago.

ARCHITECTURE

The church, designed by Karl Vitzthum and John Burns in a highly modern Gothic style, was completed in 1953. It is a five story marble edifice fitted onto a narrow lot between downtown high-rises. The Franciscan Friary is situated above the church.

TREASURE

A nineteenth century German monstrance.

SS. PETER AND PAUL

12433 S. Halsted St., West Pullman

PATRON

Ss. Peter and Paul are often revered together as the two leading Apostles of the early Church. Peter, formerly known as Simon, was chosen by Jesus as the head of the Church. Paul, formerly known as Saul, persecuted the early Christians until he was miraculously converted. He became the most vigorous missionary of the early Church. Both were martyred in Rome about 64 or 65 AD.

HISTORY

Founded as a Lithuanian parish in 1913. The parish began serving a wide variety of ethnic groups in the 1950s. Parish membership began to decline in the 1970s as descendants of the original parishioners moved to the suburbs.

ARCHITECTURE

The modern church, designed by Fox and Fox, was completed in 1959. It was the last church building authorized by Cardinal Stritch and one of the first dedicated by Cardinal Meyer.

TREASURE

The stained glass window over the front entrance, "Christmas Throughout the Year," was designed by Michaudel Stained Glass Studio in Chicago.

SS. PETER AND PAUL

3745 S. Paulina St., McKinley Park

PATRON

SS. Peter and Paul are often revered together as the two leading Apostles of the early Church. Peter, formerly known as Simon, was chosen by Jesus as the head of the Church. Paul, formerly known as Saul, persecuted the early Christians until he was miraculously converted. He became the most vigorous missionary of the early Church. Both were martyred in Rome about 64 or 65 AD.

HISTORY

Founded in 1895 as a Polish parish. The founding pastor was Rev. Paul Rhode, later an auxiliary bishop and then bishop of Green Bay. It remained a national parish until 1950, serving Polish immigrants who worked in the Union Stockyards or the Central Manufacturing District. The parish currently serves people of all backgrounds, but the parish and neighborhood are predominantly Latino.

ARCHITECTURE

The church, designed in a Roman Renaissance style, was completed in 1907.

TREASURE

Six Tiffany glass windows are "portraits" of Polish saints.

ST. PETER CANISIUS

5057 W. North Ave., Austin

PATRON

Peter Canisius (1521–1597) was educated in Cologne, Germany. He became a Jesuit and travelled and worked with Saint Ignatius of Loyola. He led the Counter-Reformation in German lands, founding universities and attending the Council of Trent..

HISTORY

Founded in 1925. The parish served a congregation of many different European ethnic origins. In recent years the area has become primarily African-American and Latino. Mass is celebrated in English and Spanish.

ARCHITECTURE

The church, designed in a modernized Romanesque style by Meyer & Cook, was completed in 1936.

TREASURE

A statue of St. Peter Canisius.

ST. PHILIP NERI

2132 E. 72nd St., South Shore

PATRON

Philip Neri (1515-1595) came from an impoverished noble family of Florence, Italy. Experiencing a religious conversion as a young man, he moved to Rome and began to care for the sick and for impoverished pilgrims. He became a priest and founded the Congregation of the Oratory in 1575.

HISTORY

Founded in 1912 to serve the upwardly mobile Irish Catholics of South Shore. Since the 1960s the parish and neighborhood have been predominantly middle-class African-American.

ARCHITECTURE

The church, designed in a modernized Gothic style by Joseph W. McCarthy, was completed in 1928. The cruciform church is one of the largest in the archdiocese and it reputedly had the longest Communion rail in the city.

TREASURE

Golden mosaic Stations of the Cross.

ST. PHILOMENA

1921 N. Kedvale Ave., Hermosa

PATRON

Philomena was a virgin martyr about whom nothing at all is known, not even the date of her death. Her tomb was discovered in the early 19th century and she became a popular saint throughout that century, primarily through the influence of St. John Vianney, the Curé of Ars.

HISTORY

Founded as a mission of St. Aloysius in 1888, it became a German parish in 1894. The parish ceased to be German after World War I as the surrounding neighborhood was settled by Poles and Italians. Since the 1970s the parish and neighborhood have been predominantly Latino.

St. Philomena

ARCHITECTURE

The church, designed in a Gothic style by Hermann J. Gaul, was completed in 1923. New shrines to Puerto Rico's Our Lady of Divine Providence and Mexico's Virgin of Guadalupe were recently added.

TREASURE

Dominican artist, Father Angelo Zarlenga, created a large bronze crucifix for the altar as well as marble statues of Mary and Joseph.

ST. PIUS V

1919 S. Ashland Ave., Lower West Side

PATRON

Michael Ghislieri (1504-1572), a member of the impoverished Italian nobility, became a Dominican priest. As a bishop and cardinal he combated the Reformation. Elected Pope in 1565 he chose the name Pius V and vigorously applied the reforms of the Council of Trent.

HISTORY

Founded in 1874. The parish was primarily Irish into the early 20th century when it became predominantly Polish. The Dominican Order began administering the parish in 1922 and they remain today. Since the 1970s the parish has been primarily Latino.

ARCHITECTURE

The church, designed in a Romanesque style by James J. Egan in 1885, was completed in 1893. In 1929 a shrine to St. Jude was erected in the church, and it became an object of great devotion throughout the Depression and long afterwards.

TREASURE

The mural of St. Jude and Our Lady of Guadalupe, designed by local artists Aurelio Diaz and Jose Moya, was completed in 1978.

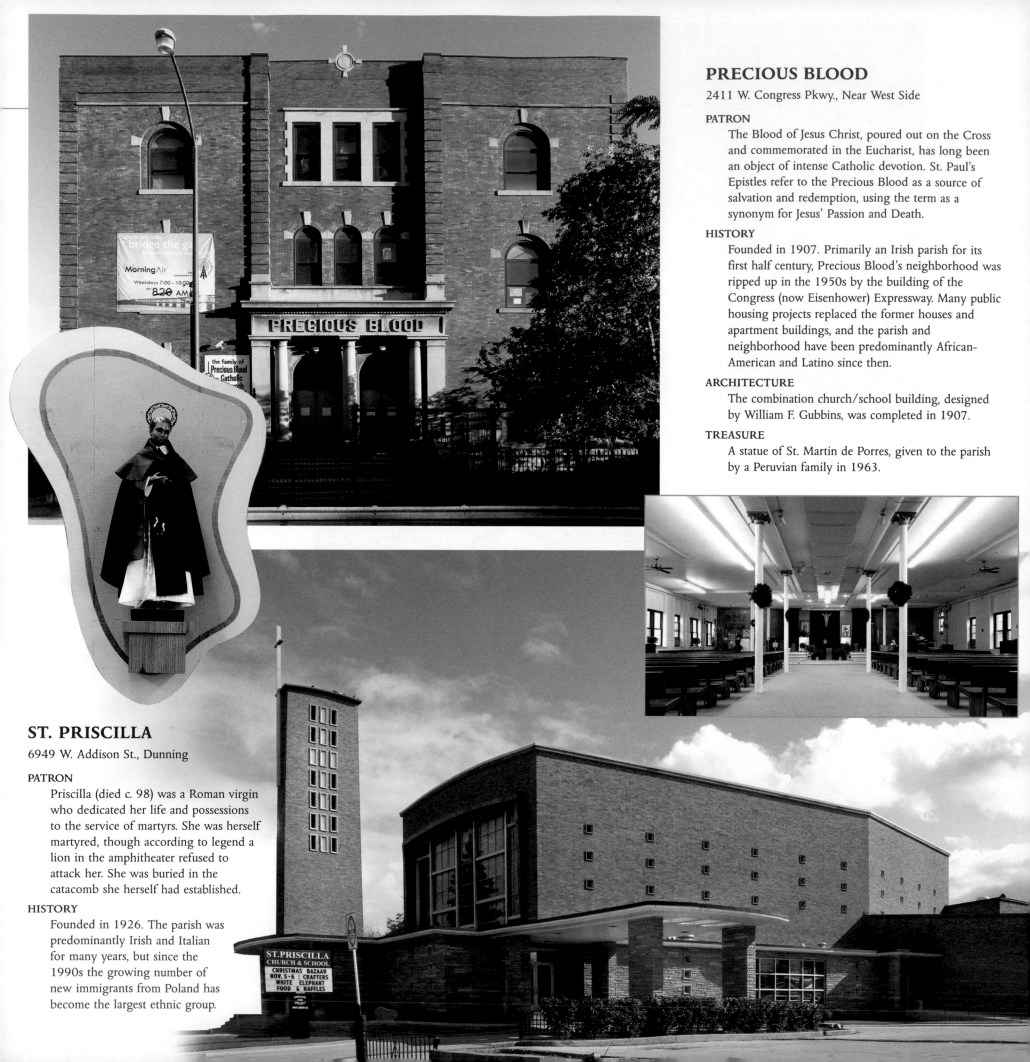

PRECIOUS BLOOD

2411 W. Congress Pkwy., Near West Side

PATRON

The Blood of Jesus Christ, poured out on the Cross and commemorated in the Eucharist, has long been an object of intense Catholic devotion. St. Paul's Epistles refer to the Precious Blood as a source of salvation and redemption, using the term as a synonym for Jesus' Passion and Death.

HISTORY

Founded in 1907. Primarily an Irish parish for its first half century, Precious Blood's neighborhood was ripped up in the 1950s by the building of the Congress (now Eisenhower) Expressway. Many public housing projects replaced the former houses and apartment buildings, and the parish and neighborhood have been predominantly African-American and Latino since then.

ARCHITECTURE

The combination church/school building, designed by William F. Gubbins, was completed in 1907.

TREASURE

A statue of St. Martin de Porres, given to the parish by a Peruvian family in 1963.

ST. PRISCILLA

6949 W. Addison St., Dunning

PATRON

Priscilla (died c. 98) was a Roman virgin who dedicated her life and possessions to the service of martyrs. She was herself martyred, though according to legend a lion in the amphitheater refused to attack her. She was buried in the catacomb she herself had established.

HISTORY

Founded in 1926. The parish was predominantly Irish and Italian for many years, but since the 1990s the growing number of new immigrants from Poland has become the largest ethnic group.

St. Priscilla

ARCHITECTURE

A combination church/school building served the parish until the modern church, designed by Barry and Kay, was completed in 1959.

TREASURE

The large sanctuary, with its marble floors, Eucharistic altar, and Holy Family altar, leads to a dramatic marble crucifix that is framed from ceiling to floor by a marble wall and brass screen.

ST. PROCOPIUS

1641 S. Allport St., Lower West Side

PATRON

Procopius (c. 980–1053) was a priest and hermit. He evangelized the people in the duchy of Bohemia where he remains a special patron.

HISTORY

Founded in 1875 as a Bohemian (Czech) parish. The Benedictine Fathers administered the parish, beginning in 1885, but in recent years the Jesuits have administered it. Since the 1960s the parish and neighborhood have been predominantly Mexican. The logo designed for the 125th anniversary neatly summarizes the parish history, with pictures of the Infant of Prague and Our Lady of Guadalupe as well as symbols of the two religious orders that have served the parish.

ARCHITECTURE

The church, designed by Paul Huber in a Romanesque style, was completed in 1883.

TREASURE

Capilla and mosaic of Our Lady of Guadalupe dedicated in 1963.

PROVIDENCE OF GOD

717 W. 18th St., Lower West Side

PATRON

The parish name commemorates the Divine Providence, or fatherly care, of God.

HISTORY

Founded in 1900 as a Lithuanian parish. It remained a Lithuanian parish until the 1960s, when the building of the Dan Ryan expressway displaced many parishioners. The parish and neighborhood are now predominantly Mexican.

ARCHITECTURE

The church, designed in a Romanesque style by Leo Strelka, was completed in 1927. Its twin steeples are landmarks for motorists zooming by only a few hundred feet away on the expressway.

TREASURE

Stained glass windows from Munich's F. X. Zettler Studios.

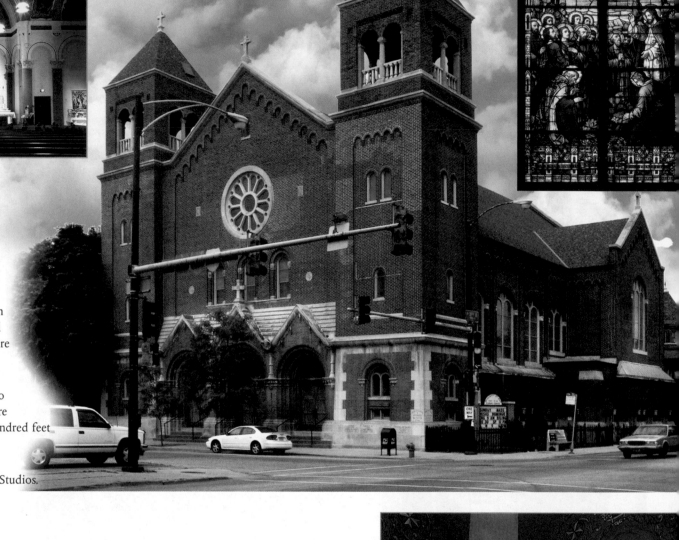

QUEEN OF ALL SAINTS

6280 N. Sauganash Ave., Forest Glen

PATRON

Since the Blessed Virgin Mary was assumed into heaven after her death, by the power of her Son, Jesus Christ, she is the first, and therefore the Queen, of all the saints in heaven.

HISTORY

Founded in 1929 in a lightly settled area on the far northwest side of the city. The neighborhood filled up as a residential area after World War II. The parish and neighborhood have a wide diversity of European ethnic groups, and include many police, fire, and city workers.

ARCHITECTURE

The church, designed in a modernized Gothic style by Meyer & Cook, was completed in 1960. The magnificent, cathedral-like church was raised to the dignity of a basilica by Pope John XXIII in 1962.

Queen of All Saints

QUEEN OF ANGELS

4412 N. Western Ave., Lincoln Square

PATRON

The Blessed Virgin Mary was assumed into heaven after her death, by the power of her Son, Jesus Christ, and thus is the Queen of all saints and angels in heaven.

HISTORY

Founded in 1909, in a residential neighborhood opened up by the completion of the Ravenswood L line in 1907. The parish has served a wide variety of ethnic groups. The neighborhood is prosperous and gentrified including a growing Hispanic population.

ARCHITECTURE

The church, overlooking Welles Park, was first planned by Henry J. Schlacks in 1924, but construction stalled through the 20s and 30s. Since architect Schlacks had died in the meantime, the firm of McCarthy, Smith and Eppig redesigned the church in a modernized Gothic style and it was completed in 1940.

TREASURE

German mahogany in the towering baldachino and cross over the altar.

QUEEN OF THE UNIVERSE

7114 S. Hamlin Ave., West Lawn

PATRON

The Blessed Virgin Mary was assumed into heaven after her death, by the power of her Son, Jesus Christ, and thus is the queen of all in heaven, earth, and throughout the universe.

HISTORY

Founded in 1955 by Fr. Stanley L. Ryzner. Though the parish was a territorial one in a new residential area on the outskirts of the city, the majority of the parishioners were Polish-Americans who had moved from the inner city. The school opened in 1957. The parish and neighborhood are now predominantly Latino. Mass is celebrated in English and Spanish.

ARCHITECTURE

The combination church/school building, constructed in 1956, was originally intended to be temporary; but it was renovated in 1970 with stained glass windows and appropriate decorations and still serves the parish. A shrine of Our Lady Queen of the Universe was dedicated in 1979. Since the church lies in the flight path of Midway Airport, jet noise was always a problem during Mass until the government finally installed soundproofing in 2002

TREASURE

A mosaic of Our Lady of Guadalupe was installed in 2005 at the Golden Jubilee of the parish.

ST. RENE GOUPIL

6949 W. 63rd Pl., Clearing

PATRON

Rene Goupil (1606–1642) was one of the North American Martyrs. A Frenchman with a medical degree, he offered to work as a medic for the Jesuit missionaries laboring among the Huron Indians in Canada and upper New York State. He was captured, tortured, and martyred by the Iroquois, enemies of the Hurons. St. Rene Goupil is the patron saint of anesthetists.

HISTORY

Founded in 1959 by Fr. Edward M. Flannery as the city grew on the far southwest side beyond Midway Airport. The parish and neighborhood were settled by a mixture of ethnic groups (mainly Polish, Irish, and Italian) who had moved from the inner city. The Sisters Servants of the Immaculate Heart of Mary from Monroe, Michigan taught in the parish school for many years.

ARCHITECTURE

The original church/school building was designed by Joseph W. McCarthy & Associates. The new church was designed in a modernized Romanesque style by Guy D. Gehlausen and completed in 1989.

TREASURE

The marble outdoor statue of St. Rene Goupil has welcomed people to the parish since its founding.

St. Rene Goupil

RESURRECTION

3043 N. Francisco Ave., Avondale

PATRON

Resurrection of the Lord Jesus Christ is the central belief of the Christian Faith. Resurrection of the body after death by the power of Christ is also the goal of all Christians.

HISTORY

Founded in 1991 through a merger of St. Francis Xavier, a formerly German parish, and St. Veronica, a formerly Irish parish. The new parish and the surrounding neighborhood are predominantly Latino and are newly prosperous and gentrifying.

ARCHITECTURE

The church building is the former St. Francis Xavier church, designed in a Gothic style and completed in 1929.

TREASURE

A statue of St. Veronica from the former parish.

ST. RICHARD

5030 S. Kostner Ave., Archer Heights

PATRON

Richard of Chichester (1197–1253) was educated at Oxford, Paris, and Bologna. He became chancellor of Oxford in 1235. He became a priest in 1242 and was installed as bishop of Chichester in 1245 after a dispute with the King of England. He was considered a model diocesan bishop by his contemporaries.

HISTORY

Founded in 1928 as a territorial parish created to serve the needs of parishioners from varied ethnic and racial backgrounds who had moved to Archer Heights from the inner city. The parish and neighborhood retain a strong Polish presence while welcoming a growing Hispanic community. Mass is celebrated in English and Polish.

ARCHITECTURE

The combination church/school building, designed by Joseph W. McCarthy & Associates, was completed in 1960.

TREASURE

A prayer of St. Richard inscribed on the exterior of the church.

LORD JESUS CHRIST+
MAY WE KNOW YOU MORE CLEARLY+ LOVE YOU MORE DEARLY+ AND FOLLOW YOU MORE NEARLY+ DAY BY DAY+

ST. RICHARD OF CHICHESTER

ST. RITA OF CASCIA

6243 S. Fairfield Ave., Chicago Lawn

PATRON

Rita of Cascia (1377–1447) was born in Umbria and was convinced to marry against her wishes. After her husband died a violent death, she became an Augustinian nun around 1407. Rita lived 40 years in the convent, spending her time in prayer and charity, and working for peace in the region.

HISTORY

Founded in 1905 by the Augustinian Order, who still administer the

parish. The parish was an adjunct of St. Rita College (now high school). The parish was predominantly Irish for many years. However, since the 1970s the parish and neighborhood have been predominantly Hispanic and African-American.

ARCHITECTURE

The church, designed by A.F. Moratz in a modernized Romanesque style, was completed in 1950.

TREASURE

A pillow from the tomb of St. Rita in Cascia, Italy.

St. Rita of Cascia

ST. ROBERT BELLARMINE

4646 N. Austin Ave., Portage Park

PATRON

Robert Bellarmine (1542–1621) was born in Tuscany. He became a Jesuit and was ordained a priest in 1570. He taught theology at Louvain and then at the Roman College. Named a Cardinal in 1598, he lived an austere life in Rome. He became prefect of the Vatican Library and wrote many books of devotion.

HISTORY

Founded in 1930 on the far northwest side of the city. The neighborhood filled up as a residential area after World War II. The parishioners come from a wide variety of European ethnic origins. The parish supports a vibrant school which continues to expand its programs and remains faithful to its Catholic identity.

ARCHITECTURE

The first church was designed by McCarthy, Hundreiser & Associates and completed in 1970, but burned down in 1988. The new church, designed by Ben Nelson and Associates, took its place in 1989 with a full basement to serve as a parish hall with all necessary facilities.

TREASURE

The Holy Family shrine.

ST. ROMAN

2311 S. Washtenaw Ave., South Lawndale

PATRON

Roman, or Romanus, (died c. 258) was a martyr in Rome. Nothing certain is known of his life or death, though he is alleged to have been converted by St. Laurence.

HISTORY

Founded in 1928 as a Polish parish. By the middle of the 20th century, the parish had begun to serve many different ethnic groups, and since the 1960s, the parish and neighborhood have been predominantly Mexican.

ARCHITECTURE

The church, designed in a Spanish Mission style by Sandel and Strong, was begun just before the stock market crash of 1929 and completed in 1930.

TREASURE

The domed ceiling has a mural of Polish saints surrounding the Trinity.

ST. SABINA

1210 W. 78th Pl., Auburn Gresham

PATRON

Sabina (died late 3rd century) was a wealthy Roman lady converted to Christianity by her servant Serapia. Serapia was martyred during the persecutions of emperor Hadrian, and Sabina about a month later.

HISTORY

Founded in 1916 as a predominantly Irish parish. It developed a very active youth ministry after the construction of its community center in 1937. Since the 1960s, the parish and neighborhood have been predominantly African-American. St. Sabina is currently one of the premier black Catholic parishes in the city.

St. Sabina

ARCHITECTURE

The church, designed in an English Gothic style by Joseph W. McCarthy, was completed in 1933. The bell tower rises 135 feet and can be seen throughout the neighborhood.

TREASURE

A huge mural of a dark-skinned Jesus between the hands of God the Father fills the wall behind the altar. It is a sanctuary that celebrates African-American culture and art.

SACRED HEART

2864 E. 96th St.,
East Side

PATRON

St. Margaret Mary Alacoque (1647-1690), a French nun of Paray-le-Monial, France, was primarily responsible for spreading devotion to the Sacred Heart of Jesus. Since the 17th century, this has been one of the most popular of all Catholic devotions, common to many different ethnic groups.

HISTORY

Founded in 1913 as a Croatian parish. Franciscan priests have administered the parish since 1919. This working-class parish and neighborhood remains predominantly Croatian.

ARCHITECTURE

The modern church, designed by Fox & Fox, was completed in 1964.

TREASURE

A statue of the Sacred Heart.

ST. STEPHEN KING OF HUNGARY

2015 W. Augusta Blvd., West Town

PATRON

Stephen of Hungary (c.975–1038) was born a pagan but was baptized with his father, the duke of Hungary, at age 10. Succeeding his father in 997, he completed the evangelization of his duchy and in 1001 he was crowned King of Hungary by the Holy Roman Emperor with the approval of the Pope. He founded many dioceses and monasteries and gave generously to the poor.

HISTORY

Founded in 1934 as a Hungarian parish. The parish was originally named St. Emeric, for the son of St. Stephen, but was renamed in 1938. The parish also served some Polish families, but the Hungarian element was reinforced after Communist suppression of an uprising in 1956. Mass is celebrated in English and Hungarian.

ARCHITECTURE

The church building was purchased in 1939 from the Emmanuel Slovak Baptist Church.

TREASURE

An oil painting of King Stephen is the artistic work of a member of Hungary's nobility who had been a parishioner.

ST. SYLVESTER

2157 N. Humboldt Blvd., Logan Square

PATRON

Sylvester (d. 335) was named Pope in 314, during the reign of Emperor Constantine, who first declared Christianity the state religion of the Roman Empire. He sent delegates to the Council of Nicaea and approved the council's affirmation of both the divinity and the humanity of Jesus.

HISTORY

Founded in 1884 to serve the English-speaking (mainly Irish) Catholics in a predominantly Protestant neighborhood. The parish served a wide variety of European ethnic groups over the years, and since the 1970s the parish and neighborhood have been predominantly Latino. The area is newly prosperous and gentrifying.

ARCHITECTURE

The church, designed by Egan and Prindeville in a Romanesque style, was completed in 1907. Both the bell tower and the peak of the church are topped by Celtic crosses.

TREASURE

Brilliant stained glass windows, perhaps influenced by Celtic spirituality, honor many saintly women, such as the Virgin Mary, Catherine of Siena, Rose of Lima, and Margaret Mary Alacoque.

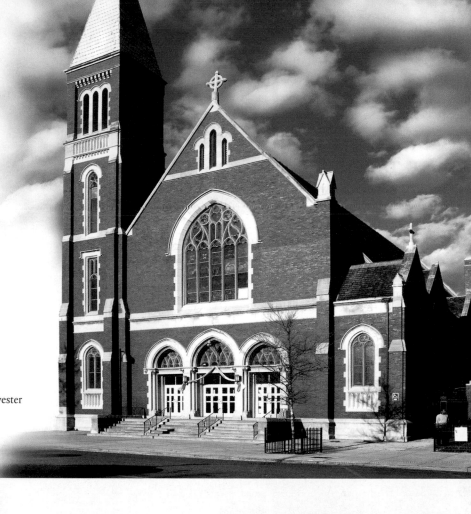

St. Sylvester

ST. SYMPHOROSA

6135 S. Austin Ave., Clearing

PATRON

Symphorosa was martyred with her seven sons at Tibur (Tivoli) towards the end of the reign of Emperor Hadrian (117–138). Nothing else is known for certain about her life or death.

HISTORY

Founded in 1927 as a multi-ethnic American parish for English-speaking Catholics in the far southwest corner of Chicago. The neighborhood filled up with residences after World War II. Today, the parish proudly continues its historical mandate as it serves a multi-ethnic congregation.

ARCHITECTURE

The church, designed in a modernized Gothic style by George S. Smith, was completed in 1957 and renovated in 2003.

TREASURE

The original church building, constructed in 1928, now serves as the Father Sharp Social Center. The cornerstone of this building, which ties the community to its past, will be laid in a place of honor when a new parish center is constructed.

ST. THECLA
6725 W. Devon Ave., Norwood Park

PATRON

Thecla of Iconium (first century AD) was one of the first virgin martyrs of the early Church. She was converted to Christianity by St. Paul. She spent the rest of her life as an ascetic, removed from the world. She died and was buried in Syria.

HISTORY

Founded in 1925. It was a territorial parish but its congregation was predominantly Polish. The ethnic makeup has become more heterogeneous over the years. Because of its location at the edge of the city, it is home to many police, firefighters, and other city workers.

ARCHITECTURE

The modern brick church, designed by Meyer and Cook, was completed in 1963. Renovations of the interior were completed in 2005.

TREASURE

Altar carving of the Last Supper.

ST. THERESE
218 W. Alexander St., Armour Square

PATRON

Therese of Lisieux (1873-1897) was born to a middle-class French family. She became a Carmelite nun at age 15. She died young of tuberculosis. Her life illustrates the potential for sanctity in the most ordinary routines of daily life. She has been widely revered as "The Little Flower," and has been declared a Doctor of the Church and a patroness of the Missions.

HISTORY

Founded as a Chinese Catholic mission in 1947 in the growing Chinese district of what was then "Little Italy." As the area developed into the city's "Chinatown," the Chinese parish took over the former Italian church of Santa Maria Incoronata when that parish was consolidated with Santa Lucia in 1960.

ARCHITECTURE

The church building, formerly the parish church of Santa Maria Incoronata, was designed in a Renaissance style by William F. Gubbins in 1904. When the parish became Chinese, giant fu dogs were added to guard the entrance.

TREASURE

A silk and gold tapestry depicts Mary as a Chinese empress. The tapestry translates into Chinese cultural terms the old name of the church, Santa Maria Incoronata, i.e., Mary Queen of Heaven.

ST. THOMAS THE APOSTLE

5472 S. Kimbark Ave., Hyde Park

PATRON

Thomas (died c. 72), also called Didymus (the twin), was one of the Twelve Apostles. He is usually referred to as "Doubting Thomas," since he was absent when Jesus first appeared to the Apostles after the Resurrection, and he doubted the story of his appearance until Jesus showed Himself again. Nothing is known for certain about his life after Pentecost, but a persistent tradition holds that he evangelized and was martyred in India

HISTORY

Founded in 1869 in what was then the independent township of Hyde Park. The area was predominantly Protestant and Catholics were not welcomed. The neighborhood took on new importance, shortly after its annexation to Chicago in 1889, when the University of Chicago was founded in 1892. The parish has always served a diverse congregation and is now racially and ethnically integrated.

ARCHITECTURE

The church, designed in a radically modern style with strong Spanish and Moorish influences by Francis Barry Byrne, was completed in 1924. Byrne, a disciple of Frank Lloyd Wright, broke with the tradition of historical revivals when he designed what has been called "the first modern church in America."

TREASURE

Heroic bronze Stations of the Cross were designed by Alfeo Faggi, and terrracotta by Alfonso Ionelli.

ST. WILLIAM

2600 N. Sayre Ave., Montclare

PATRON

William (died 1142) was born in Piedmont in northern Italy. After a pilgrimage to St.
James' shrine in Compostela, he became a hermit in the mountains of the south of Italy.
He founded a congregation of monks that followed the Benedictine rule.

HISTORY

Founded in 1916 for German and English speaking Catholics. It has served a wide variety
of ethnic groups since then in a semi-suburban residential area.

ARCHITECTURE

The modern church, designed by Belli and Belli, was completed in 1960. The statue of
St. William on the façade of the church is carved from a single, massive block of marble.

TREASURE

A shrine of the Holy Family, Jesus, Mary, and Joseph.

The Archdiocese of

CHICAGO

SUBURBAN
PARISHES

Alsip

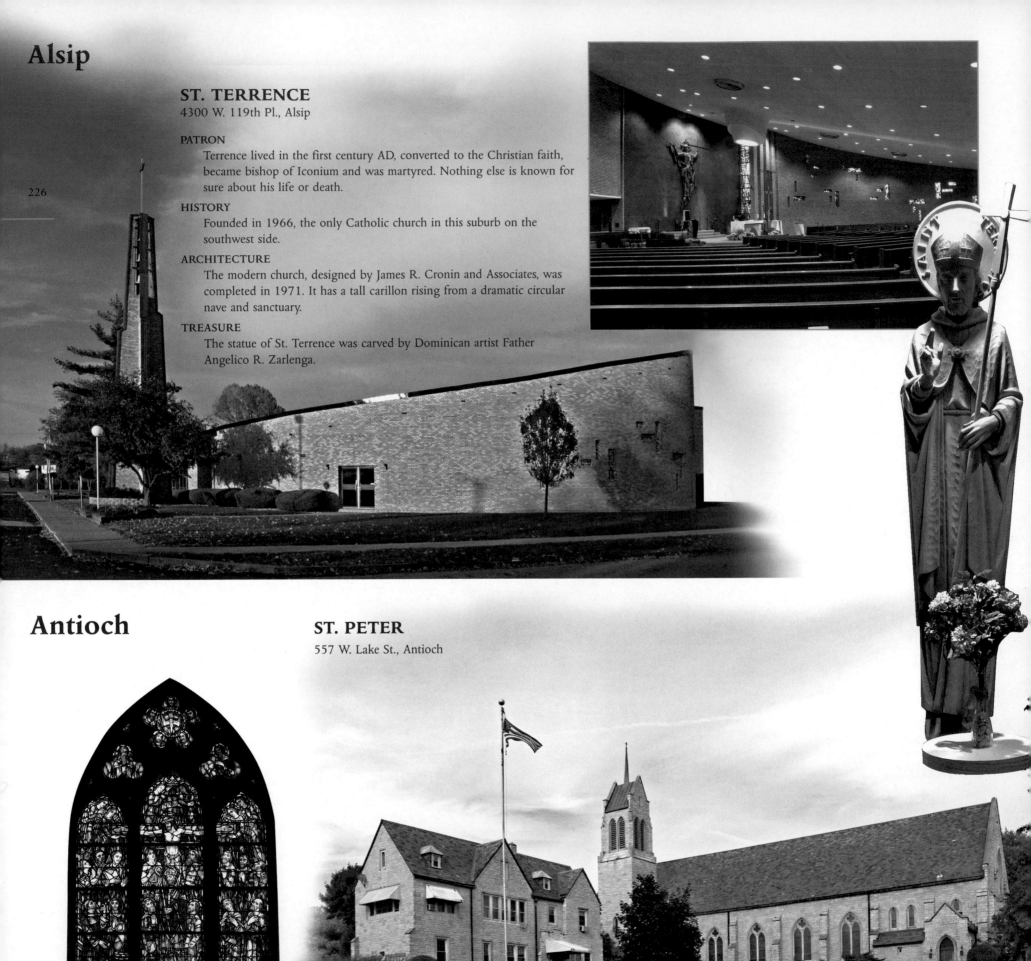

ST. TERRENCE
4300 W. 119th Pl., Alsip

PATRON

Terrence lived in the first century AD, converted to the Christian faith, became bishop of Iconium and was martyred. Nothing else is known for sure about his life or death.

HISTORY

Founded in 1966, the only Catholic church in this suburb on the southwest side.

ARCHITECTURE

The modern church, designed by James R. Cronin and Associates, was completed in 1971. It has a tall carillon rising from a dramatic circular nave and sanctuary.

TREASURE

The statue of St. Terrence was carved by Dominican artist Father Angelico R. Zarlenga.

Antioch

ST. PETER
557 W. Lake St., Antioch

PATRON

Peter (died c. 64) was one of the Twelve Apostles. Originally named Simon, he and his brother Andrew were fishermen, called by Jesus to follow Him. Jesus renamed him Peter, which means Rock, and designated him as the foundation or head of the early Church. Peter was thus the first Pope and was martyred in Rome.

HISTORY

Founded about 1897 as a mission of St. Patrick in Wadsworth, this church near the Illinois-Wisconsin border became a parish in 1905. Though the surrounding area was originally farmland and lake resorts, it has become more suburban in recent years, increasing the permanent congregation of the parish.

ARCHITECTURE

The church, designed in an English Gothic style by Leo Strelka, was completed in 1930.

TREASURE

The stained glass windows with wood tracery by Rambush Studios are modeled after those of 13th century Chartres.

Argo

ST. BLASE

6101 S. 75th Ave., Argo

PATRON

Blase, or Blaise (died c. 316), was a bishop of Sebaste in Armenia who was martyred for the Faith. Little is known for certain about his life, but a popular legend says that he was a healer of men and animals. On one occasion he is said to have saved a child from choking on a fishbone. This story led to the custom of the blessing of throats on his feast day, February 3rd.

HISTORY

Founded as a mission of St. Joseph, Summit in 1916, it became a Polish parish in 1924. It remained a working-class Polish parish for a long time, but in recent years it has also counted many Latino parishioners. Mass is now celebrated in English, Polish, and Spanish.

ARCHITECTURE

The modern church, designed by Strelka, Tobolski and Strelka, was completed in 1963.

TREASURE

A replica of a historic statue of Our Lady of San Juan de los Lagos, presented by a Mexican bishop to the parish in 1998 (pictured here), and a depiction of Our Lady of Czestochowa hold equal prominence in the church.

Arlington Heights

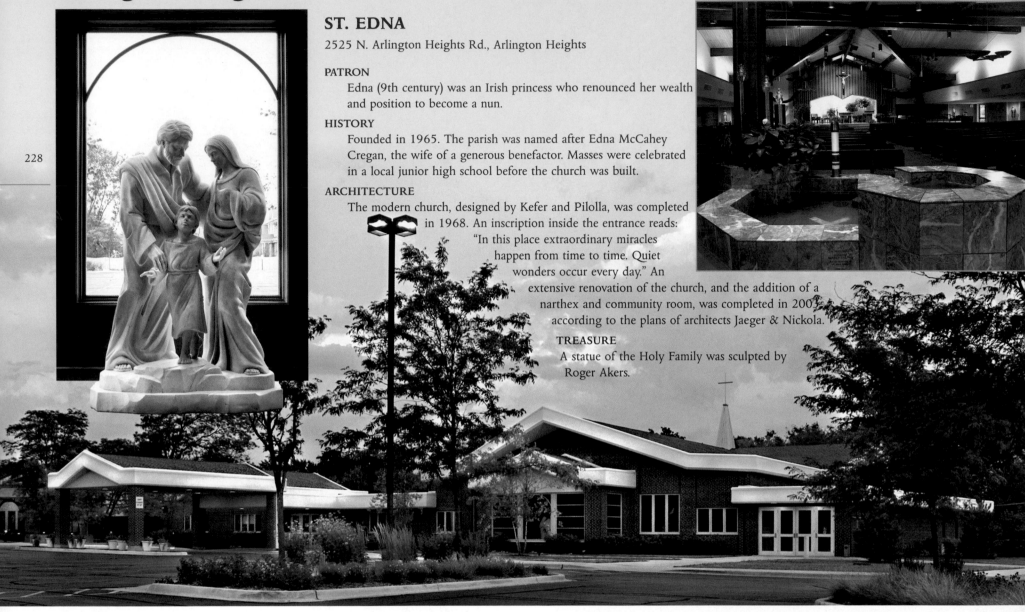

ST. EDNA

2525 N. Arlington Heights Rd., Arlington Heights

PATRON

Edna (9th century) was an Irish princess who renounced her wealth and position to become a nun.

HISTORY

Founded in 1965. The parish was named after Edna McCahey Cregan, the wife of a generous benefactor. Masses were celebrated in a local junior high school before the church was built.

ARCHITECTURE

The modern church, designed by Kefer and Pilolla, was completed in 1968. An inscription inside the entrance reads: "In this place extraordinary miracles happen from time to time. Quiet wonders occur every day." An extensive renovation of the church, and the addition of a narthex and community room, was completed in 2003 according to the plans of architects Jaeger & Nickola.

TREASURE

A statue of the Holy Family was sculpted by Roger Akers.

ST. JAMES

820 N. Arlington Heights Rd., Arlington Heights

PATRON

Two of the Twelve Apostles were named James. One, usually called James the Greater, was the son of Zebedee and the brother of John. He was the first Apostle to be martyred, in 44 AD. The other, usually called James the Less, was the son of Alphaeus. He became first bishop of Jerusalem and was martyred there about 62 AD. The parish was named for James the Less, since the first Mass was celebrated in the community on his feast day, May 3rd. The parishioners also identify with him in their efforts always to "try harder".

HISTORY

The Catholics of the Arlington Heights area were served by priests from surrounding parishes as early as the 1880s. From 1902 until 1922 it was a mission of St. Mary's in DesPlaines; thereafter it was an independent parish. When the population of the northwest suburbs soared after World War II, St. James was divided into new parishes on several occasions. The parish currently has over 1000 volunteers in 101 active ministries.

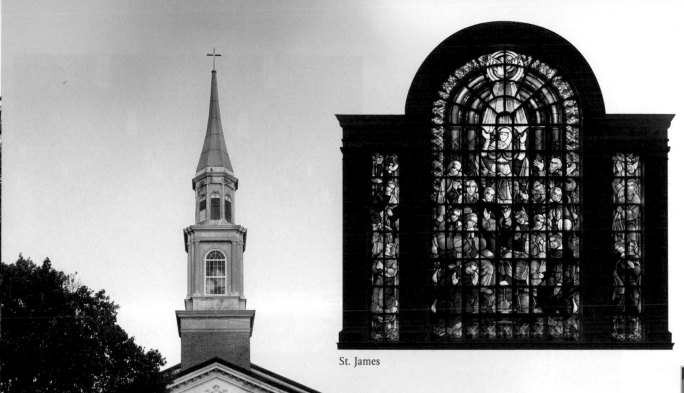

St. James

ARCHITECTURE

The church, designed in a colonial style modeled after the main chapel at St. Mary of the Lake Seminary, was completed in 1952.

TREASURE

The original stylized stained glass windows, designed by a priest from Holland, rise 30 feet along the nave.

MISION SAN JUAN DIEGO

2323 N. Wilke Rd., Arlington Heights

PATRON

Juan Diego (died c. 1548) was a Mexican peasant who converted to Christianity at about the age of fifty. On December 9, 1531, the Blessed Virgin appeared to him on Tepeyac Hill, leaving him with an image known as Our Lady of Guadalupe.

HISTORY

Founded in 1961 as a mission church for Spanish-speaking farm workers in the area. The parish's patron was canonized in July 2002 by Pope John Paul II.

ARCHITECTURE

Cardinal George dedicated the mission's new church and offices in 2003 after members of the congregation renovated the former Scandinavian Club in Arlington Heights.

Mision de San Juan Diego

TREASURE

The "Genesis" mural, painted by Leonardo Nierman.

Beach Park/Zion

OUR LADY OF HUMILITY

10655 W. Wadsworth Rd., Beach Park/Zion

PATRON

The parish name refers to one of many titles of Mary invoked in the Litany of the Blessed Virgin. Cardinal Stritch suggested the name in honor of the Marian Year, which was being celebrated in 1954, and in memory of the chapel of Our Lady of Humility in which he had prayed as a seminarian at the North American College in Rome.

HISTORY

Founded in 1954 in the far northeastern corner of the Archdiocese. It is a geographically sprawling, ethnically diverse parish.

ARCHITECTURE

The modern church, designed by Joseph L. Bennett, was completed in 1956. The church was "turned around" in 2004, thus aligning the altar with Marian windows that had previously been beside the entrance doors

TREASURE

A new rose window depicting Our Lady of Humility is now above the altar.

Bellwood

ST. SIMEON

430 Bohland Ave., Bellwood

PATRON

Simeon (died c. 107) was a kinsman of Joseph and Mary and an early follower of Jesus. When the Apostle James the Less, the first bishop of Jerusalem, was martyred in 62 AD, Simeon succeeded him, serving until his own martyrdom at an advanced age.

HISTORY

Founded in 1930 as a Polish parish. The parish became more ethnically diverse over the years, with many Irish and Italian members, and more recently the parish and suburb have included many African-Americans and Latinos.

ARCHITECTURE

The church, a modern fan-shaped structure designed by C. I. Krajewski, was completed in 1966. It has one of the largest, single-themed stained glass windows in the world, measuring 144 feet by 20 feet.

TREASURE

A jeweled ciborium, paten, and chalice were made from jewelry donated by a parish member, Rose Polka.

St. Simeon

Berwyn

ST. LEONARD

3318 S. Clarence Ave., Berwyn

PATRON

Leonard was a Frankish noble of the 6th century, who became a hermit. Nothing is known for certain of his life or death.

HISTORY

Founded in 1918 as a mission of St. Mary, Riverside, it became a parish in 1923. The parish has always had a diverse congregation.

ARCHITECTURE

The church, designed by George S. Smith in a modernized Gothic style, was completed in 1951.

TREASURE

The stained glass windows, designed and executed in the Clinton Glass studios of Chicago, have facets with antique and cathedral glass from Belgium, Germany, France, and England.

Berwyn

ST. MARY OF CELLE

1428 S. Wesley Ave., Berwyn

PATRON

The parish name means "house of Mary." The parish is named after the shrine to Our Lady of Mariazell, established by Benedictine monks in Austria in 1157.

HISTORY

Founded in 1909 as a Bohemian parish, but with territorial boundaries and open to all. Bohemian Benedictines from St. Procopius Abbey, Lisle IL. administered the parish until 1979. It has always been a diverse parish, and in recent years Latinos have become predominant.

ARCHITECTURE

The church, designed in a Spanish Mission-style by Meyer and Cook, was completed in 1931. Several symbols of Benedictine spirituality are included in the design.

TREASURE

Recently discovered original tiles and decorative wood elements have been used in a new baptismal font and shrine area as well as to enhance the altar of sacrifice.

ST. ODILO

2244 S. East Ave., Berwyn

PATRON

Odilo (962-1049) was a member of the French nobility who became a Benedictine monk and later the abbot at Cluny. He promoted the Truce of God whereby military hostilities were suspended at certain times and which guaranteed sanctuary to those who sought refuge in a church. He instituted the feast now know as All Soul's Day.

HISTORY

Founded in 1927, to relieve overcrowding at St. Leonard' parish. The parish became a center of prayer for the souls in Purgatory, following the lead of the parish patron. The parish has always served a diverse congregation from many different ethnic origins.

ARCHITECTURE

The modern church, designed by Andrew G. Stoecker, was completed in 1963.

TREASURE

A striking bronze depiction of the tormented Souls in Purgatory.

St. Odilo

Blue Island

ST. BENEDICT

2339 York St., Blue Island

PATRON

Benedict of Nursia (480-547) was the twin brother of St. Scholastica. He founded the monastery at Monte Cassino, where he wrote the Rule of his order. He is considered the father of Western monasticism.

HISTORY

Founded as a mission by Benedictine Fathers in 1861, it became a parish in 1886. Diocesan priests began administering the parish in 1904. Originally a German parish, it soon included Irish, Poles, and Bohemians as well. In recent years the parish and neighborhood have become predominantly Latino.

ARCHITECTURE

The modern church, designed by James R. Cronin and Associates, was completed in 1970.

TREASURE

The cross hanging over the altar.

Brookfield

ST. BARBARA

4008 Prairie Ave., Brookfield

PATRON
Barbara was a virgin martyr (died c. 235), but little is known of her life. This parish was named for the mother of Konrad Ricker, a real estate developer who donated the land for the church.

HISTORY
Founded as a mission of St. Francis Xavier, La Grange, in 1912, it became a parish in 1916. The parish has always served a congregation of diverse ethnic origins. Mass is celebrated in English and Spanish.

ARCHITECTURE
A modern, circular church, designed by Joseph L. Bennett, was completed in 1970. It is complemented by a free-standing, three-belled carillon. Parishioners sacrificed several houses, just south of the rectory, to make room for this church.

TREASURE
Stations of the Cross in Venetian mosaic glass.

Buffalo Grove

ST. MARY

10 N. Buffalo Grove Rd., Buffalo Grove

PATRON
The Blessed Virgin Mary, wife of St. Joseph, Mother of Jesus.

HISTORY
Mass was celebrated for German farm families in Buffalo Grove as early as 1847. From 1852 the church became a mission of St. John the Baptist in Johnsburg, McHenry County. St. Mary was established as a parish in 1869. The parish lost its exclusively German character after World War I, but it remained a country parish until the 1950s, when the area began to be subdivided for suburban residences.

ARCHITECTURE

A Gothic church, designed by William J. Brinkmann, was completed in 1900; and in 1980 a modern, semi-circular annex was added, according to plans by Hundrieser-Gutowsky and Associates. A simple altar bridges the transition between the old and new structures.

TREASURE

The original Gothic reredos, which once stood behind the main altar, is now a shrine.

Burbank

ST. ALBERT THE GREAT

5555 W. State Rd., Burbank

PATRON

Albert the Great (1206–1280) was a Dominican priest. He taught theology at Cologne and at Paris, and was the mentor of St. Thomas Aquinas. He introduced Greek and Arabic science and philosophy to medieval Europe, most notably the works of Aristotle.

HISTORY

Originally founded as a mission of St. Gerald, Oak Lawn in 1949, it became a parish in 1951. Though the area was divided several times into new parishes, St. Albert's continued to grow. It serves a large and diverse congregation.

ARCHITECTURE

The modern church, designed by Bartolomeo and Hansen, was completed in 1965. It has a 45 foot bell tower.

TREASURE

A stained glass window depicting the parish patron, St. Albert the Great, and his most famous pupil, St. Thomas Aquinas.

St. Mary

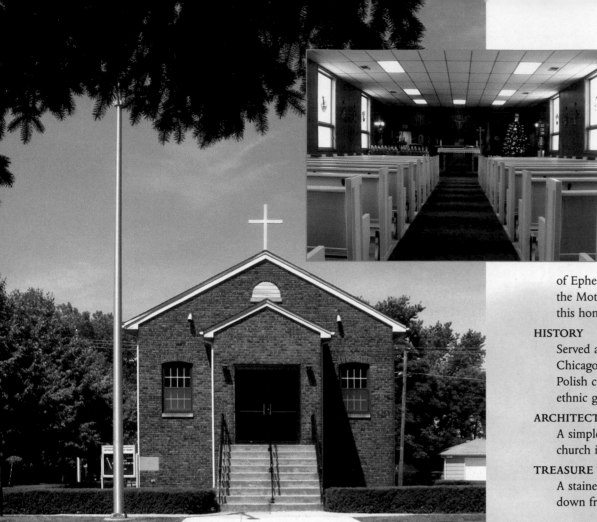

Burnham

MOTHER OF GOD

14207 S. Green Bay Ave.,
Burnham

PATRON
The Blessed Virgin Mary, wife of St.
Joseph, Mother of Jesus. The Council
of Ephesus (431) definitively declared Mary to be
the Mother of God, refuting heretics who denied her
this honor and title.

HISTORY
Served as a mission of St. Florian, in the Hegewisch section of
Chicago. It was founded as a parish in 1956, serving a primarily
Polish congregation. The parish now serves a variety of different
ethnic groups.

ARCHITECTURE
A simple brick church, constructed in 1946, may be the smallest
church in the archdiocese.

TREASURE
A stained glass medallion depicting Mary receiving Jesus's body
down from the cross.

Calumet City

ST. ANDREW THE APOSTLE

768 Lincoln Ave., Calumet City

PATRON
Andrew (died c.60) was one of the Twelve Apostles, a fisherman
and the brother of Simon Peter. He preached in Asia Minor and
Greece and possibly as far north as modern Russia (where he is
revered as the national patron). He is said to have been crucified
on an X-shaped cross, which has become his symbol and is also
used as an emblem for Scotland on the Union Jack flag.

HISTORY

Founded in 1892 as a Polish parish. It has remained a predominantly working-class parish of Polish, Italian, and Irish families.

ARCHITECTURE

The church, designed in a Romanesque style by Sandal and Strong, was completed in 1931.

TREASURE

The beautiful marble baptistery, with a carving of St. John the Baptist.

St. Andrew the Apostle

OUR LADY OF KNOCK

501 163rd St., Calumet City

PATRON

The parish name refers to an apparition of the Blessed Virgin Mary at St. John the Baptist Church, Knock, County Mayo, Ireland, in 1879. The founding pastor, Rev. Martin J. Neary, chose this name to honor his parents who had been born near Knock.

HISTORY

Founded in 1957 to serve Catholics in a new subdivision of Calumet City. The parish serves a number of different ethnic groups, but despite the name of the church Poles outnumber Irish.

ARCHITECTURE

The modern church, designed by Fox & Fox, was completed in 1958.

TREASURE

Melville P. Steinfels' dramatic mosaic representation of the 1879 Marian apparition at Knock.

ST. VICTOR

553 Hirsch Ave., Calumet City

PATRON

Victor (died c. 198) was a Pope and martyr. It is believed he was a native of Africa and, therefore, one of the first black Popes, reigning from about 189 A.D. St. Jerome refers to him as the first theologian of the Church who wrote in Latin, rather than Greek. Only a treatise concerning the celebration of Easter has survived.

HISTORY

Founded in 1925 as a territorial parish, since the only previous parish in the area was exclusively Polish. The original makeup of St. Victor was heavily Polish with strong currents of second generation Italian, German, Slavic, and Irish. The ethnic makeup is still a mix of Caucasian ethnicities, as well as Hispanic, African-American, and Nigerian.

ARCHITECTURE

The church, designed in a Romanesque style by James Burns, carrying the theme of many old Roman churches, was completed in 1928. Ten stained glass windows, designed and manufactured by the Tyrolese Art Glass Co. of Innsbruck, Austria, were installed in 1930; and seven additional windows were installed later.

TREASURE

The outdoor Fatima shrine was donated by schoolchildren in 1959.

Calumet Park

SEVEN HOLY FOUNDERS

12400 S. Ada St., Calumet Park

PATRON

The Seven Holy Founders of the Servite Order were wealthy merchants of Florence, Italy who founded a new order of friars, called the Servants of Mary, in 1233.

HISTORY

Founded in 1949, as a mission of St. Donatus, Blue Island, to serve a rapidly developing suburban area just beyond the southern border of Chicago. It was the first church of any denomination in the town. It remained a mission until 1974. The parish was predominantly Irish and Polish at first, but the town and the parish have become predominantly Latino and African-American.

ARCHITECTURE

A combination church/school building, designed by Edo J. Belli, was completed in 1955.

TREASURE:

A shrine to Our Lady of Guadalupe.

Chicago Heights

ST. AGNES

1501 Chicago Rd., Chicago Heights

PATRON

Agnes (died c. 304) was a virgin martyr of Rome. On her feast day of January 21, two lambs are sheared in Rome and palliums for newly consecrated bishops are made from the wool in honor of St. Agnes.

HISTORY

Founded in 1895 in a newly established industrial suburb, St. Agnes is the mother church of Chicago Heights. The parish was primarily Irish at first, but has evolved as a welcoming, diverse community.

ARCHITECTURE

The combination church/school building was completed in 1926, and renovated in 1995. The building is in a classical Roman style.

TREASURE:

Reredos with painting of St. Agnes behind the high altar.

ST. KIERAN

724 W. 195th St., Chicago Heights

PATRON

Kieran (or Ciaran) of Clonmacnoise (c. 512–c.545) was an Irish monk. He founded the monastery of Clonmacnoise, on the Shannon River, but died at an early age before completing the buildings. This monastery was known for centuries as a center of religious scholarship.

HISTORY

Founded in 1960. Soil from Clomnacnoise and water from the River Shannon were sealed in the cornerstone of the church.

ARCHITECTURE

The modern church was completed in 1984, replacing a combination church/school structure that had served since 1962.

TREASURE

A copy of one of the Irish High Crosses from the ruins of St. Kieran's monastery in Clonmacnoise was commissioned for the new church in 1984. The Cross of the Scriptures on the East wall of the church lobby is dedicated to all who helped to build the new church.

ST. PAUL

206 E. 25th St., Chicago Heights

PATRON

Paul the Apostle (died c. 65) was originally named Saul. He was a Jew of Tarsus, a tentmaker by trade, who persecuted the early Christians. On his way to Damascus to arrest another group of them, he was knocked to the ground and struck blind by a heavenly light. He converted to Christianity and became such an effective preacher throughout the Roman world that he is known as the Apostle of the Gentiles. He was martyred in Rome.

St. Paul

HISTORY

Founded in 1927 as a Slovak parish in an industrial enclave of Chicago Heights. The parish was named in honor of Fr. Paul Shiska, a Wisconsin priest who encouraged the Slovaks to organize their own parish.

ARCHITECTURE

The combination church/school building was completed in 1929.

TREASURE

A shrine depicting the Souls in Purgatory imploring the aid of Mary and Jesus.

Chicago Ridge

OUR LADY OF THE RIDGE

10811 S. Ridgeland Ave., Chicago Ridge

PATRON

The Blessed Virgin Mary is invoked as patron under a title that refers to the village of Chicago Ridge, which was incorporated in 1914.

HISTORY

The parish was founded in 1948 to serve the increasing faith communities of Chicago Ridge and Worth after World War II. Though predominantly Irish at its founding, today the church serves a multi-ethnic congregation.

ARCHITECTURE

The first church building was a former grocery story at 106th and Ridgeland, now the home of the VFW. In 1964, the school auditorium was extended to provide a worship space. In 2000, a new church, designed by John Voosen, was dedicated.

TREASURE

The Adoration Chapel, located in the parish center (formerly the convent), opened as a 24-hour Eucharistic chapel in 2002. The same building houses and feeds the homeless during the winter months.

1510 S. 49th Ct., Cicero

PATRON

Anthony of Padua (1195-1231) was a Franciscan friar, born in Lisbon, Portugal. He spent the latter part of his life in Italy and was called to teach theology at the University of Padua. A popular preacher in his own time, he has been a very popular saint among many ethnic groups and individuals. He is sometimes invoked as the patron saint of lost articles.

HISTORY

Founded in 1911 as a Lithuanian parish. The parish remained primarily Lithuanian for many years, but since 1975 has become predominantly Mexican. Mass is celebrated in English, Lithuanian, and Spanish. An outdoor dramatization of the Via Crucis is enacted every Good Friday, and the other great popular celebration is the Feast of Our Lady of Guadalupe in December.

ARCHITECTURE

The church, designed by Leo Strelka in a Romanesque style, was completed in 1926. Archbishop George Matulaitis of Lithuania, who was attending the Eucharistic Congress in Chicago, performed the dedication. The front portico was added in 1954.

TREASURE

Relics of Archbishop George Matulaitis who dedicated the church.

ST. FRANCES OF ROME

1428 S. 59th Ct., Cicero

PATRON

Frances of Rome (1384-1440) was a Roman aristocrat who devoted herself to aiding the city's poor. When her husband died after forty years of marriage, she became a nun and founded the Oblates of Mary.

HISTORY

Founded in 1923. As a territorial parish in a city with many national parishes, St. Frances has always served many different ethnic groups.

St. Frances of Rome

ARCHITECTURE

A combination church/school building, designed in a Spanish Mission style, was completed in 1924. This building was razed in 1990, and Mass has been celebrated since then in a chapel at the former Middle School.

TREASURE

A statue of the patroness was carved by Italian artisans from rare marble.

ST. MARY OF CZESTOCHOWA

3010 S. 48th Ct., Cicero

PATRON

The parish name commemorates an image of the Blessed Virgin Mary at the shrine of Jasna Gora, near Czestochowa, Poland. The icon is often referred to as the Black Madonna, for the dark color of the wood on which it was painted. Our Lady of Czestochowa is revered as the patroness of Poland, and her image was credited with helping the Poles defeat an invading Swedish army in 1655.

HISTORY

Founded in 1895 as a Polish parish. It remained primarily Polish but in recent years the parish has also embraced many Latino families. Mass is celebrated in English, Polish, and Spanish.

ARCHITECTURE

The church, one of the few Polish churches designed in a Gothic style, was completed in 1918. A mosaic of Our Lady of Czestochowa is framed in the high altar, and the parish patroness is honored every year in late August with special Masses, an outdoor procession, a special religious service, and a social gathering.

TREASURE

A side chapel holds a painting of Our Lady of Czestochowa done in Poland and given by the former Primate of Poland, Cardinal Wyszynski, to an alumnus of the parish school, Bishop Aloysius Wycislo of Green Bay WI.

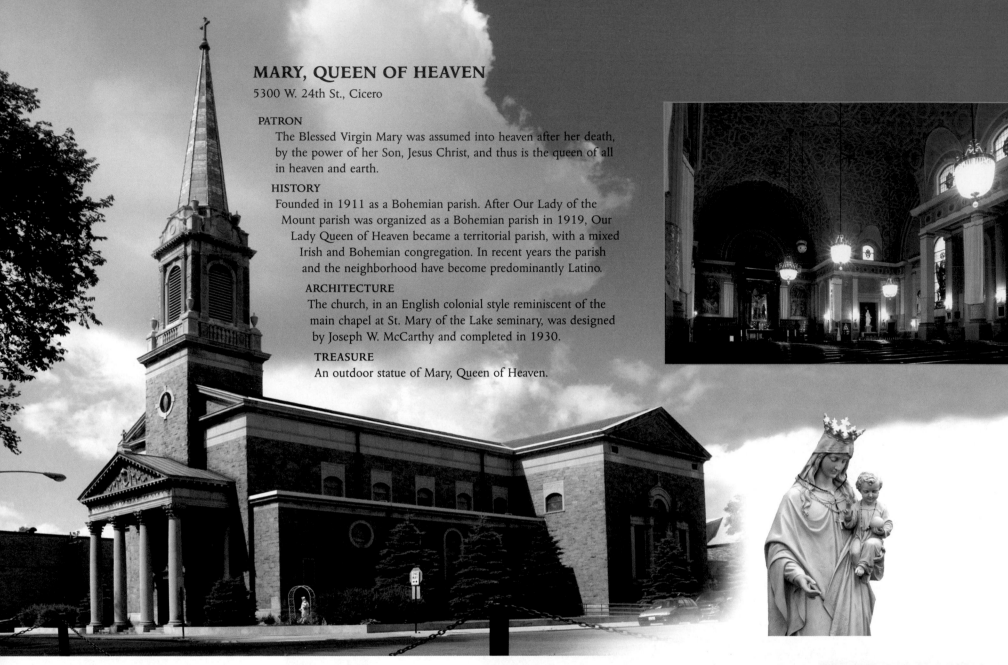

MARY, QUEEN OF HEAVEN

5300 W. 24th St., Cicero

PATRON

The Blessed Virgin Mary was assumed into heaven after her death, by the power of her Son, Jesus Christ, and thus is the queen of all in heaven and earth.

HISTORY

Founded in 1911 as a Bohemian parish. After Our Lady of the Mount parish was organized as a Bohemian parish in 1919, Our Lady Queen of Heaven became a territorial parish, with a mixed Irish and Bohemian congregation. In recent years the parish and the neighborhood have become predominantly Latino.

ARCHITECTURE

The church, in an English colonial style reminiscent of the main chapel at St. Mary of the Lake seminary, was designed by Joseph W. McCarthy and completed in 1930.

TREASURE

An outdoor statue of Mary, Queen of Heaven.

OUR LADY OF CHARITY

3600 S. 57th Ct., Cicero

PATRON

The parish name refers to a miraculous statue of the Blessed Virgin Mary, discovered in Cuba around 1608. Our Lady of Charity is the patroness of Cuba.

HISTORY

Founded as a mission of St. Dionysius, Cicero, in 1943, it became a parish in 1954. The parish has always been ethnically diverse, and it remains so today with the older parishioners of eastern European origin and the newcomers mostly Latino.

ARCHITECTURE

The original combination church/school structure was renovated and enlarged, according to plans by Naess & Murphy, in 1954.

TREASURE

An ornate antique chalice bequeathed to the parish by a former pastor, Fr. Maurice B. Kennedy.

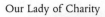

OUR LADY OF THE MOUNT

2414 S. 64th Ave., Cicero

PATRON

The parish name refers to the "Holy Mount" near the village of Pribam, south of Prague, in the Czech Republic.

HISTORY

Our Lady Queen of Heaven parish had been founded for the Bohemians of Cicero in 1911, but after World War I many of the Bohemians had already moved farther west so a new parish was organized for them in 1919 and the former church became a territorial parish. The parish remained primarily Bohemian, but some Italian, Polish, and Latino parishioners also joined them. Mass is celeberated in English, Czech, and Spanish.

ARCHITECTURE

The church, designed by Rezny & Krippner in a Romanesque style, was completed in 1926.

TREASURE

A stained glass window of Our Lady of the Mount.

Country Club Hills

ST. EMERIC

4330 W. 180th St., Country Club Hills

PATRON

Emeric (1007-1031) was a prince of Hungary, the son of St. Stephen, Hungary's first Christian king. He did not live to inherit St. Stephen's throne, as he died in a hunting accident. The first pastor, Fr. Stephen Ryan, chose this youthful patron saint since Country Club Hills was a youthful community.

HISTORY

Founded as a mission of St. Joseph's, Homewood, in 1959 it became a parish in 1960. This suburban parish has served a wide variety of ethnic groups over the years and is now part of a racially integrated community. An annual Mass on the Grass is celebrated, highlighting both the multicultural richness of the community and the pleasantly landscaped grounds.

ARCHITECTURE

The modern church, designed by Fox & Fox, was completed in 1963. The stained glass windows were designed by David Wiskirchen.

TREASURE

A statue of St. Emeric.

Deerfield

HOLY CROSS

724 Elder Lane, Deerfield

PATRON

The Cross on which Jesus Christ died has always been an object of devotion for Christians, especially since relics of the True Cross were discovered by St. Helena in the early fourth century.

HISTORY

Organized in 1909 as a mission church, when Mass was first celebrated in a private home and then in a simple frame church, it became a parish in 1929. This suburban area expanded rapidly after World War II.

ARCHITECTURE

The modern church, designed by Barry & Kay was completed in 1957, and was originally intended as a temporary church. A gymnasium and community center were added in 1986 when it had become obvious that the church was to be permanent. The church was renovated and expanded in 2005.

TREASURE

The Holy Cross is, appropriately, the main focus of attention in the church, with the crucifix from the old church hanging over the altar.

Holy Cross

Des Plaines

ST. MARY

794 Pearson St., Des Plaines

PATRON

The Blessed Virgin Mary, wife of St. Joseph, Mother of Jesus.

HISTORY

Founded as a mission in Arlington Heights. The first church building was relocated to Des Plaines in 1883, and the community became a parish in 1906. The parish and neighborhood remained small until the suburban housing boom after World War II. Though it has been divided several times to form new parishes, St. Mary remains a large and diverse community. Mass is celebrated in English and Spanish.

ARCHITECTURE

After several small, country church buildings became inadequate, the parish worshiped in a converted bowling alley from 1936 to 1970. The modern church was completed in time for Christmas Mass in 1970.

TREASURE

Various stained glass windows that date back to 1906.

ST. JOAN OF ARC

9248 N. Lawndale Ave., Evanston (Skokie)

PATRON

Joan of Arc (1412-1431) was a shepherd girl of France. During the Hundred Years War against the English, she received visions from saints urging her to find and support the true king of France. She led troops in battle and secured the throne for Charles VII. She was then captured and executed by the English. She has been one of the most popular saints of the last few centuries, and not just in France.

HISTORY

Founded in 1951 in a rapidly growing section between Skokie and Evanston. The surrounding area is one of the most ethnically diverse communities in Chicagoland.

ARCHITECTURE

The combination church/school, designed by Meyer and Cook, was completed in 1954 and renovated in 2001.

TREASURE

The statue of Joan of Arc.

ST. MARY

1012 Lake St., Evanston

PATRON

The Blessed Virgin Mary, wife of St. Joseph, Mother of Jesus.

HISTORY

Founded in 1866 as a mission church attended from St. Henry, Chicago or St. Joseph, Grosse Pointe, it became a parish in 1872. It has been an anchor in "downtown" Evanston ever since, with a diverse congregation.

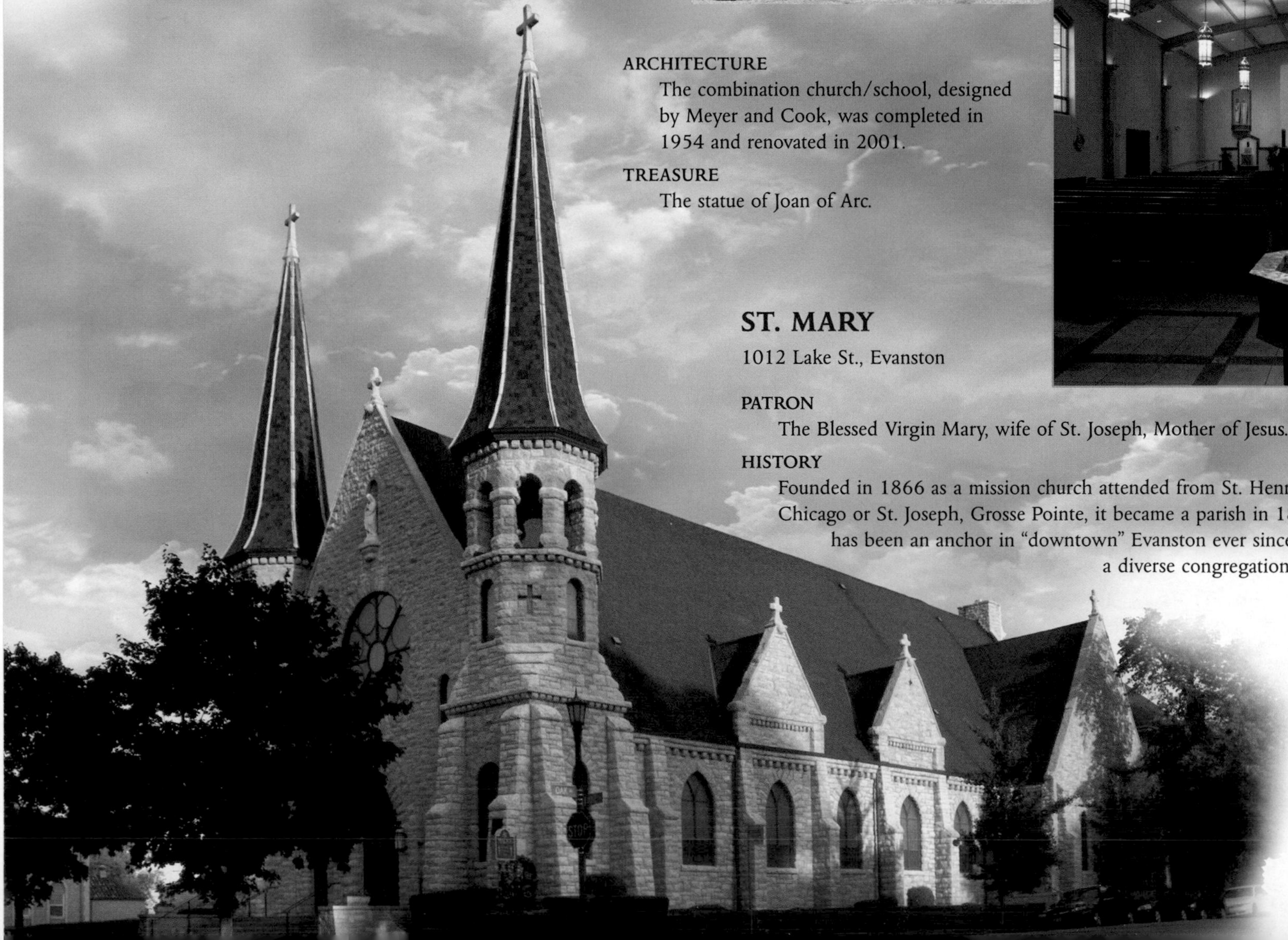

ARCHITECTURE

The church, designed by a parishioner, Steven Jennings, was completed in 1892. The Gothic church is constructed of Lemont limestone, the same building material used on the exterior of Holy Name Cathedral.

TREASURE

The rose window over the choir loft depicts the Eight Beatitudes.

St. Mary

ST. NICHOLAS

806 Ridge Ave., Evanston

PATRON

Nicholas was a fourth century bishop of Myra, in Asia Minor. Though little is known for certain about his life, many popular legends have grown up about him. Supposedly his provision of a dowry for poor girls led to the Santa Claus tradition of gift-giving.

HISTORY

Founded in 1887, one of a string of country churches for German-speaking Luxembourgers. It remained a German-speaking parish until 1927 and became quite diverse after World War II. Its congregation now includes Latino, African-American, Haitian, and Asian parishioners.

ARCHITECTURE

The church, designed in Gothic style by Hermann J. Gaul, was completed in 1906. Nearly a century later, John Voosen, Gaul's great nephew and the inheritor of his architectural practice, designed the interior renovation.

TREASURE

A painting of Our Lady of Guadalupe by Octavio Ocampo.

Flossmoor

INFANT JESUS OF PRAGUE

1131 Douglas Ave., Flossmoor

PATRON

Devotion to the Child Jesus has been popular in the Catholic Church at least since the Middle Ages, but it was especially intense in Spain. The exact origin of the famous Infant Jesus statue is not known, but it was probably hand carved in Spain about 1340. A Spanish noblewoman presented it to the Carmelite church in Prague in 1628, and it has thus been revered as the Infant Jesus of Prague

HISTORY

First organized in 1952, it became a full-fledged parish in 1957 with the appointment of Fr. Richard Hills as the first resident pastor. The parish has grown to over 2000 families that reside in Floosmoor, Olympia Fields, and the surrounding suburbs. The parish's diverse population is very proud of its school and its service to the community

ARCHITECTURE

The church, designed in a Romanesque style, was completed in 1956. The rose window over the front entrance has the Infant Jesus at its center. In 2004, a major renovation was completed, continuing the style but bringing the choir near the altar and remodeling the sanctuary to include a beautiful corpus of Jesus and an adoration area.

TREASURE

A statue of the Infant Jesus of Prague.

Forest Park

ST. BERNARDINE

7246 W. Harrison St., Forest Park

PATRON

Bernardine of Siena (1388-1444) was a Franciscan monk. He traveled throughout Italy as a preacher and he promoted devotion to the Holy Name of Jesus.

HISTORY

Founded in 1911. Though the parish had territorial boundaries, it was predominantly German until World War I. The parish and suburb grew rapidly after World War II, and the Congress (Eisenhower) Expressway cut right in front of the church.

ARCHITECTURE

The original church building was a portable wooden structure, nicknamed The Ark, which had previously served in several West Side parishes. A combination church-school building was erected in 1915. The present church, designed by McCarthy, Smith, and Eppig in a Spanish Mission style, was completed in 1939.

St. Bernardine

TREASURE
 Twelve painted shields representing the Twelve Apostles.

Franklin Park

ST. GERTRUDE

9613 Schiller Blvd., Franklin Park

PATRON
 Gertrude (1256-1302) was a Benedictine nun in Germany. She experienced numerous mystical visions and helped spread devotion to the Sacred Heart of Jesus.

HISTORY
 Founded in 1901, on land donated by the community's founder, Lesser Franklin. It was originally a farm and railroad community, and the parish had a German predominance. The area filled up with suburban residences after World War II.

ARCHITECTURE
 The modern church, designed by Belli and Belli, was completed in 1954.

TREASURE
 A massive stained glass window tells the awesome story of the Apocalypse with Christ as Judge, the Four Evangelists, and the awe-inspiring Four Horsemen.

ST. GILBERT

301 E. Belvidere Rd., Grayslake

PATRON

Gilbert of Sempringham (c.1083-1189) was the son of a Norman father and an Anglo-Saxon mother, born shortly after the Norman Invasion of England. He studied in France and became a priest, managing churches on his father's estates and organizing the care of the poor and sick. He founded an order of nuns. He lived to be over 100 years old.

HISTORY

Founded in 1930 in a farming and summer-cottage area. The community became largely suburban after World War II.

ARCHITECTURE

The original, colonial-style church, built in 1930, has been refurbished and is used for baptisms, weddings, and as a day chapel. The modern church was completed in 1965 and renovated in 2004.

TREASURE

The gorgeous stained glass panorama behind the altar.

Grayslake

Gurnee

ST. PAUL THE APOSTLE

6401 Gages Lake Rd., Gurnee

PATRON

Paul the Apostle (died c. 65) was originally named Saul. He was a Jew of Tarsus, a tentmaker by trade, who persecuted the early Christians. On his way to Damascus to arrest another group of them, he was knocked to the ground and struck blind by a heavenly light. He converted to Christianity and became such an effective preacher throughout the Roman world that he is known as the Apostle of the Gentiles. He was martyred in Rome.

St. Paul the Apostle

HISTORY

Founded in 1991 in a rapidly growing suburban area near Six Flags Great America amusement park and many corporate headquarters.

ARCHITECTURE

Mass was celebrated in the gym of a local public school until the modern church, designed by Hammel, Green and Abrahamson, was completed in 1997.

TREASURE

The night light in St. Paul's cupola can be seen for miles.

Hanover Park

ST. ANSGAR

2040 Laurel Ave., Hanover Park

PATRON

Ansgar (801-865) was a French nobleman and a Benedictine monk. King Harold of Denmark, a convert to Christianity, invited Ansgar to evangelize his kingdom. He also founded the first Christian church in Sweden. He later served as archbishop of Hamburg, Germany (which included the city of Hanover, after which Hanover Park was named). He is revered as the patron saint of Denmark.

HISTORY

Founded in 1968 in the far western section of the county and archdiocese. Parishioners submitted three names for the new parish, and Cardinal Cody chose Ansgar — "he will be a suitable patron." The parish serves a very diverse congregation and celebrates Mass in English, Spanish, and Filipino.

ARCHITECTURE

The multi-purpose church building, designed without fixed seating, was completed in 1978. An addition, connected to the main church by a glass atrium, was constructed in 1997. Several artifacts were salvaged from schools and churches that had closed, e.g., the presider's chair and holy water receptacle from All Saints in Chicago; the vestment case and marble altar from the Augustinian Seminary; and the tabernacle from the chapel at Aquinas High School.

TREASURE

A baptistery was salvaged from Holy Name Cathedral after its renovation.

Harvey

ASCENSION—ST. SUSANNA

15234 Myrtle Ave., Harvey

PATRON

Christ ascended into heaven forty days after his Resurrection, a pledge and a promise of the bodily resurrection and ascension of all faithful Christians.

Susanna was a Roman martyr of the 3rd century. Nothing certain is known of her life and death, but a Roman church has borne her name since the 5th century.

HISTORY

The parish was formed from a merger in 1985 between Ascension (founded 1894) and St. Susanna, the Polish parish of Harvey (founded 1927). The parish worships at the church building that formerly served Ascension. The congregation consists of Polish, Irish, African-American, and Latino families.

ARCHITECTURE

The former Ascension church, designed in a Gothic style, was completed in 1911.

TREASURE

A stained glass window depicting Jesus's Acension into Heaven.

ST. JOHN THE BAPTIST

15746 Union Ave., Harvey

PATRON

John the Baptist was a cousin of Jesus Christ, the son of Zachary and Elizabeth. He preached a message of repentance, baptizing his followers in the Jordan River, and announcing the imminent coming of the Messiah. He was martyred by King Herod circa 30 AD.

HISTORY

Founded in 1914 as a Polish parish. Poles remain a significant portion of the parishioners, but the parish also serves many Mexican immigrants and African Americans.

ARCHITECTURE

The church, designed in a modernized Romanesque style, was completed in 1958.

TREASURE

The shrine to Our Lady of Guadalupe.

267

Harwood Heights

ST. ROSALIE

4401 N. Oak Park Ave., Harwood Heights

PATRON

Rosalie was a Sicilian noblewoman of the 2nd or 3rd century who lived most of her life as a hermit. Her relics were credited with saving the city of Palermo from the plague and she is revered now as the patron saint of the city.

HISTORY

Founded in 1960 on land purchased from the Ridgemoor Country Club. The parish, in a suburb surrounded by the city of Chicago and the suburb of Norridge, serves a congregation of diverse European origins, especially Italians and Poles. Mass is celebrated in English and Polish.

ARCHITECTURE

The modern church, designed by A. J. Del Bianco and Robert Schwartz, was completed in 1961. A magnificent cross, designed by one of the parishioners, marks the center of the church.

TREASURE

A statue of the patron saint in the sanctuary.

Hazel Crest

ST. ANNE

16802 S. Lincoln St., Hazel Crest

PATRON

Anne (or Ann) is traditionally revered as the mother of the Blessed Virgin Mary. Nothing certain is known of her life, though apocryphal sources give her name and that of her husband St. Joachim. Devotion to Anne increased during the Middle Ages along with devotion to Mary.

HISTORY

Founded in 1911 as a mission of St. Joseph's, Homewood. It became a parish in 1949 when the area began to fill up with suburban residences. The parish and community are now racially diverse.

ARCHITECTURE

The combination church/school building was completed in 1957.

TREASURE

The outdoor stations of the cross, called the Prayer Walk, built by the men of the parish in 1958.

Hickory Hills

ST. PATRICIA

9050 S. 86th Ave., Hickory Hills

PATRON

Patricia (died c.371) was a niece of the Roman emperor Constantine. To maintain her vow of virginity, she fled Constantinople and died at Naples where she is the patron saint.

HISTORY

Founded in 1959 in a rapidly expanding area on the southwest side. Father Thomas V. Brody was the founding pastor. The Sisters of the Holy Family of Nazareth have taught in the parish school since 1960.

ARCHITECTURE

The modern church, designed by Emil Mastandrea, was completed in 1961. Originally intended as a temporary church that could be converted to classrooms, it was built in the exact same style as the school. The parishioners consider the school, which has been handing on the Faith for forty-five years to thousands of children, the greatest treasure of the parish.

TREASURE

An outdoor statue of the parish patron.

St. Patricia

Highland Park

IMMACULATE CONCEPTION

770 Deerfield Rd., Highland Park

PATRON

The Immaculate Conception is the dogma of faith stating that the Blessed Virgin was from the first instant of her conception, by a singular privilege and grace of God, preserved from all stain of original sin. Shortly after this dogma was defined by Pope Pius IX in 1854, Our Lady appeared to Bernadette Soubirous at Lourdes in 1858, describing herself as the Immaculate Conception. Devotion to Mary under this title became widespread thereafter.

HISTORY

Originally a country church named St. Mary of the Woods, it was a mission of St. Joseph's Wilmette from its founding in 1846 until it received its first resident pastor in 1893. The name was changed to Immaculate Conception in 1916. The original parishioners were Irish but many Italians also settled in this area. In recent years, Mass has been celebrated in English, Spanish, and Korean.

ARCHITECTURE

The first church was a log cabin. This was followed by a frame church, then a brick church. The modern church, designed by Barry and Kay, was completed in 1967 and remodeled in 1997. An Italian-style piazza was also added in the 1997 renovation with a life-sized statue of the Immaculate Conception (modeled after one in Rome).

TREASURE

Tiffany crystal chandeliers and stained glass windows.

Hometown

OUR LADY OF LORETTO

8925 S. Kostner Ave., Hometown

PATRON

The parish name recalls the legendary "holy house" of Mary, which was allegedly transported miraculously from Nazareth to the field of Loretto in Italy. The founding pastor of this parish, Patrick J. Ronayne, chose this name since Our Lady of Loretto is patroness of aviators and homes, and this area of small homes was near Midway Airport.

HISTORY

Founded in 1951 in a new subdivision just west of Evergreen Park. A tornado ripped through town in 1967, destroying many homes and the parish rectory. The parish serves a congregation of diverse European ethnic origins.

ARCHITECTURE

The modern church, designed by Vitzthum & Kill, was completed in 1969.

TREASURE

A simple, elegant adoration chapel.

Homewood

ST. JOSEPH

17951 Dixie Hwy., Homewood

PATRON

Husband of the Blessed Virgin Mary and foster-father of Jesus. Descended from the house of David, he was a carpenter of Nazareth. He is revered as the patron saint of workers.

St. Joseph

HISTORY

Founded in 1914 in a still rural area in south Cook County. The parish and community filled up with suburban residences after World War II. The parish serves a diverse congregation of commuters to Chicago as well as workers in nearby industries.

ARCHITECTURE

The modern church, designed by Fox and Fox, was completed in 1955.

TREASURE

A golden monstrance with an image of St. Joseph in the base.

ST. MARY OF VERNON

236 U.S. Highway 45, Indian Creek

Indian Creek

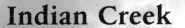

PATRON

The parish is dedicated to the Blessed Virgin Mary. The name "Vernon" was added to distinguish it from the surrounding St. Mary parishes and to express the location in the newly developing area of Vernon Township.

HISTORY

Founded in 1978 by Fr. John P. Finnegan, the parish has grown from a few hundred very young families to over two thousand households of diverse ages, ethnic and cultural backgrounds. Emphasizing the themes of the Second Vatican Council, St. Mary of Vernon strives to be welcoming and inclusive, with particular dedication to outreach and service ministries.

ARCHITECTURE

The original worship center, designed by Carl Hundrieser and completed in 1981, now provides the entranceway and narthex for the church. Designed by Bob Nickola of Jaeger, Nickola Architects, the new church was completed in December 2005 and dedicated in February 2006.

TREASURE

The statue of Mary as a simple young woman was designed locally by Deacon Ellsworth Cordesman of Highland Park and was carved in Italy out of linden wood.

ST. FRANCIS XAVIER

124 N. Spring Ave., La Grange

PATRON

Francis Xavier (1506-1551) was a nobleman from the Basque reqion of Spain. He studied at the University of Paris where he met St. Ignatius of Loyola and joined his Society of Jesus (Jesuits). He sailed to Goa, India as a missionary in 1541 and evangelized throughout India, the East Indies, and Japan, until his death ten years later.

HISTORY

Founded in 1890 in the railroad suburb of LaGrange. The parish and community grew explosively after both World Wars, and the parish has been divided several times. The area is heavily Catholic. In recent years three separate Masses have been necessary to accommodate First Communions, and these First Communion classes include as many students from the public school across the street as from the parish school.

ARCHITECTURE

The church, designed by Joseph W. McCarthy in a Renaissance style, was completed in 1931. Its huge dome over the crossing of the nave lends a Byzantine touch to the design.

TREASURE

A relic of St. Francis Xavier.

La Grange Park

ST. LOUISE DE MARILLAC

1144 Harrison Ave., La Grange Park

PATRON

Louise de Marillac (1591-1660) was from an aristocratic French family. After the early death of her husband in 1625, she devoted her life to service of the poor, under the influence of St. Vincent de Paul. She founded the Daughters of Charity, who tend the poor and the sick in hospitals and orphanages.

St. Louise de Marillac

HISTORY

Founded in 1955. Though the archdiocese had purchased property in the area in the 1920s, the community did not grow until after World War II. The parish serves a diverse congregation of European ethnic origins in LaGrange Park and Brookfield.

ARCHITECTURE

The modern church, designed by Barry & Kay, was completed in 1957. The architecture is marked by long, graceful lines, a majestic cross-topped cupola, and a beckoning cross above the main entrance.

TREASURE

A statue of Louise de Marillac giving the Book of the Gospels to one of her Daughters of Charity, is located in the lobby of the new parish center.

Lake Forest

ST. MARY

175 E. Illinois Rd., Lake Forest

PATRON

The Blessed Virgin Mary, wife of St. Joseph, Mother of Jesus.

HISTORY

Founded in 1875. Fr. James McGovern, the first Chicago-born priest in the diocese, was the founding pastor. The congregation was predominantly Irish during the early years of the parish, but has become much more diverse over the years.

ARCHITECTURE

The original frame church, built in 1875, was torn down in 1909 since it was in danger of collapsing. The current church, designed in a Romanesque style by Henry Lord Gay, was completed in 1910.

TREASURE

The church has many hand-forged, silver sacred objects, some dating back 80 to 90 years.

Lansing

ST. ANN

3010 Ridge Rd., Lansing

PATRON

Ann (or Anne) is traditionally revered as the mother of the Blessed Virgin Mary. Nothing certain is known of her life, though apocryphal sources give her name and that of her husband, St. Joachim. Devotion to Ann increased during the Middle Ages along with devotion to Mary.

HISTORY

Founded in 1913 as a mission of St. John's, Glenwood. It became a parish in 1941. The area filled up with residences after World War II, and the parish now serves a diverse congregation.

ARCHITECTURE

One of the newest churches in the archdiocese, the modern mission-style structure was designed by Prisco, Cerina and Sturm of Northbrook in the late 1990s.

TREASURE

A large stained glass window of St. Ann and her child Mary was salvaged from the Niles Seminary chapel.

Lemont

ST. ALPHONSUS

210 E. Logan, Lemont

PATRON

Alphonsus Liguori (1696–1787) was a nobleman of Naples who first studied law, but then became a priest and preacher. He founded the Redemptorist religious order in 1732 and published numerous theological and devotional works.

HISTORY

Founded as a mission of St. Michael's, the German Redemptorist church in Chicago, in 1867. It became a German parish in 1874, with the majority of its parishioners from Luxembourg or Alsace. Polish and Bohemian families also attended until they formed parishes of their own. It remained a German country parish until recent years.

St. Alphonsus

ARCHITECTURE

The church, designed in a Gothic style by Charles L. Wallace of Joliet, was completed in 1921. Standing on a bluff overlooking the DesPlaines River, it can be seen for miles around. The original bells have been tolling the Angelus for 75 years.

TREASURE

The glorious stained glass windows.

SS. CYRIL AND METHODIUS

608 Sobieski St., Lemont

PATRON

Cyril (826–869) and Methodius (c815–885) were brothers, born of Greek nobility, who became priests in Constantinople. They evangelized the Slavic nations, translated the liturgy into Old Slavonic, and made numerous converts. They are jointly revered as the Apostles of the Slavs.

HISTORY

Founded in 1884 as a Polish parish. The surrounding area was called Jasna Gora, in memory of the immigrants' roots in Poland. The parish continues to offer Mass in both English and Polish.

ARCHITECTURE

The church, designed in a Romanesque style by E. Bielmaier and Sons of Milwaukee, was completed in 1929, replacing a former church that burned down in 1928. Some of the highlights are the beautiful original rose window, the new entryway, and the church's steeple, which is the highest elevation in Cook County.

TREASURE

An icon of Our Lady of Czestochowa was enshrined in 1999.

OUR LADY OF MOUNT CARMEL

1101 N. 23rd Ave., Melrose Park

PATRON

The parish name commemorates the apparition of Our Lady to the founder of the Carmelite Order, St. Simon Stock, in 1251. During this apparition, Our Lady gave St. Simon the scapular, two pieces of cloth to be worn under ordinary clothing in devotion to Mary. The wife of an Italian farmer in the area that became Melrose Park brought a statue of Our Lady of Mt. Carmel from Naples in 1894 and that statue is still in the parish today.

HISTORY

Founded in 1903 as an Italian parish. It has been administered by the Scalabrini Fathers from 1905 until the present. The congregation remains primarily Italian but is also more diverse. Masses are celebrated in English, Italian, and Spanish.

ARCHITECTURE

The modern church, with its "tent style" peaked roof, was built by Belli and Belli Architects and completed in 1968.

TREASURE

The Our Lady of Mount Carmel statue, with a crown of gold and precious stones, around which the parish was built.

SACRED HEART

819 N. 16th Ave., Melrose Park

PATRON

St. Margaret Mary Alacoque (1647–1690), a French nun of Paray-le-Monial, France, was primarily responsible for spreading devotion to the Sacred Heart of Jesus. Since the 17th century, this has been one of the most popular of all Catholic devotions, common to many different ethnic groups.

HISTORY

Founded in 1893 as a German parish. It has always served a number of different ethnic groups, such as Italians, Poles, and Slovenians, as well. The parish grew rapidly in the suburban expansion after World War II.

ARCHITECTURE

The modern church, designed by Pirola & Erbach, was completed in 1955.

TREASURE

A marble statue of the Risen Christ, with his Sacred Heart exposed, stands high above the rear of the sanctuary.

Midlothian

ST. CHRISTOPHER

14641 S. Keeler Ave., Midlothian

PATRON

Christopher was a 3rd century martyr. Nothing is known for certain about his life or death. The legend that he carried the Christ Child across a raging river, earning him the name "Christ-bearer", or Christopher, has made him the patron of travelers.

HISTORY

Founded in 1922 in a still rural area of south Cook County. The area filled up with suburban residences after World War II. The parish was administered by Franciscan priests until 1972. Though many of the original parishioners were Polish, the parish and community have always been ethnically diverse. The annual parish fiesta and carnival has been bringing together people of many different backgrounds for over 50 years.

ARCHITECTURE

The original frame church was burned to the ground by the Midlothian Fire Department in 1961 in preparation for a new church building. The modern church, designed by Fox and Fox, was completed in 1962. The church has a distinctive octagonal bell tower.

TREASURE

A stained glass window of Christ's Agony in the Garden, from the original church.

Morton Grove

ST. MARTHA

8523 Georgiana Ave.,
Morton Grove

PATRON

Martha was a member of a family in Bethany that Jesus was especially fond of. She was the sister of Lazarus, whom Jesus raised from the dead, and of Mary. According to the Gospels, Martha was the busy, pragmatic, efficient sister in the family whereas Mary was the quiet, contemplative one.

HISTORY

Founded as a mission church for a Luxembourger farm community in 1919, it became a parish in 1922. The area filled up with suburban residences after World War II. Parishioners say it still retains some of the feel of a country parish, "like a a little church in Wisconsin."

ARCHITECTURE

The English Gothic church, designed by Arthur Foster, was completed in 1923.

TREASURE

A painting of St. Martha.

ST. CECILIA

700 S. Meier Rd., Mount Prospect

PATRON

Cecilia was a Roman martyr of the 3rd century. Legend portrays her as a young noblewoman. She has been revered as the patron of sacred music since the 16th century because it is said that on her wedding day she "sang in her heart a hymn of love for Jesus."

Mount Prospect

HISTORY

Founded in 1967 in a fast-growing section of Mount Prospect. The parish has grown to 1500 registered families of diverse ethnic backgrounds. It also serves as the site for the Mt. Prospect Area Hispanic Ministry. The parish has many active ministries, and numerous annual events, such as Lenten Soup Suppers, a rummage sale, parish picnic, and Paczki/Mardi Gras/Tamale party.

ARCHITECTURE

The modern church, shaped like a sea shell, was completed in 1970. A gathering space, wake room, and portico were added in 1997.

TREASURE

A relic of St. Cecilia enclosed in an antique reliquary.

ST. EMILY

1400 E. Central Rd., Suite 101, Mount Prospect

PATRON

Emily de Rodat (1787–1852) was born in the south of France. She taught in the local school and became aware of the obstacles to education facing poor children. With several other teachers, she founded the Congregation of the Holy Family, dedicated to educating the poor.

HISTORY

Founded in 1960 in an unincorporated area later annexed to Mount Prospect. The parish has grown very large as the area has filled up with residences.

ARCHITECTURE

The modern, circular church was completed in 1971.

TREASURE

An awe-inspiring crucifix suspended over the altar.

ST. RAYMOND DE PENAFORT

301 S I-Oka Ave., Mount Prospect

PATRON

Raymond de Penafort (c. 1180–1275) was a member of the nobility of Aragon and Catalonia, educated at Barcelona and Bologna. He joined the Dominican order in 1222 becoming Master General in 1238. He was noted for his writings in theology and canon law. The founding pastor of this parish, Fr. Thomas O'Brien, chose the name in honor of his mentor, Fr. (late Auxiliary Bishop) Raymond Hillinger.

HISTORY

Founded in 1949 in a rapidly growing suburban area. The parish serves a diverse congregation, including many descendants of Poles and Italians who moved from the northwest side of Chicago.

ARCHITECTURE

The modern church, designed by Pirola and Erbach, was completed in 1962. Theodore Erbach, one of the architectural partners, was a parishioner.

TREASURE

A dozen stained-glass windows, designed and executed by Robert Harmon in 1988, tell the Jesus story from Incarnation to Last Judgment in abstract sweeps of color.

ST. THOMAS BECKET

1321 N. Burning Bush Lane, Mount Prospect

PATRON

Thomas Becket (1118–1170), also known as Thomas of Canterbury, was an English lawyer. Named Chancellor of England by King Henry II, he eventually opposed the king's interference in ecclesiastical matters. Knights of the king murdered him at the cathedral of Canterbury.

St. Thomas Becket

HISTORY

Founded in 1968 in an unincorporated but rapidly growing section of Mount Prospect. Today, the parish serves a diverse congregation, including many Polish families who moved from the northwest side of Chicago and others newly emigrated from Poland.

ARCHITECTURE

In the early years, the people gathered and worshiped in the gymnasium of Maryville Academy, and then in the school across the street (Indian Grove Elementary). A modern multi-purpose building, designed by James R. Cronin and Associates and completed in 1980, now serves as church and religious education center.

TREASURE

A hand-woven tapestry of the patron saint, made by an order of Benedictine nuns in England, was donated to the parish. There are only two of these tapestries in existence.

Mundelein

SANTA MARIA DEL POPOLO

116 N. Lake St., Mundelein

PATRON

The parish name refers to a 15th century image of Mary in Carrara, Italy, which was credited with saving the town on a number of occasions. The parish was named for Santa Maria del Popolo (St. Mary of the People) because it was the titular church in Rome for George Cardinal Mundelein, for whom this town was named.

HISTORY

Founded in 1935 in a small suburban town near St. Mary of the Lake Seminary, which Cardinal Mundelein had founded in the 1920s. The Cardinal took a personal interest in the parish, contributing to the fund for building a church and suggesting the colonial American style that was adopted. The parish and town filled up with suburban residences after World War II. Mass is celebrated in English and Spanish.

ARCHITECTURE

A modernized colonial-style church, designed by McCarthy, Smith & Eppig, was completed in 1935. The current red brick church/school building was designed by Hal Chambers in 1964.

TREASURE

An oil painting of St. Mary of the People, donated by Cardinal Mundelein, is in the parish chapel.

OUR LADY OF RANSOM

8624 W. Normal Ave., Niles

PATRON

The parish name commemorates an appearance of Our Lady in 13th century Spain, in which Mary carried two bags of coins to ransom Christians imprisoned by the Moors. This apparition is also referred to as Our Lady of Mercy.

HISTORY

Founded in 1960 in a fast growing section of Niles, Our Lady of Ransom parish has continued to grow and reflects a diversity of cultures, ethnicities in its ministries and membership.

ARCHITECTURE

In 1962 a combination school/church building with lower parish hall and convent was designed and constructed. The church initially was designated to become a gymnasium in the event that a new church could be built on the parish grounds. In 2006 a church renovation/construction project was completed establishing a permanent church in place of the original one. This building was designed by Serena, Sturm Architects and built by Frederick Quinn Construction. Cardinal Francis George dedicated this new church on the Feast of Pentecost, June 3, 2006. While somewhat contemporary in structural design, the elements in this church reflect a much more traditional environment for our place of worship.

TREASURE

The new altar which has become the focal point of our renovated church is truly the treasure of this sacred space. It originally was the altar which adorned the church of St. Angela on the west side of Chicago. In receiving this gift from the archdiocese, the relics from our temporary altar as well as those from St. Angela's altar were placed underneath the new mensa of our altar, reflecting the history of St. Angela's parishioners and those of Our Lady of Ransom Parish.

Norridge

DIVINE SAVIOR

7740 W. Montrose Ave., Norridge

PATRON

The parish name recalls that Jesus Christ, who died on the cross, is the Savior of the world.

HISTORY

Founded as a mission of St. Francis Borgia in 1950, it became a parish in 1955. Norridge was a rapidly growing suburb completely surrounded by the city of Chicago. The two major Catholic ethnic groups from Chicago's northwest side, Poles and Italians, form the majority of the parishioners.

Divine Saviour

ARCHITECTURE

The combination church/school building, designed by Gaul and Voosen, was completed in 1957.

TREASURE

The chancel mosaic was executed in Venetian glass by Dominican artist Father Angelico Rinaldo Zarlenga and installed in 1977.

North Chicago

QUEEN OF PEACE

910 14th St., North Chicago

PATRON

Our Lady has been venerated as a peacemaker, or Queen of Peace, since the Middle Ages. During World War I, Pope Benedict XV added the title Queen of Peace to the litany of the Blessed Virgin. The title was chosen for this parish because the Gulf War was raging in the Middle East when this parish was founded.

HISTORY

Founded in 1991 in a merger of Holy Family (founded in 1901) and Holy Rosary (a Polish parish founded in 1904), both in North Chicago, and Mother of God (a Croatian and Slovenian parish founded in 1903) in Waukegan. The parish worships in the former Holy Rosary church. The congregation is Anglo, Latino, and African-American.

ARCHITECTURE

The former Holy Rosary church building, in the Romanesque style, was built in 1925. The interior of the church was renovated and restored to its original design in 1992.

TREASURE

A stained glass window in the Founders' Chapel to the east of the sanctuary incorporates symbols from the three parishes that merged to form Queen of Peace.

North Riverside

MATER CHRISTI

2431 S. 10th Ave., North Riverside

PATRON

Mater Christi means Mother of Christ in Latin. The parish is named for the Blessed Virgin Mary.

HISTORY

Established as a mission church of St. Mary in Riverside, it became a parish in 1953. The area soon filled up with suburban residences, and the parish serves a diverse congregation, including many Bohemians who moved from the West Side of Chicago. Characterized by a family spirit, this small community has taken to heart St. Paul's words: "Let us not grow weary of doing good."

ARCHITECTURE

The modernized colonial church, designed by Belli and Belli, was built on the top of a small hill in 1953.

TREASURE

The outdoor shrine of the Mother of Mothers was dedicated in 1956, and continues to inspire through the unique relationship of Christ's Mother to all mothers.

Northbrook

ST. NORBERT

1809 Walters Ave., Northbrook

PATRON

Norbert (c1080–1134) was a German noble who lived a worldly life, but was converted and became a priest. He founded the Premonstratensian order of Augustinian canons and was named archbishop of Magdeburg. He was influential in reforming the lives of the clergy.

St. Norbert

HISTORY
The parish was founded as the Mission of the Holy Ghost in 1899, an adjunct of the Society of the Divine Word's monastery and seminary at Techny. In 1914 a combination church/school building was erected on the seminary grounds at Techny and the parish was named St. Norbert. After the Second World War, as the surrounding area filled in with suburban residences, the Divine Word Fathers moved the parish to its present location in Northbrook, and in 1953 they relinquished administration of the parish to diocesan priests. Originally a German parish, St. Norbert's now serves a suburban congregation of over 2000 families.

ARCHITECTURE
The modern church, designed by Holmes and Fox of Des Plaines, was completed in 1965.

TREASURE
The statue of the Sacred Heart.

OUR LADY OF THE BROOK
3700 Dundee Rd., Northbrook

PATRON
The parish name honors the Blessed Virgin Mary, invoking her under a title that recalls the name of the town and was selected by popular vote of the parishioners.

HISTORY
Founded in 1968 in a rapidly growing section of Northbrook. The parish has over 1000 families and serves a diverse congregation.

ARCHITECTURE
The multi-purpose Worship Center, designed by Sunshine, Jaeger & Kupritz, was completed in 1972.

TREASURE
The triple stained glass window behind the altar in the sanctuary.

ST. PHILIP THE APOSTLE

1962 Old Willow Rd., Northfield

PATRON

Philip was one of the Twelve Apostles, and probably a disciple of John the Baptist before being called by Jesus. He himself brought Nathanael, another of the Twelve, to Jesus. After Pentecost he preached in Greece and Asia Minor and was martyred late in the 1st century.

HISTORY

Founded in 1947. The parish has grown up along with this suburban community.

ARCHITECTURE

The modern church, designed by Alexander H. Bacci of Schmidt, Garden & Erickson's architectural firm, was completed in 1963. The church has a 48 foot high entrance wall. A 15 foot tall oak crucifix with 8 foot lindenwood corpus, carved in Florence, Italy, hangs prominently in the sanctuary.

TREASURE

The entire east wall of the baptistery consists of a stained-glass window vividly portraying the Baptism of Our Lord by John the Baptist.

Northlake

ST. JOHN VIANNEY

46 N. Wolf Rd., Northlake

PATRON

John Vianney, also known as the Curé of Ars (1786–1859), was the son of a farmer in the south of France.

Though he desired to become a priest, his poor grades prevented his ordination until age 30.

Assigned to the parish of Ars, a tiny village near Lyons, he became a renowned preacher and confessor. He is revered today as the patron saint of parish priests.

HISTORY

Founded as a mission of St. Gertrude, Franklin Park in 1941, it quickly became a parish in 1942 because many defense workers were living and working in the area. The community filled in with residences after World War II. The parish serves a diverse congregation and Mass is celebrated in English, Spanish, and Filipino.

ARCHITECTURE

The modern church, designed by Joseph Bagnuolo in 1965, is shaped like a fish. Its cornerstone contains five pieces of granite from the parish church in Ars, France, home of the parish's patron

TREASURE

A 35 foot high stained glass window of the Sacred Heart in the sanctuary.

Oak Forest

ST. DAMIAN

5250 W. 155th St., Oak Forest

PATRON

Damian (3rd century), twin brother of Cosmas, took up the practice of medicine, becoming a skilled doctor. He and his brother were martyred for the Faith. Damian was chosen patron of the parish because of its proximity to the county hospital around which the town of Oak Forest grew up.

HISTORY

Founded in 1962 by Fr. Stanley Shaw in a rapidly growing suburb southwest of the city. St. Damian day school opened in 1963 and it has been a two-time recipient of the U.S. Department of Education Blue Ribbon of Excellence, in 1992 and 2005.

ARCHITECTURE

The modern church, designed by Gaul and Voosen, was completed in 1969, enlarged in the 1970s, and renovated in 1994. Stained glass windows, handcrafted by the late Rev. Richard R. Grimmel, adorn the Eucharistic chapel. The church façade was remodeled in 2001, and the convent was converted into new parish offices.

TREASURE

St. Damian Grotto of the Saints, featuring Mary, Joseph, and Patrick, where loved ones are remembered and special occasions celebrated.

Oak Lawn

ST. CATHERINE OF ALEXANDRIA

4100 W. 107th St., Oak Lawn

PATRON

Catherine of Alexandria was a fourth century virgin and martyr. She is the patroness of Christian philosophers and students of philosophy. Her feast day is November 25.

HISTORY

Founded in 1957 in a new subdivision of Oak Lawn. The parish serves a congregation of diverse European ethnic origins.

ARCHITECTURE

The combination church/school building, designed by John L. Bartolomeo and Associates, was completed in 1958.

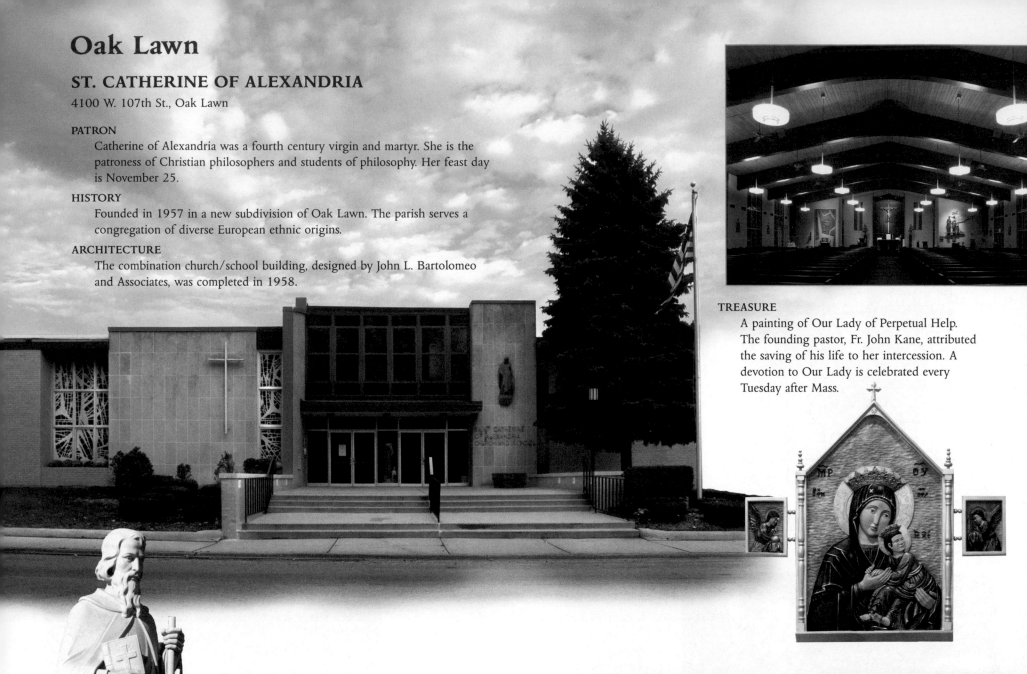

TREASURE

A painting of Our Lady of Perpetual Help. The founding pastor, Fr. John Kane, attributed the saving of his life to her intercession. A devotion to Our Lady is celebrated every Tuesday after Mass.

ST. GERALD

9310 S. 55th Ct., Oak Lawn

PATRON

Gerald (died c. 732) was a native of Northumbria, who became a monk at Lindisfarne, Ireland. He founded the monastery at Mayo, which became known as Mayo of the Saxons for most of its monks were from England. The monastery became a noted center of learning and holiness under Gerald's leadership as abbot.

HISTORY

Organized as a mission in 1921, it became a parish in 1934. The parish and community filled up with suburban residences after World War II. The parish serves a congregation of diverse European ethnic origins, a growing group of immigrant Hispanics, and a small number of Polish-speaking parishioners.

St. Gerald

ARCHITECTURE

The modern church, designed by Pirola and Erbach, was completed in 1958. In a 2004 remodeling, the original rectangular worship space was configured into a broad semi-circle, moving the sanctuary to another wall and bringing in more natural light.

TREASURE

A statue of St. Gerald stands outside the entrance of the church.

ST. GERMAINE

9711 S. Kolin Ave., Oak Lawn

PATRON

Germaine (1579–1601) was a poor French peasant who was neglected and mistreated by her family. She was pious and considerate of others, helping those who were even more needy than herself. She is venerated as the patroness of abused children.

HISTORY

Founded in 1962 in a rapidly growing section of Oak Lawn. The boundaries agreed upon with pastors of surrounding parishes makes St. Germaine an exact square mile in territory. The parish serves a congregation of diverse European ethnic origins.

ARCHITECTURE

The modern church, designed by Ralph H. Burke, Inc., was completed in 1966.

TREASURE

A relic of St. Germaine is venerated in the church.

Orland Hills

ST. ELIZABETH SETON

9300 W.167th St., Orland Hills

PATRON

Elizabeth Bayley Seton (1774–1821) was the first
American-born saint. Married to William Seton, she was the
mother of five children. After her husband's death in 1805,
she converted from Episcopalianism to Catholicism. She
founded the Sisters of Charity in 1809, the first American
religious community for women, and opened the first
Catholic school in Baltimore, Maryland.

HISTORY

Founded in 1987, by Rev. William T. O'Mara, in a fast growing suburban area.

ARCHITECTURE

The modern church, designed by Belli and Belli, was completed in 1990, and
expanded in 2000, according to plans of Jaeger and Nikola. Brother Joe Aspell,
S.M., and Jim Bacigalupi, fashioned the liturgical furnishings for the church,
highlighted by the Processional Cross.

TREASURE

The statue of Mary, Seat of Wisdom, by Brother Joe Aspell. Mary is portrayed as
an older woman, at the moment of Pentecost, when she helps the first Christian
community receive the Holy Spirit.

Orland Park

ST. FRANCIS OF ASSISI

15050 S. Wolf Rd., Orland Park

PATRON

Francis of Assisi (1181–1226) was the son of a wealthy cloth
merchant. Captured during a war between Assisi and
Perugia, he experienced a religious conversion and took
the Gospels as the rule of his life, Jesus Christ as his
literal example. He dressed in rough clothes, begged
for his sustenance, and preached purity and peace. In
1212, he founded the Franciscan religious order
and, two years later, Clare of Assisi became his
spiritual student and founded the women's order
of Franciscans.

St. Francis of Assisi

HISTORY

Founded in 1990 in a rapidly growing area in the far southwestern corner of Cook County and the Archdiocese. The parish serves a congregation of diverse European ethnic origins, many of whom moved from the South Side of Chicago.

ARCHITECTURE

The modern church, designed by Prisco, Serena and Sturm, was completed in 1996. The free-standing catechetical center, designed by Domenella Architects, opened in 2005.

TREASURE

The dramatic oak altar was designed by John Buscemi of Chicago. The statue of Mary, titled "Mother and Disciple", was designed by Anna Koh and Jeffrey Varilla. Both won awards from *Modern Liturgy Magazine*.

ST. MICHAEL

14327 Highland Ave., Orland Park

PATRON

Michael, whose name means "Who is like to God?", is one of the three archangels mentioned in the Bible. He led the army of God against Lucifer and the rebel angels and is thus usually depicted in warrior garb.

HISTORY

Organized as a country mission church for Luxembourger farmers in 1867, it did not receive a resident pastor and become a parish until 1926. The area filled up with suburban residences after World War II. The parish serves a congregation of diverse European ethnic origins, including many Irish parishioners who moved from the South Side of Chicago.

ARCHITECTURE

The modern church, designed by John L. Bartolomeo, was completed in 1969 and reconfigured by architect Paul Strake in 1985

TREASURE

Distinctive sculptures in metal and stone.

Palos Heights

ST. ALEXANDER

7025 W. 126th St., Palos Heights

PATRON

Alexander (died c. 116) was a Roman citizen. He became Pope during the reign of Emperor Trajan and was martyred by beheading. The founding pastor of this parish, Fr. Joseph R. Hanton, chose the name in honor of his father and brother, both named Alexander.

HISTORY

Founded in 1959 in a rapidly growing sector of southwestern Cook County. The founding pastor purchased a ranch house as a rectory and converted the garage into a chapel for daily Mass. Sunday Masses were first offered in a local funeral home. The parish has grown rapidly and serves a congregation of diverse European ethnic origins.

ARCHITECTURE

The modern church, which stretches out at ground level much like a ranch house, was designed by Bartolomeo and Associates and completed in 1961

TREASURE

A stained glass window of Jesus and the little children.

INCARNATION

5757 W. 127th St., Palos Heights

PATRON

The parish name commemorates the mystery by which the Second Person of the Blessed Trinity became Man.

HISTORY

Founded in 1962 in a rapidly growing area of southwest Cook County. The parish has grown rapidly and serves a congregation of diverse European ethnic origins. The parish has sponsored and built the church of San Francisco in Moquequa, Peru.

ARCHITECTURE

The modern, octagonal church, designed by Ben Nelson, was completed in 1996. It was the last church dedicated by Cardinal Joseph Bernardin before his death. The gymnasium, the Bernardin Center, had been the first parish facility dedicated by the Cardinal after his arrival in the city in 1982.

TREASURE

Stained glass windows tell the story of Creation.

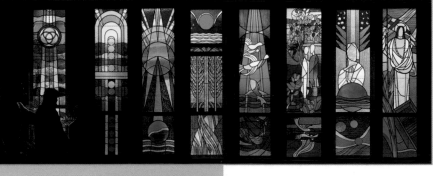

Incarnation

Palos Hills

SACRED HEART

8245 W. 111th St., Palos Hills

PATRON

St. Margaret Mary Alacoque (1647–1690), a French nun of Paray-le-Monial, France, was primarily responsible for spreading devotion to the Sacred Heart of Jesus. Since the 17th century, this has been one of the most popular of all Catholic devotions, common to many different ethnic groups.

HISTORY

Organized as a mission church in 1872 for the German and Irish farmers in the surrounding area. The area filled up with suburban residences after World War II and Sacred Heart became a parish in 1968.

ARCHITECTURE

The modern octagonal church, designed by Ware Associates, was completed in 1994.

TREASURE

Treasured artifacts from three previous church buildings in the parish, and precious items from closed South Side churches have been tastefully incorporated into the new church.

ST. VINCENT FERRER

1530 Jackson Ave., River Forest

PATRON

Vincent Ferrer (1350–1419) was a Valencian Dominican whose vocation as a scholar, teacher, and papal advisor was transformed after surviving the plague. He took to the roads becoming one of the most famous itinerant preachers in Europe. His mission crusade preached conversion, repentance, and a readiness for the Last Judgment.

HISTORY

Founded in 1931 by the Dominican Fathers in the neighborhood of their House of Studies in River Forest. The parish serves the suburban North Avenue corridor – Elmwood Park as well as River Forest. Italians and Irish were the first families of the parish; now Polish, Filipinos, Latinos, plus many other ethnic groups make up the faith assembly.

ARCHITECTURE

The present church building is the third place of worship on the property. Designed in an English Gothic style by Frank J. Ellert, the church was completed in 1956. Recent upgrading has brightened and refreshed the massive interior, which seats a thousand worshippers.

TREASURE

The sixteen stained glass windows of the Rosary are notable. Designed and executed by Richard Stoettner of T. C. Esser Company of Milwaukee, each panel depicts an Old Testament story alluding to one of the traditional fifteen mysteries of the Rosary.

River Grove

ST. CYPRIAN

2601 N. Clinton St., River Grove

PATRON

Cyprian (c. 200–258) was born in Carthage and became an orator and teacher of rhetoric. He converted to the Faith and became a priest and the Bishop of Carthage. His theological writings earned him renown as one of the Latin Fathers of the Church. He was martyred by beheading

HISTORY

Founded in 1927 as suburban development was beginning in the area. The community filled in with residences after World War II. The parish serves a diverse congregation of mainly European origins.

ARCHITECTURE

The church, in an American colonial style, reminiscent of the chapel at St. Mary of the Lake Seminary, was designed by Pirola and Erbach and completed in 1951.

TREASURE

A stained glass wall, reminiscent of the work of Chagall, was designed by parishioner Raymond Toloczko, and executed by brother priests, Fathers Richard and Arthur Douaire.

Riverdale

QUEEN OF APOSTLES

207 W. 145th St., Riverdale

PATRON

The feast of the Queen of Apostles was established on the first Saturday after the Ascension by the Sacred Congregation of Rites at the request of the Pallottine Fathers. Mary initiated her mission as Queen of Apostles when she gathered with the Apostles in the upper room after Jesus's Ascension, waiting with them for the coming of the Holy Spirit on Pentecost.

HISTORY

Founded in 1953 in a new subdivision south of Chicago. The small parish has a congregation of predominantly European ethnic origins.

ARCHITECTURE

The modern church, designed by Fox and Fox, was completed in 1954. It features a large Gothic arch over the entranceway.

TREASURE

A large stained glass window over the choir loft depicts Mary, Queen of Apostles.

Riverside

ST. MARY

126 Herrick Rd., Riverside

PATRON

The Blessed Virgin Mary, wife of St. Joseph, Mother of Jesus.

HISTORY

Organized as a mission church in 1875, it became a parish in 1885. The community was a planned suburb, laid out by landscape architects Frederick Law Olmsted and Calvert Vaux along the Burlington railroad line. The area had few Catholics until new subdivisions were established after World War II.

ARCHITECTURE

The church, designed by Harry F. Robinson, a parishioner, was completed in 1926. Robinson had formerly worked for Frank Lloyd Wright and he incorporated a number of Prairie School architectural features in the church.

TREASURE

Six stained glass windows depicting lives of Jesus and Mary on either side of the nave.

Rolling Meadows

ST. COLETTE

3900 S. Meadow Dr., Rolling Meadows

PATRON

Colette (1381–1447) was the daughter of a French carpenter. She was orphaned at age 17 and became a Franciscan hermit. She reformed her branch of the Franciscans to the original austerity of Francis and Clare. The order became known as the Poor Clares. The founding pastor of this parish, Fr. James Halpin, had been closely associated with the Poor Clares in Chicago.

HISTORY

Founded in 1957 in a newly incorporated suburb in the far northwestern sector of Cook County. The parish grew rapidly and now serves a diverse congregation. Masses are celebrated in English and Spanish.

ARCHITECTURE

The modern church, designed by Hermann J. Gaul, was completed in 1959, then renovated in 1978 and 1992.

TREASURE

The church doors contain depictions of the Eight Beatitudes

Rosemont

OUR LADY OF HOPE

9711 W. Devon Ave., Rosemont

PATRON

Devotion to Our Lady of Hope originated in the Dark Ages of Europe following the breakup of Charlemagne's empire. Numerous shrines to Our Lady of Hope proliferated. A French priest, Paul-Marie Prudhomme, was largely responsible for reviving devotion to Mary under this title in the 19th century.

HISTORY

Founded in 1957 in an area of south Des Plaines, later incorporated into Rosemont.

ARCHITECTURE

The combination of church building and parish center are designed in a modernized version of the Midwestern prairie style that is welcoming, functional, and efficient.

TREASURE

The chapel, used for morning and noon liturgies, has a dramatic stained glass window which creates an atmosphere of prayer. A meditation garden is planned for the 50th anniversary of the parish in 2007.

OUR LADY OF HOPE

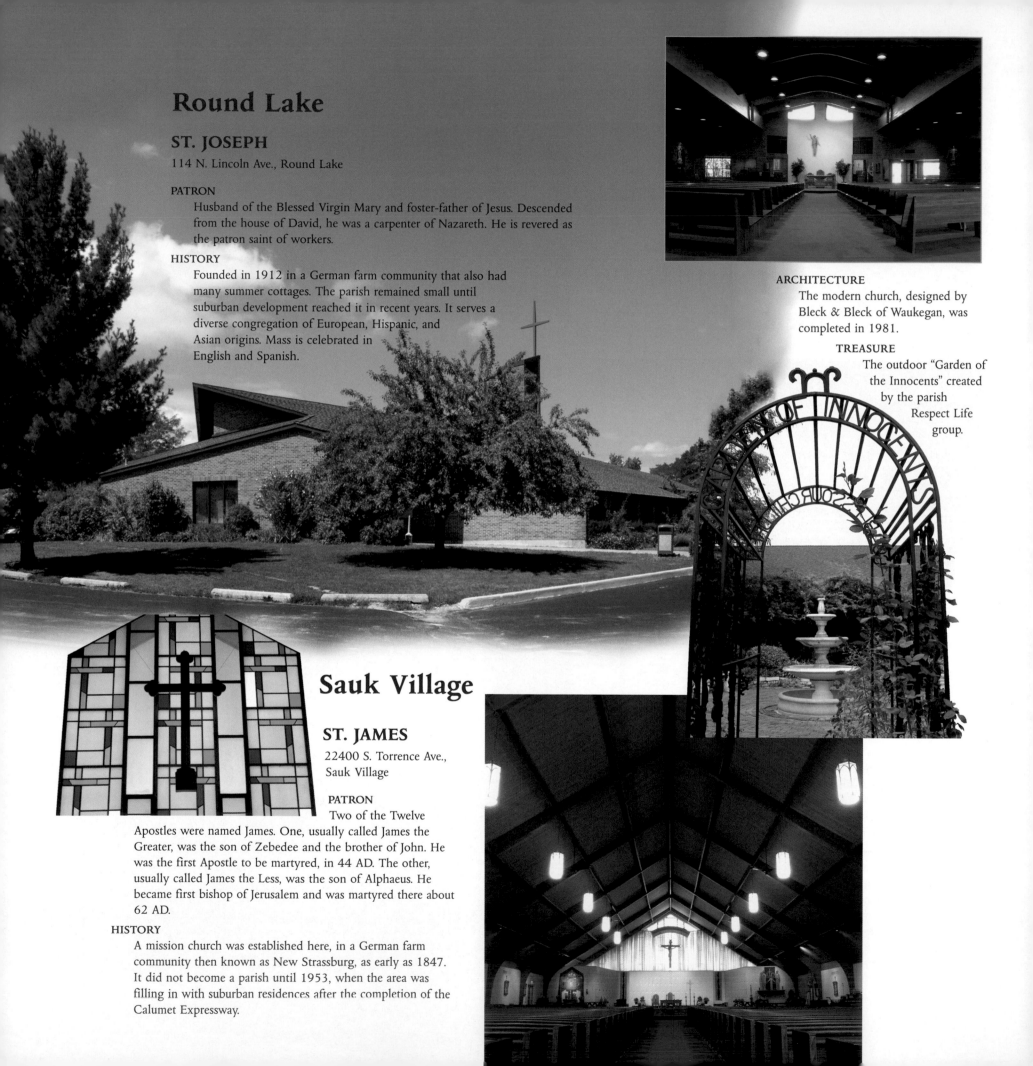

Round Lake

ST. JOSEPH

114 N. Lincoln Ave., Round Lake

PATRON

Husband of the Blessed Virgin Mary and foster-father of Jesus. Descended from the house of David, he was a carpenter of Nazareth. He is revered as the patron saint of workers.

HISTORY

Founded in 1912 in a German farm community that also had many summer cottages. The parish remained small until suburban development reached it in recent years. It serves a diverse congregation of European, Hispanic, and Asian origins. Mass is celebrated in English and Spanish.

ARCHITECTURE

The modern church, designed by Bleck & Bleck of Waukegan, was completed in 1981.

TREASURE

The outdoor "Garden of the Innocents" created by the parish Respect Life group.

Sauk Village

ST. JAMES

22400 S. Torrence Ave., Sauk Village

PATRON

Two of the Twelve Apostles were named James. One, usually called James the Greater, was the son of Zebedee and the brother of John. He was the first Apostle to be martyred, in 44 AD. The other, usually called James the Less, was the son of Alphaeus. He became first bishop of Jerusalem and was martyred there about 62 AD.

HISTORY

A mission church was established here, in a German farm community then known as New Strassburg, as early as 1847. It did not become a parish until 1953, when the area was filling in with suburban residences after the completion of the Calumet Expressway.

St. James

ARCHITECTURE

The modern, combination church/school building, designed by Cronin and Cronin, was completed in 1962.

TREASURE

A mission Cross from 1885 was found in the rafters of Old St. James church by Fr. Tom Conde in 2000. It has been restored to its original color and finish and now hangs in the church.

Schaumburg

CHURCH OF THE HOLY SPIRIT

1451 W. Bode Rd., Schaumburg

PATRON

The parish is dedicated to the Third Person of the Blessed Trinity.

HISTORY

Founded in 1972 in a rapidly growing area in the far northwest corner of Cook County. The founding pastor, Fr. George Kane, served the parish for 24 years. The parish continues to grow on many levels, and now serves a congregation of Anglos, Hispanics, Filipinos, and other immigrant groups. An annual Country Fair brings this diverse community together for five days of food, fun, music and prayer. Mass is celebrated in English and Spanish each week in the church and bilingually outdoors at the Fair

ARCHITECTURE

The modern church, designed with Midwestern prairie school elements, was completed in 1974 and renovated in 1985.

TREASURE

A painting of Our Lady of Guadalupe, patroness of the Americas.

South Holland

HOLY GHOST

700 E. 170th St., South Holland

PATRON

The parish is dedicated to the Third Person of the Blessed Trinity.

HISTORY

Founded in 1962 to relieve overcrowding in St. Jude Parish, South Holland.

ARCHITECTURE

The modern church, designed by Loebl, Schlossman, Bennett & Dart, was completed in 1971. After complaints from parishioners, the founding pastor, Fr. Thomas Gorman, added a huge crucifix above the tabernacle, saying "We need a traditional symbol in our modern church." A forty foot long vigil light structure was also erected at the back wall of the church, depicting the Seven Gifts of the Holy Spirit.

TREASURE

A large stained glass window of Jesus and the children, the work of Munich artisan Max Guler, from the closed Ss. Cyril and Methodius church, is at the baptistery. Two other windows from that church, an angel and a symbolic representation of the Holy Trinity, have also been preserved.

ST. JUDE THE APOSTLE

880 E. 154th St., South Holland

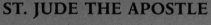

PATRON

Jude, sometimes known as Jude Thaddeus, was one of the Twelve Apostles. Little is known of his life or where he was martyred. In recent years he has become popular as the "patron saint of lost causes," supposedly because no one prayed to him for centuries due to the similarity between his name and that of the traitor Judas.

St. Jude the Apostle

HISTORY

Founded in 1957 in a rapidly growing south suburb. An empty barn served as the first church. The parish serves a diverse, racially integrated congregation.

ARCHITECTURE

The combination church/school building, designed by Joseph L. Bartolomeo, was completed in 1958.

TREASURE

Stained glass windows.

Stickney

ST. PIUS X

4314 S. Oak Park Ave., Stickney

PATRON

Giuseppe Sarto (1835–1914) was born into a poor family in northern Italy. He became a parish priest, the bishop of Mantua, and Patriarch of Venice. He was elected Pope in 1903, taking the name Pius X. He is revered for restoring the age of First Communion to 7 instead of the later ages previously common.

HISTORY

Founded in 1954, just after the canonization of Pius X, it may have been the first parish in the U.S. named for him. The parish was in a fast growing suburban area just outside the southwestern edge of the city. It serves a congregation of diverse origins, including many Bohemians from the southwest side of Chicago and a growing Hispanic population.

ARCHITECTURE

The modern church, designed by Thomas E. Cook, was completed in 1955.

TREASURE

Stained glass window of the parish patron, Pope St. Pius X.

Westchester

DIVINE INFANT

1601 Newcastle Ave., Westchester

PATRON

Devotion to the Infant Jesus has been popular in the Catholic Church at least since the time of St. Francis Assisi, who introduced the Christmas crib in the 13th century. An image of Jesus called the Infant Jesus of Prague has been venerated since 1628.

HISTORY

Founded in 1947 by Fr. Charles Langan as the western suburbs grew rapidly in the postwar building boom. The parish and its school serve a diverse congregation.

ARCHITECTURE

The modern church, designed by Thomas W. Cooke, was completed in 1963. Celtic and Byzantine mosaics decorate the ceiling of the sanctuary. Many stained glass windows depict events in the life of Jesus from the Annunciation to the Ascension, with a modern Nativity scene and Jesus's biblical lineage in vibrant colors at the back of the sanctuary.

TREASURE

A shrine to the Divine Infant.

DIVINE PROVIDENCE

2550 Mayfair Ave., Westchester

PATRON

The parish name commemorates the Divine Providence, or Fatherly Care, of God.

Divine Providence

HISTORY
Founded in 1956 by Fr. Walter McInerney, the second parish in Westchester, which filled up with residences after World War II. The parish serves a diverse congregation.

ARCHITECTURE
After worshipping at the High Ridge Public School and then in a combination church/school building, the parishioners celebrated the opening of a modern church in 1986. Noteworthy is the stained glass window in the Baptistery area.

TREASURE
A statue of the Risen Christ under a skylight in the sanctuary.

Western Springs

ST. JOHN OF THE CROSS
5005 S. Wolf Rd., Western Springs

PATRON
John of the Cross (1542–1591) was born of an impoverished noble family in Spain. He became a Carmelite priest at age 25 and experienced numerous mystical experiences. Along with St. Teresa of Avila he organized a reformed branch of the Carmelites, known as the Discalced, or barefoot, friars.

HISTORY
Founded in 1960 in a rapidly growing area of western Cook County. The parish serves a congregation of 3548 households. While many parishioners have moved from the south and west sides of the city, over 60 families have been in the area for three generations.

ARCHITECTURE
The modern church, designed by Edward Dart, was completed in 1977.

Inspired by the humble life Jesus lived, the architect used simple materials such as brick, tile, wood, and textured concrete in a building reminiscent of the stable where the Christ Child was born.

TREASURE
A bronze statue of St. John of the Cross holding up the Sacred Host, designed by William Thompson, stands in the vestibule.

Wheeling

ST. JOSEPH THE WORKER

181 W. Dundee Rd., Wheeling

PATRON

Husband of the Blessed Virgin Mary and foster-father of Jesus. Descended from the house of David, he was a carpenter of Nazareth. He is revered as the patron saint of workers.

HISTORY

Founded in 1957 in a rapidly growing area of northwestern Cook County. Despite the suburban location, the parish is very diverse. Sunday Masses are celebrated in English, Spanish, and Polish, and there is also a large contingent of Filipino parishioners.

ARCHITECTURE

The combination church/school building, designed by Joseph L. Bennett, was completed in 1958.

TREASURE

St. Joseph adoration chapel.

Wilmette

ST. FRANCIS XAVIER

524 Ninth St., Wilmette

PATRON

Francis Xavier (1506–1551) was a nobleman from the Basque region of Spain. He studied at the University of Paris where he met St. Ignatius of Loyola and joined his Society of Jesus (Jesuits). He sailed to Goa, India as a missionary in 1541 and evangelized throughout India, the East Indies, and Japan, until his death ten years later.

HISTORY

Founded in 1904 as an English-speaking parish. Though predominantly Irish at first, it serves a diverse congregation in this North Shore suburb.

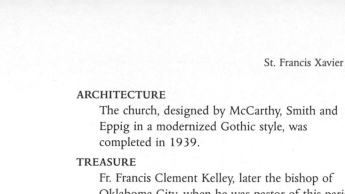

St. Francis Xavier

ARCHITECTURE

The church, designed by McCarthy, Smith and Eppig in a modernized Gothic style, was completed in 1939.

TREASURE

Fr. Francis Clement Kelley, later the bishop of Oklahoma City, when he was pastor of this parish, asked parishioners to donate some of their jewelry for the fabrication of sacred vessels. A gold chalice was fashioned and jewels were imbedded in an ornate monstrance.

ST. JOSEPH

1747 Lake Ave , Wilmette

PATRON

Husband of the Blessed Virgin Mary and foster-father of Jesus. Descended from the house of David, he was a carpenter of Nazareth. He is revered as the patron saint of workers.

HISTORY

Founded in 1845 in a German farming village then known as Gross Point. It remained predominantly German into the 20th century when it became a more diverse suburban parish.

ARCHITECTURE

The church, designed in a modernized Romanesque style by McCarthy, Smith & Eppig, was completed in 1939. It was the last church dedicated by Cardinal Mundelein before his death that year. It features a soaring campanile and an elegant porte cochere.

TREASURE

The Crucifixion scene, silhouetted in front of stained glass windows, behind the main altar.

Winnetka

SS. FAITH, HOPE, AND CHARITY

191 Linden St., Winnetka

PATRON

The parish is dedicated to three virgin martyrs of Rome in the early centuries of the Church.

HISTORY

Founded in 1936 on property donated by two elderly sisters. The parish serves the two North Shore suburbs of Kenilworth and Winnetka.

ARCHITECTURE

The church, designed by Edward J. Schulte of Cincinnati in a modernized colonial style, was completed in 1963. A free-standing bell tower stands beside the church. A 24' mahogany cross is said to be one of the largest religious carvings ever created in the US.

TREASURE

A golden monstrance and the other sacred vessels for the Eucharist.

SACRED HEART
1077 Tower Rd., Winnetka

PATRON
St. Margaret Mary Alacoque (1647–1690), a French nun of Paray-le-Monial, France, was primarily responsible for spreading devotion to the Sacred Heart of Jesus. Since the 17th century, this has been one of the most popular of all Catholic devotions, common to many different ethnic groups.

HISTORY
Founded in 1897 in the Hubbard Woods section of Winnetka. Msgr. Reynold Hillenbrand, the former rector of St. Mary of the Lake Seminary, served as pastor from 1944 to 1973. Msgr. Hillenbrand was a leader in the liturgical movement and he introduced many liturgical improvements before they became general after the Second Vatican Council. The parish serves the North Shore suburbs of Winnetka and Glencoe.

ARCHITECTURE
The Gothic church was completed in 1925, and recently renovated in 1995.

TREASURE
The sculpture of The Vine and the Branches, by Joseph O'Connell.

EDWARD R. KANTOWICZ, a native Chicagoan (St. Margaret Mary parish), received a Ph.D. in history from the University of Chicago. Formerly a professor of history at Carleton University in Ottawa, Canada, he is currently an independent scholar and writer. He is co-author (with Ellen Skerrett and Steven M. Avella) of *Catholicism, Chicago Style*, and the author of *Corporation Sole: Cardinal Mundelein and Chicago Catholicism*. Most recently he was the author of two volumes on *The World in the Twentieth Century*.

CREDITS

Published by Booklink, Ireland
Publisher: Dr. Claude Costecalde

© Photographs, 2006, Tina Leto and the Archives of the Archdiocese of Chicago, except those otherwise credited

© Text, 2006, Archdiocese of Chicago, Illinois, USA

Design by Dunbar Design
and GraphicBase, Ireland

Printed in Ireland by the Universities Press